Against the Grain

An Instrument Maker's Journey

FIGURE 0.1 *Natura morta con strumenti* musicali by Bartolo Bettera (1639–1688). Photograph used with kind permission of Dorotheum, Vienna.

Against the Grain
An Instrument Maker's Journey

PAUL FISCHER

The Choir Press

First published in the United Kingdom in 2023 by
The Choir Press

ISBN 978-1-78963-336-8

An earlier version of Chapter 3 appeared in *Let the Wood Speak* by Paul Fischer, with David Nickson (Chipping Norton, 2018), and is reproduced with permission.

To my wife, Joy, without whose help and support over many years, and particularly following a major stroke, this work would never have been started or completed.

Last, but by no means least, to the patient and gifted Thérèse Wassily Saba, copy editor and contributor to this book, including some of the explanatory footnotes. I give my sincere thanks for her encouragement and the benefit of her knowledge and her wide experience of the classical guitar world.

Paul Fischer

Contents

Figures

Foreword

When the invitation came to write the Foreword to this new publication on the life and career of Paul Fischer, I was only too happy to oblige, having first met Paul shortly after his arrival at the workshop of David Rubio in 1969. Paul's skills as a luthier quite simply are second to none, not only in the field of the classical guitar but also in researching and constructing earlier 'period' plucked instruments such as the lute, vihuela and cittern. Paul's initial training in the field of harpsichord building was to stand him in good stead and all is revealed about his life in this highly interesting, entertaining and absorbing book, including his radical change of direction spending several years in the British Army; he regarded this move as an opportunity for viewing life from a very different perspective and dimension, thereby gaining many new and valuable experiences.

One might say that his early apprenticeship in life was demanding and challenging, with not only the acquisition of precise knowledge of beautiful and rare woods, plus developing the incredible skills to work in the construction of fine and delicate musical instruments, initially harpsichords, but then also the contrasting tough and much more rigorous nature of necessary training required by the armed forces. There is no small difference between, for example, the thinning down of a delicate membrane of wood for a harpsichord soundboard, compared to blasting at targets on the North German ranges with the 120 mm main armament, ensconced within a massive 65-ton Conqueror tank! Paul served with one of the most distinguished cavalry regiments in the British Army: the 11th Hussars.

His account of this time, with its rigorous training, and service partly in Berlin at the start of the Cold War, makes for fascinating reading.

Emerging from his military exploits at the end of the 1960s, during which time he married Joy, whom he had first met in 1964, Paul then entered the world of guitar building with relish and enthusiasm. He was first working within the calm and rarefied atmosphere of the Oxfordshire workshop of David Rubio, and then eventually in his own very similar premises in Chipping Norton, when Rubio decided that a move to Cambridge was called for. Paul, now within his own environment, went on to achieve a position as one of the finest instrument makers in the world.

As the 1980s unfolded, Paul was becoming increasingly concerned with the difficult supply of quality tone woods; he eventually travelled to Brazil on a Winston Churchill Travelling Fellowship to explore the possibilities of sourcing alternative timbers of similar quality with the important issues of conservation and protection of the by then increasingly threatened Brazilian rainforests. The results of this quest, Paul provides here, having sourced a number of beautiful woods and subsequently going on to produce instruments, which were both visually stunning and tonally superb.

During the 1980s, the Fischer guitar had generally been constructed along the lines of the tried and tested design used by David Rubio, incorporating the slightly arched, fan-braced top. Paul, however, always believed that the top, or soundboard, could benefit from his wider experience with other plucked instruments and developed a completely different form of bracing to create more volume and projection as well as achieving increased clarity in voicing. This was to become known in his instruments as the Taut system. How this was arrived at makes for fascinating reading, and eventually I was delighted to be able to take possession of one of these fine instruments in 2006, when Paul decided to build a small batch of guitars to celebrate fifty years of instrument making.

My own first visit to Duns Tew was in 1968, the year before Paul had arrived, and David Rubio had strongly expressed the opinion that guitarists should really make an effort to understand how the instrument was constructed and what made it work; whenever I was there, David seemed prepared to explain and clarify important constructional details. Happily, these opportunities continued with Paul and, over the years, there have been many sessions with him, not only explaining what he was doing with strutting, varnishes, various timbers, etc., but also wanting to know what players were looking for in an instrument. Indeed, Paul was one of those luthiers, like Rubio, who preferred honest feedback when a new instrument was proffered for assessment. Not for him were remarks such as 'Well, it sounds very nice', or even 'Isn't it nice and shiny'; no, if something was not working, he insisted on being told, otherwise progress could not take place.

Learning about the inner workings of guitars stimulated my interest in, for example, the eight-stringed version; indeed, Paul has completed a number of these fine instruments but, sadly, I realised for myself it was a case of 'teaching an old dog new tricks'! I reckoned it would have meant 12–18 months away from concerts to adjust to the extra strings but I would add that, if I were beginning again, I would give this instrument careful consideration because of the greater range available, particularly for Early Music and the sympathetic overtones created by the two extra bass strings.

However, I also developed a passion for antique guitars, particularly the transitional and early nineteenth-century instruments and, later, I was able to buy several of these from Paul's own collection, including a beautiful instrument attributed to François Lupot and another very interesting guitar by the late eighteenth-century London firm Longman & Broderip.

I am delighted to say that a firm and lasting friendship with Paul has matured over more than five decades, and in what must have been dozens of visits over the years, many with my wife, the guitarist Cobie Smit; these were always educational, incredibly inspirational and, of course, highly pleasurable experiences – Paul and Joy being excellent hosts. The immense success Paul Fischer has achieved in a remarkable career is, of course, not only due to his amazing gifts but also sheer hard work, his energy, combined with a passionate belief in what he wanted to create.

Therefore, with this fascinating publication, we celebrate his artistic contribution and his supreme talent.

John Mills
April 2021

FIGURE 0.2 Paul Fischer and John Mills with his restored nineteenth-century guitar.
Source: John Mills. Reproduced with permission.

Acknowledgements

This book would not have been written without the encouragement, help and generosity of so many people. The process began as a post-stroke therapy exercise but quickly turned into a spectacle of discarded, scrunched-up sheets of paper scattered across the floor. My wife, Joy, came to my aid and swiftly learnt to decipher my handwritten originals.

Those who contributed so much would naturally come from the world of the classical and flamenco guitar and include such luminaries as guitarists Gerald Garcia, Thomas Liauw, Juan Martín, John Mills and Xuefei Yang. To each of them I owe my sincere gratitude. Siegfried Hogenmüller, a long-time friend and colleague, is owed my heartfelt thanks and *dankbarkeit* for being a continuing source of historical data and inspiration. The physicist Dr Bernard Richardson has kindly provided valuable source material from his extensive work on acoustics of musical instruments (see Appendix II).

Others deserving of thanks are the guitarist–composer Gilbert Biberian, the writer Julian Roach, and luthiers Sérgio Abreu, Christopher Dean and Jasper Sender. And to my first teacher, Andrea Goble, and his daughter, Catherine, and my son, Scott, and daughter, Rachel.

Since receiving a Winston Churchill Fellowship in 1984, the Memorial Trust has remained a true source of support.

We are also very grateful for the contributions of Badi, Odair and Sérgio Assad, Anne Denis and Françoise-Emmanuelle Denis, Judicaël Perroy, Dr Martin Harris and Alan Lewis. And most importantly, I would like to thank David Nickson for his hard work on the original version of my biography and for convincing me that 'there was a book in there'.

The following individuals/organisations have kindly granted permission for photographs and text to be reproduced: BCA, Emrys

Babb, Brian Blood, The Churchill Trust, Colin Cooper, Françoise-Emmanuelle Denis, Dolmetsch Archive, Haddon Davies, Robert Dean, Paul Felix, Felipe Fittipaldi, 'Garconjon', Charles W. Griffin, Lakeland Arts, John Marshall, Rik Middleton, Norman Charles Myall, Claus Nürnburger, Maurice Summerfield and Ashley Mark Publishing, David Van Edwards and Richard Winslade.

Instrument making has always been, and should continue to be, an ongoing process of development. Each design reflects particular skills and tastes of the maker, not just a reaction to the more restricted requirements of composers or performers from the past or present. The craft of instrument making should be more than just 'reproduction', in the same way that ornamentation in music should be more than playing only what the early masters had committed to print.

Eugène Arnold Dolmetsch
(1858–1940)

Introduction

Now that we are comfortably in the twenty-first century, it is easier to examine the twentieth century and the role played by significant creative lives in its history. In 2013 Paul Fischer began the process of looking back over his long career as an instrument maker. He had been making classical guitars for over fifty years, and musical instruments for even longer.

In an interview with BBC Oxford in 2009, when Paul was celebrating his fiftieth anniversary since first starting out as a luthier, Paul explained his philosophy of instrument making thus: 'When it comes to something you feel passionate about, you demonstrate your patience because you really want to be sure that what you're doing is producing something of the very highest quality.'

One of the celebrations of this long and fruitful career was manifest in the project of the documentary filmmaker Henry Astor. The idea of this film was not only to reflect the career of one of Britain's finest instrument makers but also to reflect a broad view of his life in music, his long-term professional relationships with musicians, as well as the music itself. Thus, Henry Astor's film, *Aubade: The Last Guitar*, which was premièred on 12 February 2014 at the Chipping Norton Theatre, appropriately near to Paul Fischer's workshop, not only documents making a guitar from start to finish but also incorporates two other 'creative processes' – that of the performer, Xuefei Yang, for whom the guitar was made, and the composer William Lovelady, who wrote a piece called *Aubade* for Xuefei Yang to play on the new Paul Fischer guitar.

In 2013, as they were finishing the filming, Paul commented to Henry Astor, 'Henry, I need to have a rest. I may be some time …' Shortly after Henry left, Paul had a stroke, and by the time he reached hospital he was unconscious. He was then put in an induced coma for two weeks until he awoke naturally from this state and slowly began to take stock of what had happened. The consultant at the hospital stood at the end of Paul's bed when he awoke and said, 'Do you realise you nearly died!' Paul, of course, did not realise this, as he was unconscious while he was still at home and thought he had simply fallen asleep; when he awoke in hospital, he had no idea that two weeks had passed by.

After the initial euphoria, simply for being alive, Paul noticed that he had been left with some paralysis and also with some changes in his vocal register, moving from a tenor to a counter-tenor. He remained in hospital for a full six weeks but then had to face the reality of no longer being able to make musical instruments. Had he not suffered such a debilitating stroke, he would have continued.

Paul Fischer began his instrument-making apprenticeship on Kiln Lane, Headington, with the harpsichord maker Robert Goble (1903–1991), whose instrument-making lineage traced back to the Early Music specialist and instrument maker Arnold Dolmetsch (1858–1940). Paul later worked for many years as the chief instrument maker and manager for David Rubio in his Duns Tew studio workshop in Oxfordshire. In between this, he spent a number of years in the army, which not only included military activities but also sports training and participation in Olympic-level competitions. It was after these three formative periods of his life that he then established his own instrument-making workshop in 1975, initially within the Duns Tew studios for four years before moving to his own purpose-built premises in Chipping Norton in 1979, where he still lives to this day.

As you will read, Paul's life path is not simply one of an instrument maker; while he has achieved an international reputation for his instruments, at the same time he managed to put his need to be physically active to good use during his instrument-making career by including a busy schedule of travel, exploration, lecturing and teaching, balanced out with the discipline and solitude required by a craftsman's work. He has served as an advisor to the crafts Panel for the Southern Arts Association and also as a technical advisor and panel member of the Crafts Council of Great Britain.

Paul is an Oxfordshire man in spirit; the Arts and Crafts movement, which began in late nineteenth century in Britain, is particularly strong in the Cotswolds region and Paul has followed the approach of this movement and its philosophy in all aspects of his life and work, even down to the reclaimed Cotswold stone that he used for the building of his workshop in Chipping Norton.

In 1983 he was awarded a Winston Churchill Travelling Fellowship to extend his research of wood for use in instrument making into the rainforests of Brazil. This was quite soon after the CITES (the Convention on International Trade in Endangered Species of Wild Fauna and Flora) had entered into force on 1 July 1975. On returning from Brazil, as part of the Fellowship, he built eight classical guitars, seven with woods he had collected on his trip, and organised a public performance of these instruments to share his research with other instrument makers and performers. What I hadn't realised before collaborating with Paul on his biography was the extent to which his early life in the army, in terms of endurance and his participation in pre-selection Olympic teams during that time, had had such a great influence on his approach to life, and in particular his sense of exploration. Paul is a great admirer of Arctic and particularly Antarctic explorers. Hence, his words to Henry Astor, 'Henry, I need to have a rest. I may be some time …', had a double resonance for him because they were also the last words of Captain Titus Oates ('I'm just going. I may be some time …'). Oates was responsible for the ponies in Scott's Antarctic expedition in 1912 and, like Paul, had also been a cavalryman in the army.

In this biography, which Paul Fischer and I have worked on together for over a year, much of it during the Covid-19 lockdown via long telephone conversations several times a week, we have thoroughly enjoyed reminiscing over our shared classical guitar history. I worked as the news editor of the British monthly magazine *Classical Guitar* for nearly thirty years and interviewed him on a number of occasions. I was also fortunate to visit his exhibitions at Art in Action in Waterperry Park in Oxfordshire and naturally was at a number of the West Dean Classical Guitar festivals, which were sponsored by *Classical Guitar* magazine.

Together we reviewed Paul's fascinating life's work, debating over the essential contents of the biography, with me enthusiastically adding newly revealed details of his life, his own sense of exploration and his own training under the renowned explorer Ranulph Fiennes, his admiration for Antarctic explorers, T.E. Lawrence and the Arts and Crafts movement, his childhood encounters with C.S. Lewis ... and Paul modestly attempting to subtract details constantly. In celebration of his eightieth birthday, many of his colleagues, apprentices, clients and friends have contributed to our rather large but informative Appendices, where we have also reproduced some of Paul's guitar-making articles and an up-to-date article by Dr Bernard Richardson, including a reference list he has compiled especially for our readers. Paul Fischer's *Against the Grain: An Instrument Maker's Journey* is a celebration of the enormous breadth of experiences that one Oxfordshire man's life can encapsulate.

Thérèse Wassily Saba

FIGURE 0.3 Paul Fischer next to a huge log in the rainforest of Brazil during his Winston Churchill Trust Fellowship.

Source: ©Paul Fischer Collection.

CHAPTER 1

Growing Up and All That Jazz!

Paul Fischer was born on the Isle of Man in 1941, after the start of the Second World War in September 1939. His father served in the Royal Air Force (RAF) and was stationed at RAF Jurby on the Isle of Man, in the Irish Sea, halfway between England and Ireland. RAF Jurby had been established just before the outbreak of hostilities, at a time when they were updating from the Handley Page Heyford biplane bombers (the iconic biplanes of the 1930s) to the state-of-the-art Spitfires and Hawker Hurricanes arriving in 1942. Paul's father, Albert Fisher, built link trainers – grounded devices for training pilots – and RAF Jurby was an important strategic station during the war.[1]

Albert had joined the RAF in the late 1920s and trained as an engineer. He was mostly stationed overseas: first on the North-West Frontier of India (in Kohat, which is now in Pakistan) and then later in Iraq. In Kohat the RAF had both Westland Wapiti biplanes as well as Crossley armoured cars, serving in a reconnaissance role.

FIGURE 1.1 Albert Fisher in Kohat, India, in 1935. The elephant sign in the background is a clue to his squadron and location on the North-West Frontier. He was not a pilot but clearly had just been up in a plane, as he was wearing a flying helmet with a headset for radio communication. Copyright © Paul Fischer Collection.

[1] Paul Fischer's family name uses the more common modern English spelling, Fisher; however, as an instrument maker, he adopted the earlier English spelling of Fischer.

Paul and his son, Scott, did extensive family history research in the pre-Internet days, which included much travelling throughout the length and breadth of Britain, including London, where they found that Paul's great-great-grandfather had worked as a saddler in the Royal Mews. Some of this invaluable research has been used in this chapter.

FIGURE 1.2 Westland Wapiti biplanes lined up and 'ever-ready' in Kohat, 1930s.
Copyright © Paul Fischer Collection.

FIGURE 1.3 A photograph of the RAF's Crossley armoured cars in northern Iraq in the early
1930s; the RAF roundel (the bull's eye) on the side of the vehicle confirms this.
Copyright © Paul Fischer Collection.

Paul's parents knew each other from their youth. His mother, Nell
Clayton, was from the picturesque village of Farnsfield in Nottinghamshire,
near Sherwood Forest (of Robin Hood fame). His father grew up in the town
of Ilkestone, Derbyshire, but had moved to stay with relatives in Farnsfield
following the death of his mother from the Spanish Flu towards the end of
the First World War, when he was 18 or 19 years old.[2]

Nell Clayton trained as a district nurse at Nottingham General

---

[2] The impact of this pandemic, which began in 1918 in Spain during the First World
War, is appreciated more than ever in 2020–2022 with the Covid-19 pandemic. The
death toll from the Spanish Flu was 228,000 in Britain and over 50 million
worldwide.

Hospital and would travel around by bicycle as she did her rounds in the community, mainly in Derby. Albert had been serving in the RAF for a decade, mostly abroad, when Paul's parents decided to get married on 27 March 1937. This was one year before his father was due to come out of the RAF.[3] In that final year, he was stationed at RAF Upper Heyford, Oxfordshire, and they rented a house in Steeple Aston, near to Duns Tew, in the same county. Within the year, they moved to a rented property in Headington, Oxford, and their first child, Tony (John Antony), was born on 28 January 1938.

This return to civilian life did not last long unfortunately. In 1939, due to the onset of the Second World War, Albert was recalled into the RAF and was posted to RAF Jurby on the Isle of Man and, unusually, was able to take the whole family with him. This meant that as the war progressed, the family increased in size, with both Paul and his younger brother, Collis, born on the Isle of Man – in Ballamoar House, village of Ballaugh, near to RAF Jurby: Paul was born on 20 August 1941 and Collis on 4 August 1942.

At the end of the war, in 1946, his parents, now with their three sons, moved back to their house in Headington, Oxford, which they had managed to let during their absence. Headington today is almost a 'suburb' of the expanding city of Oxford but at that time it was a small village.

Another resident of Headington was the writer Clive Staples Lewis (1889–1964), who lived at The Kilns, at the foot of Shotover Country Park. The Kilns had been bought in 1930 by C.S. Lewis, his brother Major W.H. Lewis ('Warnie') and Mrs Jane King Moore, known affectionately as 'Minto'. Mrs Moore was the mother of his roommate, Edward Francis Moore, at Keble College, Oxford, who had been killed during the First World War (1914–1918).[4] Lewis fulfilled the promise they

---

[3] Paul and Joy got married on exactly the same date exactly thirty years later.

[4] Keble College was being used for army recruitment when C.S. Lewis joined the University Officers' Training Corps during the First World War. Lewis's college, however, was University College, University of Oxford; later he held an academic position at Magdalen College, University of Oxford, from 1925 to 1954.

had made to look after each other's family should anything happen to either of them; C.S. Lewis took care of Moore's mother, adopting her as 'family'. The Kilns was a short distance from Paul's family home, and his mother, who was a state-registered nurse, worked for C.S. Lewis at The Kilns, taking care of the by then elderly Mrs Moore.

The Kilns was a smallholding with red-brick outbuildings surrounding a courtyard, and its extensive grounds included a large orchard, a lake and woods.[5] Those woods provided inspiration for C.S. Lewis's *The Lion, the Witch and the Wardrobe* (1950) and were also Paul and his brothers' playground as young children. They were not the first children to enjoy the surrounds of The Kilns: during the Second World War, when many children were evacuated from London to avoid the bombs – just as in *The Lion, the Witch and the Wardrobe* – the Lewises took in evacuees. Oxford was considered 'safe'; it was not bombed during the war, as there was an agreement between Germany and Britain not to bomb university cities – despite Spitfire parts being built in Oxford.

In the summer months, during the school holidays, Paul and his younger brother, Collis, would accompany their mother to The Kilns and, while she worked, they were allowed to play freely in the woods and the outbuildings. They would often encounter C.S. Lewis and his brother, who were always kind. There was, however, one not-so-happy encounter, which remains permanently engraved on Paul's memory. Chickens were also allowed to roam freely in the courtyard of The Kilns, and in the panic of being chased by Paul, one died! Naturally, Paul's mother was distressed and embarrassed by this. When she went to Mr Lewis to inform him of what had happened, he said he wanted to see Paul, who would have to 'face the music'. Aged 7, Paul did not fully understand what was meant by this, but did as he was told. He knocked at the door of the house and went inside. There, he was given a military-style, stiff

---

[5] The lake behind The Kilns was manmade; it was a flooded clay pit, from which the clay had been extracted for the former brickworks to create the red bricks used to build most of the houses in the area. These had been built in around 1920, so they were all relatively new.

talking to, coincidentally while standing in front of an upright piano. Paul, in his innocence, assumed this was what was meant by having to 'facing the music'!

Mrs Moore died on 12 January 1951 and, thus, Paul's mother returned to full-time nursing at The Slade Hospital, Oxford. Remarkably, her children were still allowed to visit The Kilns and play and swim in the lake. Decades later, when the biographical film *Shadowlands* (1993), about C.S. Lewis's time with his wife, Joy Davidman, was made, Paul was pleased to see that the gardener, Fred Paxford, whom he remembered from his childhood, appeared momentarily in the film.[6]

As an engineer, after leaving the RAF Paul's father found work easily in industry working for a private company. The post-war period, however, was a difficult time and it took many years for the country to recover. Paul was unaware of the level of difficulties, both because of his childhood innocence and being protected by his parents. His mother was an excellent cook and they never seemed to lack anything, even during the war.

Another death brought great change: the death of King George VI on 6 February 1952; his daughter, Elizabeth, succeeded him to the throne. Queen Elizabeth II's coronation ceremony was held one year later on 2 June 1953. This was the first time a coronation was being televised. Like so many Britons, the Fishers bought a television set a few months before the coronation. On Coronation Day, church bells rang for hours in celebration throughout Oxford. Paul, however, was not at home with his parents; instead, he was away with the Boy Scouts on what was called a 'Coronation Camp'.

They camped near the beautiful River Evenlode in the village of North Leigh, with extensive woods on the opposite riverbank. As it was late spring, they were woken at 4 am by the magical sound of the birds' morning chorus. The range of bird species – including water fowl – such

---

[6] The film *Shadowlands* (1993) was directed by Richard Attenborough, with Anthony Hopkins as C.S. Lewis and Debra Winger as Joy Davidman.

as the baritone-ranged moorhens, coots and ducks combined with the higher-pitched, sweeter-toned woodland birds and the dissonant cry of the pheasants, all contributed to this chorus, creating an enduring full orchestral experience, which Paul still remembers in all its fine detail.

Once up and about, a few boys would walk to the nearby farm to collect 'very' fresh milk, which they would carry back in a churn. The farmer, whose cows provided the milk, allowed the boys the freedom to roam on his land. As well as enjoying swimming and canoeing in the river, this also gave them access to a Roman villa in the adjoining field to their camp, where they could examine the beautiful and detailed Roman mosaics, which they had studied at school; this was Paul's introduction to living history.[7]

In the wintertime there was also fun to be had indoors and the large screens of the cinemas in those days brought escape and pleasure to all. When Paul was only 9 years old, he saw the film *Scott of the Antarctic* (1948) at the cinema in Headington. Robert Falcon Scott (1868–1912) was a Royal Navy officer who led two expeditions to the Antarctic, the second of which – the Terra Nova Expedition – had the added drama of becoming an international race to be the first to reach the South Pole; they arrived on 12 January 1912, but the Norwegian explorer, Roald Amundsen, had pitched the Norwegian flag there on 14 December 1911 and had lived to tell the tale. Sadly, Scott and his remaining three colleagues died on their return journey.

The music as well as the drama of the film left an indelible impression on Paul; the score was written by Ralph Vaughan Williams and Paul can still remember its details vividly to this day. He realised how important music was for expressing the drama of life; it was extremely haunting for a mere 9-year-old – almost frightening – as the intrepid, and ultimately doomed, explorers faced the harshness of the Antarctic blizzards.

Paul felt a strong connection with explorers and was hungry for more

---

[7] There are a number of surviving Roman villas in the Cotswolds and, even in Chipping Norton, Roman artefacts are occasionally uncovered.

knowledge. When he was 13 years old, he was excited to hear that the British Army officer, Colonel John Hunt, who had led the first successful ascent of Mount Everest by the British expedition in 1953, was to give a lecture in the centre of Oxford. It was that expedition in which Edmund Hillary and Tenzing Norgay reached the summit of Mount Everest – the world's highest peak – on 29 May 1953.[8] Paul went to the lecture straight from school on his own. It was as exciting as he had anticipated, as it was illustrated with film footage shot during the expedition, and he felt honoured to be in the presence of such a heroic figure.[9]

At home Paul's father often spoke of T.E. Lawrence – 'Lawrence of Arabia' – who grew up and was educated in Oxford. When Paul's brother was given T.E. Lawrence's *The Seven Pillars of Wisdom* as a prize in school, Paul was curious and attempted to read it, wanting to know more about this heroic figure.[10] Lawrence was a national hero in those days. Coincidentally, Paul's father had served in the Royal Air Force before the war, at the same time as Lawrence's service as Aircraftsman Shaw and he

---

[8] In fact, the news that Edmund Hillary and Tenzing Norgay had made it to the summit of Mount Everest arrived on Coronation Day, 2 June 1953. The Queen presented the fourteen members of the expedition with special-edition Coronation medals with the extra wording 'Mount Everest Expedition'.

[9] The beginning of the twentieth century was the 'Heroic Age of Antarctic Exploration' and the Antarctic explorer Ernest Shackleton (1874–1922), who led three British expeditions to the Antarctic, is another of Paul's heroes, particularly after reading Margery and James Fisher's book *Shackleton* (1957). James Fisher (not related to Paul) was an ornithologist, and he and Sir Peter Scott, the son of Robert Falcon Scott, were both artists. Together they produced many television programmes on wildlife during the 1950s and early 1960s, which Paul and his family watched avidly. Sir Peter Scott set up the Wildlife and Wetland Trust at Slimbridge in Gloucestershire; it opened in November 1946, just after the end of the Second World War.

[10] It remains a special book for Paul, so much so that he bought himself a first edition of Lawrence's *The Seven Pillars of Wisdom* from a local bookshop – at some expense. T.E. Lawrence was commonly referred to as 'Lawrence of Arabia' after the end of the First World War because of the close relationship he had forged with the tribespeople and his knowledge of their customs and the land and tribes. It was a title that later haunted him, as he felt he had betrayed those who had trusted him, without any such intention. Even today the repercussions of this continue to impact life in the Middle East.

often spoke of Lawrence's time in the RAF and his daring exploits.[11] Paul's father and Lawrence had both served on North-West Frontier in India at roughly the same time, although they were not at the same RAF station.[12]

There are particular aspects of Lawrence's life that resonate with Paul for their connections with his own. Lawrence lived in a little woodman's cottage called Clouds Hill near Bovington in Dorset, purchased for him by a group of friends, including Winston Churchill. The fact that Paul had spent some of his service life at Bovington and Lulworth Gunnery School tank training and that the Winston Churchill Trust had become an important part of his life later has added further resonance to those connections.[13]

Paul's mother belonged to a book club, and as C.S. Lewis had been her employer when his *Surprised by Joy* was published in 1955, it was on the book club's reading list. She then passed the book on to Paul, who was extremely curious and wanted to learn more about the man he had sometimes met. This autobiographical work, where Lewis discusses both his conversion to a belief in God as well as his experience of 'joy', also includes the fine details of his life as a young boy. Paul delighted in the

---

[11] T.E. Lawrence was a friend of George Bernard Shaw and, hence, adopted his name for the RAF. Lawrence's first application to the RAF as Shaw was refused on the grounds that he was not using his real name. However, on a second application, again using the name Shaw, he was allowed to join. Robert Graves also visited him at his home at Clouds Hill.

[12] T. E. Lawrence ('Lawrence of Arabia') was stationed in India as well, but not in Kohat; he was in Kurachi and Miramshah. Lawrence was there from 1926 to 1928, which was about the same time Paul's father was there. In the early 1920s, T. E. Lawrence had joined the RAF as an ordinary aircraftsman rather than an officer (as he had been in the army); he joined not using his own name but as Aircraftsman Shaw. Lawrence was a very private person and didn't enjoy the hero status he had achieved after returning from the Middle East.

[13] The details of Lawrence's tragic death remain clearly in Paul's mind to this day. Sadly, soon after leaving the RAF in 1935, Lawrence was killed in a motorbike accident when returning to Clouds Hill. On 19 May he was riding on one of his Brough Superior motorcycles, which had been named Boanerges, an Arabic word meaning 'Son of Thunder'. He was only 46 years old.

colourful stories of Lewis and his brother being severely reprimanded as children by their father, thinking of his own experience, described earlier, of having to 'face the music'.

There was always music at home. Paul's love of music was something he shared with his elder brother, Tony, who had received piano and clarinet lessons and enjoyed playing music. Paul also had piano lessons, but after breaking a finger in an unfortunate accident with a door jam, he used this as an excuse to stop lessons, as he had become more interested in woodwind instruments. His brother taught him to play the clarinet and Paul occasionally sat in for some playing experience with his brother's jazz band, The Dixieland Foot Warmers. He and his brother would go together to the second-hand shops in Oxford and purchase old, simple system clarinets, which they would then restore. These exciting expeditions were also used to purchase wind-up gramophones, which many people were discarding at that time, being cheap enough to buy second hand with their limited pocket money.[14]

Paul was introduced to jazz through the records they bought to accompany these wind-up gramophones, particularly those of pre-war jazz and 'swing' music that were available on the old shellac, 78rpm discs, and to which Paul and his brother would play along.

At school he was often pulled up for daydreaming and staring out of the window, except in the subjects he enjoyed, such as history, music and art. As Paul says, usually you like a subject when you like the teacher. The music master was a particularly colourful character and a nurturing and inspiring teacher. Mr Babb had four children of his own, whom he would deliver to school each morning on his tandem bicycle with an accommodating sidecar before arriving at his own school to teach; his 'regular' tandem bicycle was powered by pedal with a 49cc power pack driving the front wheel, much to the amusement of his pupils.

---

[14] This gives some idea of the inventiveness of their childhood activities. Paul's brother Tony even built a fully functioning television camera at home. He later became a lecturer in electronics at Victoria University, Wellington, New Zealand.

One of his most memorable music classes was a pre-Christmas rehearsal of carols for the end-of-year concert. Mr Babb was at the piano and Paul and his fellow pupils were playing on their Dolmetsch recorders. As Paul was already beginning to enjoy traditional and mid-Atlantic jazz, he couldn't resist swinging the rhythm. Mr Babb became aware of this and ordered him to go and stand by the piano. Paul prepared for a reprimand. He was greatly surprised when Mr Babb continued on the piano but then started swinging the rhythm also!

Mr Babb wanted to know why Paul was playing with a swing rhythm and he confessed that he had a collection of pre-war jazz records at home. Mr Babb asked him to bring some into school. Paul brought in a 12-inch LP of Paul Whiteman and His Concert Orchestra playing *Slaughter on Tenth Avenue* – which wasn't jazz as such, but he was playing in a swing rhythm; he also took in his *42nd Street* LP.

A 78rpm of Louis Armstrong playing *Ain't Misbehaving* was a recording from that jazz age Paul loved and still has in his collection. He even bought a C clarinet at that time because the C clarinet simple system was mostly used by pre-war American jazz musicians. Paul still plays clarinet occasionally, as well as what he regards as his personal 'theme' tune, *Ain't Misbehaving*.

It was in the spring term of 1956 – Paul's final term at Wheatley School – that the music master, Jeffrey Babb, asked his class whether there would be anyone interested in apprenticing to become a harpsichord maker. Mr Babb had made an attempt to introduce them to the sound of a harpsichord already – one day he stuck drawing pins in the hammers of the school piano and exclaimed, 'That's the sound of a harpsichord!' The resulting sound may well have tallied with the British conductor Sir Thomas Beecham's assessment of a harpsichord, that it 'sounded like two skeletons copulating on a tin roof in a thunderstorm' – a comment typical of his famous acerbic wit. Elaborating on his question, Mr Babb went on to describe what a real harpsichord was. Paul put his hand up enthusiastically: 'Yes, sir. Please, sir. Me!' In fact, Paul was the only one to have shown interest.

Mr Babb was a friend of the renowned harpsichord maker, Robert Goble, who lived and worked at Greatstones, Headington, not far from Paul's family home. And so began a new chapter in Paul Fischer's life.

FIGURE 1.4 Mr Jeffrey Babb.
Photograph by Emrys Babb. Reproduced with permission.[15]

---

[15] Jeffery Babb's dynamism continued for many years; he had been Head of Music at Wheatley School, Oxford, in 1951–1962 and then moved to Wintringham School, Yorkshire, in 1962–1988. He conducted the Grimsby, Cleethorpes and District Youth Orchestra for forty years, the Grimsby Bach Choir for twenty-two years and the Youth Music Weeks from 1972 to 2003. At the celebration for his ninetieth birthday in January 2016 he conducted the concert at St Mary's Church, near his home in Hay-on-Wye. Jeffery Babb died in April 2020 at the age of 94.

CHAPTER 2

An Introduction to Early Music:

Harpsichord Apprenticeship at Goble's

Successful people, looking back to their early years, so often cite the name of a specific teacher who had a pivotal influence on their life's direction. In Paul's case, this would be his music master, Mr Jeffery Babb, who was the head of music at Wheatley School, Oxford. Paul is in good company among the long list of musicians and artists whom Mr Babb inspired and influenced.

When Mr Babb had arranged for him to attend an interview with Robert Goble, Paul, just under 15 years old, had no idea of the wealth of music history, both in instrument making and performing, that was connected to Robert Goble (1903–1991) and his wife Elizabeth Goble (1907–1981). The pioneering harpsichord maker Robert Goble was a friend of the music master, and their home and workshop at Greatstones was only half a mile from Paul's family home. He was lucky enough to have fallen into the nest of two very important figures in the Early Music world.

At his interview, Paul was taken through the large house and associated rooms, with Robert explaining the purpose of each room and how the business functioned. As well as building instruments, Robert Goble retained some of them for hire, so there was a room for the completed instruments where Paul could appreciate the artistry of the maker. The extensive house also provided a room for the decoration of instruments. In another room were Elizabeth Goble's own instruments – a harpsichord, spinet and a viola de gamba – all of which she played. The workshop proper was in a separate building very close to the house.

FIGURE 2.1 Greatstones – a view from the front lawn, circa 1957.
Photograph by Paul Fischer.

Robert Goble was the son of Harriet and John Goble. John was a wheelwright and blacksmith from the village of Thursley, Surrey, southern England. Robert, who had learnt the basic skills of woodwork and joinery from his father, had a natural talent for understanding the way things worked and was a skilled craftsman from a young age. What is more, he had great enthusiasm for restoring broken objects; he repaired a broken violin that had been at home and, when he'd finished, took lessons on that very same instrument. Like his father, Robert would turn his hand to any task he was presented with, and both of them had reputations in Thursley for their skills and craftsmanship but Robert also had abilities in playing music.

During the First World War (1914–1918), when Robert was 14 years old, the musician, researcher and instrument maker Arnold Dolmetsch and his family rented a small house in Thursley to escape from the Zeppelin air raids in London. In an interview many years later with Robert's son, Andrea Goble, he speaks of his father's upbringing in a world where 'country craftsmanship' was valued. With Robert's own father's experience and workmanship, he helped Arnold Dolmetsch find the appropriate wood he needed for the clavichords and spinets he was creating.

Arnold Dolmetsch (1858–1940) was born in France but moved to London in the 1880s, when he decided to devote his life to Early Music, not only as a musician and scholar but also as a talented instrument maker, building copies of historical instruments such as viols, lutes, recorders and a range of keyboard instruments, and then playing, performing and teaching all of these instruments.[16] The range of his abilities was phenomenal but what has made his legacy so inextricably tied to the revival of Early Music in the modern age was his generosity of spirit in sharing his knowledge. Arnold Dolmetsch had received his own training at Maison Dolmetsch-Guillouard, his parents' piano, organ and harmonium manufactory in Le Mans, France.

After a short period spent living in Thursley, the Dolmetsch family – Arnold, his wife, Mabel,[17] and their four children – moved to their own permanent home called Jesses in nearby Haslemere, Surrey, where they also established an instrument-making workshop. A few years later, in 1925, Robert Goble joined Dolmetsch's workshop. He first worked on wooden recorders; using a lathe, he would 'turn' blanks of exotic woods into the elegant form of a recorder, but the 'voicing' – the placement of the holes for an accurate pitch – remained the preserve of Arnold Dolmetsch.

The Dolmetsches used to play the whole 'family' of recorders in ensemble and they built the full range of instruments for their consorts of

---

[16] When he moved to London, Dolmetsch was very involved in the cultural life of city and among his friends and acquaintances were the artist and designer William Morris (1834–1896) and the writers George Bernard Shaw (1856–1950), W.B. Yeats (1865–1939), Ezra Pound (1885–1972) and George Moore (1852–1933), whose novel *Evelyn Innes* (1898) celebrates Dolmetsch's life and work in lightly veiled fiction.

[17] Mabel Dolmetsch (neé Johnston) (1874–1963) was a bass viol player and was his third wife; their children were Cécile, Nathalie, Rudolph and Carl.

recorders. In concert programmes dating from this period, Robert Goble regularly appears as part of the recorder consort, alongside Arnold Dolmetsch's sons, Rudolph and Carl, with Reginald Brown and Philip Cottrell.

In 1925, the same year Robert Goble began working for Dolmetsch, Arnold Dolmetsch organised the first Haslemere Festival, where all aspects of Early Music making were enjoyed, including historic dances in period costume. The Dolmetsch Foundation: An International Society for Early Music and Instruments was established in 1928.

The Dolmetsches in Haslemere created a centre of music and related activities, particularly for the Early Music movement. In the 1920s the gatherings of Early Music specialists might include Elizabeth Brown, Marco Pallis, Richard Nicholson, Tom and Diana Poulton, and Robert Donington and his sister, Margaret, among many others.[18]

The lutenist and scholar Diana Poulton also studied with Arnold Dolmetsch, but on the lute.[19] There was a constant flow of visitors to Haslemere by students and scholars, some settling there for longer periods. The pianist Elizabeth Brown, from Liverpool, who had been a student of Arnold Dolmetsch's since 1922, both on the harpsichord and the viol, was awarded a Dolmetsch music scholarship in 1928 to continue her studies with him in Haslemere.

Elizabeth Brown and Robert Goble became acquainted there and married in 1930. Robert continued to work for Dolmetsch until 1937, when he left to set up his own workshop, initially in Haslemere. One of the first harpsichords Robert Goble built was for his wife – naturally, it

[18] Robert Donington's book, *The Interpretation of the Music of the XVIIth and XVIIIth Centuries* (Novello) was published as early as 1915 and remains an important reference text. Margaret Donington later became Margaret Powell and lived in Oxford – on Kiln Lane – just a few doors away from the Gobles at the time of Paul's apprenticeship at Goble's. Paul remembers that she played a Goble harpsichord.

[19] For more on Diana Poulton's life and work, see Diana Poulton's *John Dowland* (London: Faber and Faber, 1982), as well as the biography by Thea Abbott, *Diana Poulton: The Lady with the Lute* (Norwich: Smokehouse Press, 2014), where she also writes about Arnold Dolmetsch and his circle of friends.

was made in the Dolmetsch style. By this time, Elizabeth, who had learnt to decorate soundboards from Mabel Dolmetsch, was also involved. After a decade of having their home and workshop in Haslemere, and with the end of the Second World War, they decided that a move away from Haslemere would provide a fresh start, which would benefit them all.

In 1947 they moved with their two sons, Andrea and Paul, to the very large, 1920s red-brick house called Greatstones in Headington, Oxford. The move had the successful outcome they had hoped for and the order book was filling up – so much so that the Gobles needed to employ two professional woodworkers, who were trained by Robert to create the cases for the instruments. Andrea was now nearing the end of his schooling and was expected to join the company. Once this happened, the woodworkers left.[20] It was at this point that Paul Fischer was being interviewed.

At the end of Paul's interview and tour of the workshop at Greatstones, it was decided there and then – simply and without psychometric tests, face to face, a boy and a master, both understanding perfectly what was required and what each could offer and hope for – that Paul would take on a five-year apprenticeship commitment. Robert Goble drew up the appropriate Apprenticeship Indenture, all written in the legal language of the time, with a start date of 26 August 1956, just a few days after Paul's fifteenth birthday (Figure 2.2).

Despite his young age, Paul made a clear decision at that point to train as an instrument maker, which meant foregoing further study at college. Academically, Paul was capable of the demands of further education but this apprenticeship offered an exciting opportunity to fulfil another possible plan for the future that had been on his mind. At school some of his friends had been discussing the option of studying at Rycotewood College, Thame, Oxfordshire. This was a much-admired college that was

---

[20] For the first few years at Greatstones they continued to make recorders as well as keyboard instruments, but then the decision was made to concentrate on creating early keyboard instruments. Andrea Goble, from a conversation with Thérèse Wassily Saba, 25 February 2021.

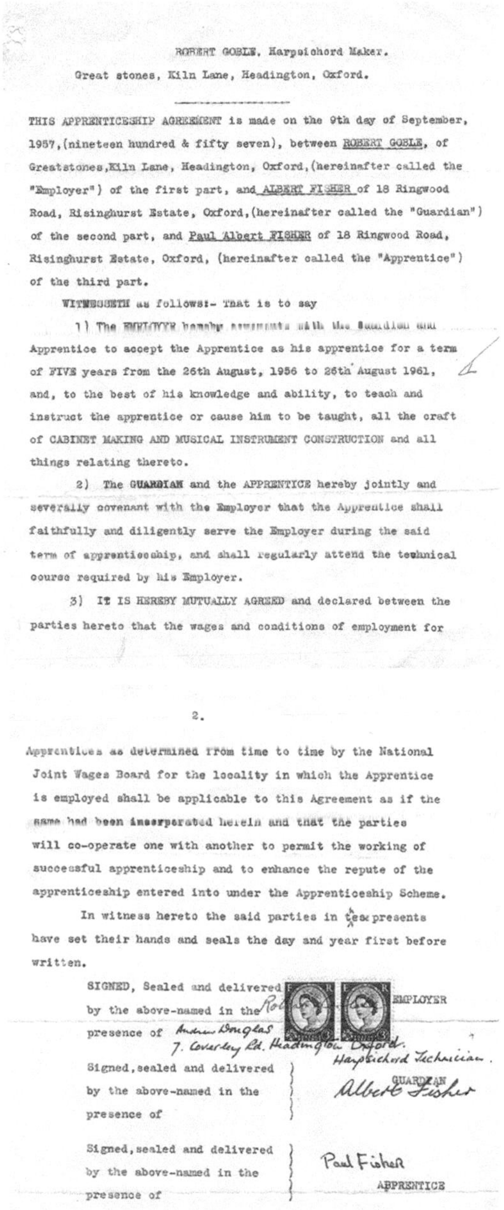

ROBERT GOBLE, Harpsichord Maker.

Great stones, Kiln Lane, Headington, Oxford.

THIS APPRENTICESHIP AGREEMENT is made on the 9th day of September, 1957, (nineteen hundred & fifty seven), between ROBERT GOBLE, of Greatstones, Kiln Lane, Headington, Oxford, (hereinafter called the "Employer") of the first part, and ALBERT FISHER of 18 Ringwood Road, Risinghurst Estate, Oxford, (hereinafter called the "Guardian") of the second part, and Paul Albert FISHER of 18 Ringwood Road, Risinghurst Estate, Oxford, (hereinafter called the "Apprentice") of the third part.

WITNESSETH as follows:- That is to say

1) The EMPLOYER hereby covenants with the Guardian and Apprentice to accept the Apprentice as his apprentice for a term of FIVE years from the 26th August, 1956 to 26th August 1961, and, to the best of his knowledge and ability, to teach and instruct the apprentice or cause him to be taught, all the craft of CABINET MAKING AND MUSICAL INSTRUMENT CONSTRUCTION and all things relating thereto.

2) The GUARDIAN and the APPRENTICE hereby jointly and severally covenant with the Employer that the Apprentice shall faithfully and diligently serve the Employer during the said term of apprenticeship, and shall regularly attend the technical course required by his Employer.

3) IT IS HEREBY MUTUALLY AGREED and declared between the parties hereto that the wages and conditions of employment for

2.

Apprentices as determined from time to time by the National Joint Wages Board for the locality in which the Apprentice is employed shall be applicable to this Agreement as if the same had been incorporated herein and that the parties will co-operate one with another to permit the working of successful apprenticeship and to enhance the repute of the apprenticeship entered into under the Apprenticeship Scheme.

In witness hereto the said parties in these presents have set their hands and seals the day and year first before written.

SIGNED, Sealed and delivered
by the above-named in the
presence of Andrew Douglas
7. Coverley Rd. Headington Oxford.
Harpsichord Technician.

EMPLOYER

Signed, sealed and delivered
by the above-named in the
presence of

GUARDIAN
Albert Fisher

Signed, sealed and delivered
by the above-named in the
presence of

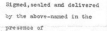

Paul Fisher
APPRENTICE

FIGURE 2.2 Paul Fischer's indenture with Robert Goble, 1956.
© Paul Fischer Collection.

17

producing very fine craftsmen in design and cabinetmaking. Some of Paul's school friends chose that option and became excellent craftsmen in their own right. The impact of visiting the Goble workshop was immediate for Paul; he knew that was exactly what he wanted. He had been lucky enough to be in the right place at the right time.

When the first day of Paul's apprenticeship with Robert Goble arrived, Paul walked briskly to Greatstones – just one month after his interview – and began on his path towards becoming an instrument maker. The house was built in an imposing nineteenth-century style but set in the gentle, wooded lower slopes of Shotover Country Park, with sweeping lawns, an orchard and a lake (Figure 2.1). It seemed a most unlikely setting for industry, but the space it offered was ideal for the workshop. Entering through the gates, Paul walked onto the circular, wide, gravel drive, with its central pond and fountain, and arrived directly at the workshop door.

The atmosphere was immediately welcoming. He was greeted by Robert Goble, who introduced him to his son Andrea and one other apprentice, Alan Almond. Alan was their first apprentice and was already two years into his apprenticeship; Paul was the second apprentice they had taken on.

Traditionally, one of the first tasks of apprentices, after having acquired the rudimentary woodworking skills, was to make themselves a tool chest, and Goble's approach was built on the best aspects of tradition in craftsmanship. The inside of these chests were very beautifully made, usually fashioned in mahogany and sometimes with decorative inlay; they had many different-sized drawers and compartments for the many and various specialised woodworking tools required for instrument making, some of which can be very small. While the tool chest could be very beautiful on the inside, on the outside it would be just painted black, as it needed to be stored alongside the workbench and would get knocked about considerably.

The setting was rural, peaceful and, most importantly, calm. There were no noisy machines; most of the work was done by hand and with heart. The workshop benches were made of beech, a very hard wood, in the style of traditional cabinet-makers' benches. They were set against the walls close to small windows, so that they could take advantage of the daylight. Paul thought it was a little dark for a workshop where such finely detailed work was required. Each artisan had a dedicated bench – Paul and Alan had theirs alongside each other – and there were also central benches, which were used to support the near-finished harpsichords (Figure 2.3).

FIGURE 2.3. Picture of the Goble workshop during Paul's time there.
Photograph ©Paul Fischer.

The work day would begin at 7.45 am, and during the winter months, whoever arrived first would light the coke-burning stove in the workshop, as it would have become very cold overnight; this drop in temperature was not helped by the workshop's concrete floor.

When Paul first started, Robert or Andrea would teach him what was required until he developed sufficient skills to continue on his own; they would only supervise when necessary. They worked until the morning tea break at 11 am, when Robert and Andrea would retire to the house for their tea and Paul and Alan would remain in the workshop. In the winter months they delighted in taking their shoes off and placing their cold feet near to the coke stove.

Although by the time of Paul's apprenticeship at Goble's they were no longer making recorders, there were earlier examples of these handcrafted instruments on the shelves set between the beams above them. Paul often took down the tenor recorder, made of beautiful rosewood, and enjoyed the pleasure of playing a wooden recorder, having only played Bakelite Dolmetsch recorders before this.[21]

Surprisingly, the Goble workshop also included the company of Silver, a resident white pigeon, and a white cat called Shandy. Silver's contribution was his christening of each new instrument after his dawn sortie – but that was something to be discovered later!

There were many elements of an earlier age and time at the Goble workshop, which reflected the style and character of the Arts and Crafts movement. The movement was against the introduction of mechanised, factory-based manufacture of the Industrial Revolution, which resulted in the loss of skilled craftspeople. In Britain the movement took its name from the Arts and Crafts Exhibition Society, a group that was founded in London in 1887. The society's aim was to bring to prominence the work of decorative artists, who had not been given the opportunity to display their works in the way that painters and sculptors had. The movement was inspired by the writings of the architect and interior designer Augustus Pugin (1812–1852), the art critic John Ruskin (1819–1900), the work of the artist and designer William Morris (1834–1896), the architect and designer Charles Robert Ashbee (1863–1942), the architect, designer and painter Charles Rennie Mackintosh (1868–1928) and the British horticulturist, garden designer, craftswoman and writer Gertrude Jekyll (1843–1932), among many others. The revival of Early Music was an

---

[21] The first Dolmetsch mass-produced school recorders, in the 1940s, were made of Bakelite, which was a precursor to plastic. These were widely used throughout schools in Britain.

important interest of the Arts and Crafts movement and it was William Morris who encouraged Arnold Dolmetsch to build his first harpsichord.[22]

As Robert and Elizabeth Goble had their beginnings with Arnold Dolmetsch, they too followed in the approach of the Arts and Crafts movement. This was a philosophy Paul would come to understand and admire more in the future, even meeting another leading figure of that magical age, such as the furniture maker Edward Barnsley (1900–1987).

Although primarily a keyboard player, Elizabeth Goble later became a founding member with Marco Pallis, of the English Consort of Viols, in which she played the viola de gamba. Elizabeth regularly performed with the English Consort of Viols at major concert venues in London and elsewhere, on the BBC and on tour in America. At the same time, Elizabeth was also involved in Robert's instrument making, as she continued to decorate the soundboards of the keyboard instruments created at Greatstones. As a couple, there was a special atmosphere of mutual support and involvement in each other's activities.

Paul experienced this supportive spirit when Elizabeth Goble would visit the workshop; she was always genuinely interested in talking to the apprentices, asking them about themselves and listening with

FIGURE 2.4 Elizabeth Goble decorating the soundboard of a harpsichord.
This photograph was taken in 1975.
Reproduced with kind permission of the Goble family.

---

[22] William Morris lived at Kelmscott House. Almost a century after his death, Paul lectured to the craft teachers of Oxfordshire in the adjoining barn, developed as a lecture theatre and performance space at Kelmscott House.

interest to their replies.[23] This was in contrast to other visitors, such as the vicar, the Reverend Head, who was a close friend of the Gobles and the vicar at their local church, Holy Trinity, Headington Quarry, where Paul's family, the Gobles and C.S. Lewis and his brother all worshipped. When the Reverend Head visited, he would drive up in his black early 1950s Triumph Mayflower, a car noted for its distinctive body design with strong angular lines, which Paul thought was appropriate for 'a man of the cloth'. Despite being part of his parish, and Paul's brother Tony (Fisher Primus) singing in the choir, the vicar ignored Paul and the other apprentice. Holy Trinity was the High Church of England, and it was the choirmaster who referred to the children, not by their first names but by their birth number in the family (in Latin): Paul was Fisher Secundus.

At the start of his apprenticeship, Paul was trained to create the many fine components in wood and metal needed for the harpsichords. These were something like the internal workings of a long case 'grandfather' clock and much patience was required. It meant he had to sit at his bench for long stretches with intense concentration and patience to create these very delicate parts for the action of the harpsichords – some needing as many as four jacks for each key on the manual. Although this was a completely new experience for him, it was a world that Paul had stepped into and felt perfectly at ease in. As was common in the workshops of the Arts and Crafts period, craftsmen could and would turn their hands to work in both wood and metal, something Robert and Andrea were both skilled at; they were consummate all-rounders and these talents would be passed on to their apprentices. How lucky Paul was to be under their guidance and influence.

The apprentices had to buy their own tools, even though their pay was low – £1 19s. – so it took a long time to acquire the full kit, and in the

---

[23] Paul also recalls the visits of Elizabeth's brother, Philip Brown, who would bring in Banbury cakes for him and Alan. For more on the history of these famous Banbury cakes and the secret recipe handed down through the generations of the Brown family, see Brown's Original Banbury Cakes www.banburycakes.co.uk.

meantime they were allowed to borrow tools from Andrea.[24] The essentials would be a jack plane, a smoothing plane, a block plane and a bullnose plane; the block and bullnose planes were the smallest needed for harpsichords. Tools were often on Paul's Christmas list. He still has those first tools he used during his apprenticeship and they are in working order, though the working chisels have become considerably shortened through sharpening and numerous replacement blades have been purchased for the planes.

Sharpening tools were vital for their work. Robert Goble taught Paul how to sharpen his tools using carborundum or natural stone in various grades, then a final finish off with a leather strap, known as a strop, or on the palm of his hand. This is a technique he continues to use to this day – Robert taught him well. The resulting edge would be so sharp that it would glisten like chromium. Robert told him that the test of sharpness would be to run the tool up the back of your arm in one stroke and remove the hairs, as if you were using a razor. Once, commenting on the state of one of Paul's tools, Robert jokingly remarked, 'Your plane is so blunt, you could ride bare-assed to London on it!' It was a congenial atmosphere to work and learn in.

Paul refers to Shandy, the cat, as one of the 'permanent residents of the workshop'. Occasionally, while Paul worked, Shandy would run up his back and position himself around his neck like a white stole. Sometimes he would bring them a present: a mouse or bird, and once even a grass snake. The extensive grounds of Greatstones provided Shandy with ideal hunting grounds and, emboldened by the choice of prey, he one day attempted to face down a weasel, a contest he was not going to win, despite the discrepancy in size. On this occasion, the White Knight (Shandy) could only show us a bloody nose.

---

[24] Of course, this pay of £1 19 shillings was standard practice considering the apprentices were being taught. In the nineteenth century apprentices were expected to sleep under their workbenches and were provided with food by their masters. At times, Paul jokingly describes his apprenticeship as being of an earlier century; however, it was not so Dickensian!

FIGURE 2.5 Paul Fischer at 17, working on a wing-shaped spinet with Andrea Goble.
Photograph from *The Oxford Times.*

The circle of Early Music performers and craftsmen was small, as was the specialised nature of skills required, so Andrew Douglas, who was also a Dolmetsch man and of Robert Goble's generation, came to work for Robert. Andrew worked in a completely separate room – the Bee Room – which was used for the stringing, voicing and tuning of the instruments; it had been used by Robert's eldest son, Andrea, for bee-keeping work, hence the name. Andrew was a voicer and tuner, a job entailing fine adjustment of the action, stringing the instrument and tuning, as Paul explains:

Voicing a harpsichord is done by cutting or scraping at the underside of the quills that pluck the strings until you get the volume, resistance and playability preferred. The goal is to make each note sound as wonderful as possible by getting each of the jacks to pluck the strings with the same resistance, so that the instrument sounds its best consistently but not uniformly, because what works for a bass string may not be suitable for a high-pitch one. Voicing is a mixture of art and science.

FIGURE 2.6 Robert and Andrea Goble in the workshop at Greatstones in 1949. Reproduced with kind permission of the Goble family.

There were only three makers in the large and spacious workshop where Paul worked. Robert Goble was mostly working in the Bee Room or in his office but would visit the workshop in order to tackle some of the more unusual jobs, such as winding the strings. This entailed putting a loop on each end of the steel strings and, using his own invention, winding on a cover of phosphor bronze wire. It was a delight to watch! On other occasions, he would make an engineering part for the complicated seven-pedal system, plus half stops. The pedals could be momentarily employed or, by pushing down and towards the right, the pedal could be locked into that position, thus offering fourteen different tonal options. Some of the Goble range of harpsichords offered effects such as a lute stop, with a raven's quill plucking the string near the tuning pin, or a harp stop, which would have a leather plectrum resembling the stroke of the ball of a finger on the string, or the 16-foot stop, which was achieved through putting a thicker winding on the strings (as the 16-foot string length was not possible).

These were modern developments of the Dolmetsch-style keyboard instruments, but such pedal systems are now rarely seen in the modern-day making of early replica keyboard instruments, as the trend is for making close copies of extant instruments. However, those instruments created by Robert Goble are still valued today. As the repertoire for the harpsichord in the twentieth and twenty-first century has expanded to include many contemporary compositions, so also has the use of the modern style of harpsichord. These are often referred to as 'revival' harpsichords, with pedals offering the performer a quick way to change the register of the instrument; they have given the harpsichord an alternate contemporary life to the Early Music approach.

As these instruments of the first half of the twentieth century were heavily strung and required a more robust carcass, tonal considerations were sacrificed for stability and reliability. These harpsichords had become something of a hybrid of the piano, with the few makers creating instruments to meet twentieth-century conditions. These included regular air transportation, air-conditioning and central heating, which could all put great stress on the light, wooden and delicate structures. Thus, there was a need to make stronger carcasses using materials that were less affected by these new conditions.

The return of the BBC's own Goble instrument for attention was a clear example of the rough treatment a beautiful instrument could suffer. The damage was usually in the form of smashed corners and broken mouldings. On one occasion, the base of every leg required the addition of a robust walnut spade foot, made to withstand the manhandling when moved around the studios.

Other changes were taking place, as many players had come from the piano and required an instrument with a similar touch to that of the piano. So lead weights were added to the keys and jacks (affecting the touch to the keys). Refinements were also made to the action, with greater facility for fine adjustment. The jacks and the addition of seven pedals with the same fine adjustment created practical benefits but also created instruments far removed from the original harpsichords that were their forebears. The Goble jack of the 1940s and 1950s did not follow the traditional jack; Goble jacks had a patented adjustment facility for the fine regulation of damper, tongue and jack height. This was an example of Robert Goble's capacity and interest in simplifying the process of voicing a harpsichord.

At that time, jacks were made of pearwood, with a tongue of holly and a hogs' bristle spring, leather plectra or sometimes ravens' quills. Raven quill plectra were obtained through the Sergeant at Arms at the Tower of London, as ravens have a historically special status there. From the very start, Paul was involved in the making of these innovative jacks.

After discovering what the 'action' of an instrument was referring to, with all the attendant fiddly details, Paul moved on to the larger stuff – the carcass. Eight-feet long and four-feet wide, it was made from iroko, beech, chestnut and spruce, all put together with equally large joints: mortice and tenons and dovetails. The same skill was required on the larger-scaled work on the carcass, even though many of the dovetails would be hidden beneath an exquisite rippled English walnut veneer, all applied in the traditional way with veneering hammers and a flat iron.

FIGURE 2.7 A Goble harpsichord from 1958, which Paul worked on.

Paul also learnt to deal with more exotic materials, such as ivory, leather, ravens' quills, hogs' bristle and tropical woods, including iroko, ebony, rosewood and African blackwood, as well as native woods, such as oak, beech, chestnut and spruce. The wood used for making harpsichords during the first half of the twentieth century did not necessarily follow those used in the originals of the seventeenth and eighteenth centuries. By the mid twentieth century, some woods and materials were becoming scarce, and it was therefore necessary to consider alternatives and, in the process, change the design from that of the seventeenth and eighteenth centuries. This attitude affected Paul's later work when looking for alternate woods for his guitars.

The most important considerations for the carcass are stability, lightness and acoustic response. The first is obvious. With the tension of so many strings pulling on a relatively light frame, the design is critical and can rightly be called 'engineering in wood', with the choice of woods being as important as the design itself. For instruments of the earlier period, the choices were interesting because of the fact that most harpsichords were highly decorated (usually with paintings) or veneered, and thus disguised the constructional woods beneath. This meant it was acceptable to use less-attractive but structurally and acoustically superior woods beneath in the knowledge that they would not be seen. Typically, poplar, spruce, sycamore and cypress were used for the carcass. Others, including holly, pear, beech and maple, came into their own when more durability, strength and stability were required. To gain the maximum benefit from these woods, careful selection and cutting was, and still is, a must, as is appropriate seasoning.

After five years, having completed his full apprenticeship, Alan Almond had to leave the Goble workshop to do his national service, which had been delayed by the obligation of his apprenticeship.[25] A few years later, in 1962, another apprentice joined the workshop, Milan Misina, who was a good craftsman and developed into a fine harpsichord

---

[25] By 1959 compulsory National Service had come to an end and, therefore, Paul was freed of this obligation.

maker. Milan had to make the 15-mile journey from Bicester each day by public transport and so would be the first to arrive; he would light the fire and let the pigeon, Silver, out for his early morning sortie. After that they would continue the previous day's tasks, which were usually devoted to making specific parts for the instruments, such as the carcass, the keyboards or the jacks, as well as veneering.

A large proportion of the work was done by hand. Some machines were used but these were mainly for the conversion of large planks into smaller, manageable dimensions; from then on, the skills of the cabinetmaker took over and again the work was done by hand.

One machine in the workshop that always amused Paul was the large pedal lathe, which was dated from 1875. It had a large cast-iron frame and an equally large cast-iron pedal wheel; the pedal wheel became redundant when Robert added an electric motor. Its other parts were beautifully made. The lathe, despite its age, produced very fine work. There were also very small machines used and these were mostly of Robert's own design and manufacture, such as the one used for winding strings, already mentioned, with a motor at one end and a free wheel at the other. It was simple but efficient!

The glue used was also traditional in character: Scotch animal glue was purchased in large slabs, much like toffee. This had to be smashed up into small pieces with a hammer and then soaked in water for several hours. When it became soft, it was placed in a container in a pan of water and heated up. Though ancient, it was a wonderful and flexible glue for instrument making. One downside was the need for it to be applied while it was hot; if it chilled, the joints became difficult to put together. This was a problem at Greatstones because during the winter months the old coke stove failed to warm the workshop enough until midday. The solution was to warm all the components in front of the stove so that the glue was not chilled by the coldness of the wood when applied. You had to work fast!

All the instruments were veneered by hand and the choice of wood varied according to the type of instrument being made. Harpsichords were nearly always veneered in exquisite rippled English walnut with inlaid line and banding, also in walnut. The smaller instruments – the wing-shaped spinet, clavichord and octavina – were also veneered in equally beautiful woods, including rosewood, cherry and satinwood – elegant and refined. These were instruments that could grace the drawing room of the grandest country house.

Paul would finish work at Goble's at 5.30 pm, but then complemented this already long day's work with further study at the Oxford College of Art and Technology in the evenings and on one full day each week (which meant working at Goble's each Saturday to compensate for this 'day off' for study). In the mid-1950s instrument-making courses did not exist, so the choice of study had to be a compromise, with the more technical elements left to Paul's other tutors, Robert and Andrea Goble. His choice was for cabinetmaking with technical drawing and wood technology – a three-year course reasonably closely related to instrument making. The combination of college and practical experience was perhaps not ideal, but it was the best that could be hoped for at the time. For one year, Paul studied at the College of Art in St Ebbes, Oxford, which Andrea Goble had also attended. Paul moved with the college to its new and hard-fought-for site in Headington, where he became one of its first students. The college – now named the Oxford College of Art and Technology – was so new that Paul's first lesson was spent unpacking the new equipment.

The Oxford School of Art in St Ebbes was an ever-evolving institution in its early history, which is reflected in its changes in name. It was part of the Oxford Schools of Technology, Art and Commerce spread over various sites throughout the city. Its first principal was John Henry Brookes, a passionate educator and disciple of the Arts and Crafts movement and later to give his name to the university, Oxford Brookes, now standing on the site of Paul's second alma mater. It would be another twenty-five years before instrument making became part of the curriculum at the London College of Furniture in 1972 – the first of its kind in the UK.

FIGURE 2.8 A Goble octavina from 1950.
Goble Family Collection. Reproduced with permission.

At Goble's, Paul was involved in the creation of a range of early keyboard instruments. Harpsichords, spinets, clavichords and octavinas were made as well. These are all plucked instruments, with the exception of the clavichord, where the string is hit by a metal 'tangent', giving a different sound, which is very quiet; but unlike the plucked keyboard instruments, the clavichord is capable of producing vibrato and variations in loudness not available to instruments in the harpsichord family.

This then was the rarefied world of Early Music instrument making in the mid-1950s, still in the early stages of its revival. The significant upturn in interest and performance of Early Music in the 1950s onwards is often referred to as the 'Revival' – which coincided with Paul's apprenticeship in instrument making.

By the end of the 1960s, a new wave of enthusiasm for Early Music performance and authenticity was gathering speed. Not only did the interpretation of the music have to be appropriate but also the details of the instruments used – that is, all instruments including plucked, bowed and blown. It was a fascinating and exciting time.

Although Paul was only just starting out as an apprentice instrument maker, he was actually working on instruments for some of the finest musicians of the day. Paul recalls many international performers arriving at the Gobles. When an instrument was required to be taken out for a concert performance, it would be all hands on deck on the drive as they all tried to lift these heavy but delicate instruments into the vehicle for transportation. If they weren't going a great distance, they were loaded onto the Goble's own Bedford Dormobile. The British harpsichordist George Malcolm was a great advocate for Goble's instruments. Other artists playing on Goble instruments included Millicent Silver, Ruth Dyson, John Francis and, of course, Thurston Dart. Leading music colleges and institutions purchased Goble instruments for their music departments, such as Nottingham University, the BBC, McGill University Montreal, Southampton University, and many others.

Paul was constantly surrounded by inspiring people while he was at Gobles. Living next door to Goble was a schoolteacher, Mr Richards, whom Paul remembers saying in a conversation, 'Read, read. I don't care what you read, but read!' Although Paul had already begun reading more broadly and his mother was a keen reader, the passion behind Mr Richards' advice left a strong impression on him. Apart from the books on Antarctic explorers and T. E. Lawrence, another figure who caught Paul's interest was Colonel Percy Harrison Fawcett – a British artillery officer and a cartographer who undertook many forays into the Amazon rainforest in the 1920s, until his mysterious disappearance on 29 May 1925; he was looking for Z, the lost city. This has been the subject of a recent film, *The Lost City of Z* (2016) by James Gray.

Paul enjoyed going to the university jazz club just off the High Street in Oxford, generally known as The High. They had two clubs: one for traditional jazz and the other for modern jazz. There he heard popular jazz musicians of the time, such as Humphrey Lyttelton, Terry Lightfoot, Chris Barber and Kenny Ball; they each had resident bands made up of local students. With his elder brother, he used to travel up to the jazz clubs in London as well, such as the Humphrey Lyttelton Club – a lot of the jazz clubs were named after the artists and there was a concentration of them around Denmark Street, near Tottenham Court Road.

Paul, now at the start of his twenties, found himself at another crossroads, trying to decide on his future life plans. His official apprenticeship and college studies were completed after five years but he had stayed on at Goble's for an extra thirteen months to give him adequate time for consideration of his future. They had been formative years but being in such a cosseted and limiting environment had done little for his social development and this needed to be addressed. And what to do about his lingering frustrations? Any opportunity for advancement was limited at Goble's, so steps had to be taken – big ones. As Paul explains:

> I'd completed my apprenticeship, and more. I had learnt a great deal and acquired a thorough grounding in instrument making but it had been gained in a nineteenth-century bubble, isolated within a closed society. I needed adventure, to get out into the wider world, and so I decided to join the British Army!

This solution, though seemingly drastic, he hoped would be short and character building all in one go. With the skills and qualifications of an instrument maker under his belt, he would be launching out on a new adventure. Robert Goble, like Paul's father, was a man of few words. There was little response when Paul made the announcement. We can only

FIGURE 2.9 A Goble clavichord from 1978.
Photograph by Paul Fischer.

FIGURE 2.10 This is a wing-shaped spinet by Robert Goble and Son from 1983. The instrument belongs to Rosalie Corn Wallis. Photograph by Paul Fischer.

imagine what his deeper thoughts were on this radical change of career direction by his apprentice.

Robert Goble and his son Andrea continued to make superb instruments for many years to come, responding to the developments in research and the changing preferences of the Early Music performers and approach to repertoire. Later, Andrea's son, Anthony Goble (1957–2000), joined the business, working with his father and

FIGURE 2.11 Greatstones in 2017, with Andrea Goble near the pond. Greatstones is very near to The Kilns, the home of C. S. Lewis. Photograph by Paul Fischer.

grandfather. Anthony was a talented musician and was taught by his grandmother Elizabeth to play both harpsichord and viola da gamba.

Although Paul had responded to the music master's question only by chance, and then only with cursory consideration of what it might mean to be involved in the unusual but fascinating profession of early instrument making, he has never regretted that decision. The early grounding in the skills and passion for the craft, and even the philosophy of the Arts and Crafts movement, would remain a constant part of his life.

CHAPTER 3

Paul Joins the Army:

11th Hussars (Prince Albert's Own)

At the age of 22, in 1963, Paul decided he needed to broaden his knowledge and horizons. Up until that time, his only experience of working had been as an apprentice in the workshop of the harpsichord maker Robert Goble.

In his schooldays he had played football and was also a very good cross-country runner. He enjoyed swimming and scuba diving and was a member of the British Sub-Aqua Club in Oxford, which he had joined as a teenager with a group of school friends.[26] They would mostly train in an indoor pool in Oxford but during the summer months made trips to the south coast of England for serious scuba-diving in the open sea. They also took advantage of the Royal Navy's HMS *Vernon*'s frogman facilities, where they were allowed to train in a special training water tank at their Portsmouth base.

Despite this, when the time came to choose between the services, Paul didn't consider the Navy, or the service of his father, the Royal Air Force (RAF). Many of Paul's school friends entered the Royal Navy or the RAF once they had finished school, which was relatively normal practice. In fact, while Paul was still at school, he had had thoughts of joining the RAF. His father, however, refused to sign the application giving permission, justifying his refusal on the grounds that once you come out of the services, what you would have learnt might not offer the skills

---

[26] At that time, the police would occasionally contact the British Sub-Aqua Club when a crime had been committed and they assumed that evidence had been thrown in The Isis, the name given to the part of the River Thames that flows through Oxford and also includes the River Cherwell.

normally required for civilian work. Therefore, his father recommended that he first qualify in a civilian profession, and if he still wished to go into the services, he could then do so safely. Paul realised his father's advice was wise and he followed it.

Paul describes his decision to join the British Army, and also to take advantage of the range of sports that were available, as a decision to 'accept the Queen's shilling' and 'join the wide world'. People in the crafts often work in remote situations, and he felt he had missed out on a lot of social development during his teenage years, although he was still in the sub-aqua club while he was working at Goble's.

However, a shock awaited him when he discovered that a minimum of six years had to be served in the British Army. He had assumed that three years was the minimum, but on hearing about life in a modern cavalry regiment, driving and commanding Centurion tanks on the North German plains and the opportunities for sport, it all seemed a little better.

The choice of regiment was the 11th Hussars (Prince Albert's Own, the 'Cherry Pickers'), one of the finest and most distinguished cavalry regiments of the British Army. It was established in 1715 as a regiment of dragoons. The regiment's nickname, the Cherry Pickers, came from an incident during the Peninsular War in which the 11th Light Dragoons (as the regiment was then named) were attacked while raiding a cherry orchard at San Martin de Trevejo, Spain. The 11th Hussars charged with the Light Brigade on 25 October 1854, commanded by their former colonel, Lord Cardigan, at Balaklava during the Crimean War. In the 1950s the regiment served in the British Army of the Rhine, close to the border with USSR-occupied Germany early in the Cold War era.[27]

The winter of 1962–1963 began in earnest in December 1962 with severe frosts followed by snow that remained until the spring – it was one of the hardest winters on record and this was precisely at the time Paul

---

[27] On 25 October 1969 the regiment was amalgamated with the 10th Royal Hussars (Prince of Wales's Own) to form The Royal Hussars (Prince of Wales's Own). Paul had been demobbed by just one year but he and his family attended the 'sad' farewell to his old regiment; the ceremony was held in Tidworth, Hampshire.

decided to join the British Army to start his basic training. He arrived at Richmond Station in Yorkshire on 12 January 1963, disembarking from the 'Catterick Flyer' together with a couple of dozen fellow recruits, where they were met and whisked away to the training depot of the 3rd Royal Tank Regiment, Cambrai and Alma Barracks.[28]

Once through the main gate, life changed abruptly. The transformation from civilian to soldier was dramatic both in speed and effect. Barked orders were to be obeyed instantly and crude imperatives were issued to do things the 'Army Way'.

From day one it was 'brasso, blanco and bull'![29] This regime continued onto the snow-covered parade ground with the hilarious spectacle of recruits sliding, falling and cursing their way through basic drill. Their curses were added to by those of the sarcastic drill instructors, demanding, 'Who gave you permission to fallout?'

This tough and rigorous existence continued without pause throughout that bleak winter. Drills, weapons training, exercises on the snow-covered and ice-covered assault course, route marches – all carried on unremittingly. The tough conditions fostered comradeship, humour and mutual support among the recruits. Paul and his fellows helped each other through those very tough first few months of the course. Not all made it: a few were 'back squadded' to begin training from scratch again, with a couple being completely dismissed from the service. This was not surprising, given the extreme conditions of that winter, which eventually gave way to a hint of the coming spring. In spring there was flooding from the melting of the accumulated snow. It gradually became possible

---

[28] The barracks were named after two campaigns: the First World War battle near the French town of Cambrai, the first in which tanks were used en masse, and the Battle of the Alma, on 20 September 1854, which took place during the Crimean War (1853–1856).

[29] Brasso was used to polish the brass on their uniforms; blanco was a paste brushed onto the webbing (belts and straps) to make it waterproof; and bull was short for bullshit! Paul's regiment used buff-coloured blanco; white blanco was used on special occasions but, unfortunately, it is not waterproof, and so if it rained on their military parade, the uniforms would end up in an awful mess.

to smile at the sadistic non-commissioned officers (NCOs) – even during the endless charades on the parade ground – especially after they had finally mastered about-turns, marching in review order and Royal Salutes.

With spring came a new training regime. This involved a move from the parade ground to the classroom, where the intricacies of the Centurion tank's 105 mm main gun and its smaller sidekick, the .30 calibre Browning machine gun, were demonstrated. Training covered the interior of a tank turret traversing, elevating, depressing and aiming This was followed by practising in the miniature indoor firing range, which used a fixed .22 rifle to fire at targets set about a model landscape. This was for the gunner to learn the firing drill and respond accordingly before going on to the ranges and firing for real. Firing a .22 rifle was precisely the gunnery drill that would be used on the Centurion tank. After this they were finally allowed out on the ranges for live use of the 105 mm gun.

This training continued for many weeks before heading off to the Royal Armoured Corps Gunnery School at Lulworth, Dorset, for the final examinations. These exams involved firing live ammunition at the hulks of Second World War tanks. Any rounds failing to hit their targets sailed through a dip in the cliffs, known as the Arish Mel gap, out into Lulworth Cove – fortunately, a safe distance away from the famous Durdle Door beach and its unsuspecting holidaymakers.

During live firing, each member of the crew had to take their turn in loading shells. In the time it took for the gunner to aim and fire, the loader was required to retrieve the next round (shell) from the rack and, cradling it in his arms, wait eagerly for the recoiling 105 mm gun to automatically open the breach ready to receive the next round. Paul was too eager to impress during the exams and prove he could have three rounds in the air at the same time. Cradling the round too close to the returning gun, the breach smashed the fuse on the high-explosive shell, and fearing it would explode, he slammed it quickly into the open breach. Nothing happened! Within seconds the shell sailed safely down the range. The error remained unmentioned but was definitely never repeated!

The pleasant, late spring trip and successful exam results were followed by a return to Catterick for the passing-out parade and embarkation leave before joining the regiment in Germany. This was the start of Paul's real career with the 11th Hussars.

Hohne Lager, previously known as Bergen-Belsen, was a camp built in 1935 to house Hitler's troops. It was first used for artillery and later, in 1938, for Panzer troops. It carried on in this role until British troops liberated the Bergen-Belsen concentration camp.[30] The survivors of Belsen were moved into Hohne, with the sick going to the Wehrmacht Hospital for treatment.

Hohne became Paul's new home, where he joined a Sabre squadron of the Regiment and was posted to 4th Heavy Troop, 'A' Squadron. This was not a Centurion-equipped troop but one using the massive 65-ton

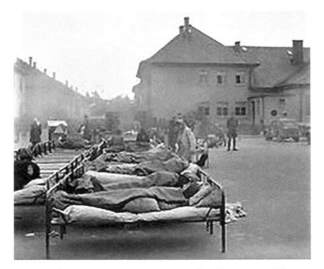

FIGURE 3.1 Bergen-Belsen as in 1945–1946, renamed Hohne in 1947. This same location became the regimental square of the 11th Hussars. The second picture shows the memorial Paul saw on his visit in 1963.

[30] Bergen-Belsen DP (Displaced Persons) camp was established in 1946, in the former German Panzer camp, after the British liberated the nearby Belsen concentration camp on 15 April 1945. The concentration camp was destroyed to prevent the spread of disease. Bergen-Belsen was later renamed Hohne Lager and became the home for the NATO armoured troops, including the 11th Hussars (PAO).

Conqueror tank (see Figure 3.2). As gunner on this new tank, Paul had to learn different firing techniques, as the main gun was 120 mm, with shells so large that they came in two parts: the propellant charge and the projectile itself. The 11th Hussars were the first regiment to receive the Centurion tank's replacement – the Chieftain – in 1965.

Joining the regiment in the same month as Paul, in May 1963, was HRH Prince Michael of Kent, who was posted to the Second Troop of the same squadron. He had entered the Royal Military School, Sandhurst, in 1961 and was commissioned into the 11th Hussars (Prince

FIGURE 3.2 One of the Conqueror tanks.
Photograph by Paul Fischer.

Albert's Own) in 1963 and became a sabre troop leader in May of that year. His grandfather, HRH King George VI, had held the post of colonel-in-chief of the regiment.

FIGURE 3.3 This historic postcard from 1909 shows the uniform of an 11th Hussar; it was known as the prettiest regiment in the British Army. Paul would wear the same uniform for ceremonial occasions, such as the presentation of the new guidon by HRH The Queen Mother in 1965.[31] Painting by Ernest Ibbetson.
Reproduced with permission of Charles W. Griffin.

[31] There is a short documentary on the 11th Hussars, dating from 1965, celebrating the 250th anniversary of the regiment's formation. HRH The Queen Mother presented them with a new guidon. Paul was in this parade. See YouTube: www.youtube.com/watch?v=B3MtE9ttTDE (accessed 12 June 2020).

Regimental life was a little more relaxed than the full-on regime of the training depot at Catterick. Soldiers were encouraged, and expected, to get involved in the many opportunities to represent their squadron and regiment in the numerous sports available. Sailing, rugby, cricket and skiing were just a few of the choices. Paul's time in Catterick and the snow-covered Yorkshire Moors had been his testing ground for cross-country running and, although the conditions had been challenging, he had enjoyed the experience.

Before plans in the sports department could be taken further, the major autumn inter-brigade exercise, Deep South, had to take precedence – in theory at least. At that time of the year, much rain could be expected and it made things rather messy. Even with tracked vehicles, soggy ground could present major challenges. 'A' Squadron had something of a reputation for 'bogging' tanks. The 50-ton weight of a Centurion tank on soggy heathland could, and often did, become bogged down. The weight caused the tank to sink until its flat bottom sat on the ground with the tracks still turning uselessly in the mud and the Rolls Royce engine roaring – but with the tank going nowhere.

RECOVERY IS NOT ALWAYS SUCCESSFUL

FIGURE 3.4 A photograph from Paul's regimental journal in 1964, showing the Centurion tank slipping beneath the Lüneburg Heath, unrecoverable![32]

---

[32] From the journal, *Hussars*, 27/3 (1964). The editor was Paul's squadron leader, Captain The Honourable George Willoughby Moke Norrie.

That particular autumn, a Centurion tank belonging to First Troop became totally bogged and, slowly, over a three-day period, it completely turned turtle and sank, never to be seen again.

Once the major annual exercise was over, its dramas and achievements providing banter for the bars and the mess, there was only a short pause before the onset of the bitter German winter. Paul was to discover that these winters were considerably colder than England's – they were much drier, with a bitter, cold wind – though somewhat easier to bear than the wet British variety.

With the onset of winter, Paul's thoughts turned once again to sports and the opportunities to head south to the snow-covered Alps. The 11th Hussars always had downhill skiing and bobsleigh trophies but this season the idea of a langlauf team was considered.[33] With the aid of a Swedish trainer, a novice team was formed and would, hopefully, be ready for competition in the New Year.

The British Army, the British Army of the Rhine (BAOR) and the Princess Marina Cup championships – one competition but with three titles – were to be held in Oberjoch, Bavaria, in late January and early February 1964. Their hard work meant that the novice team could be entered to gain valuable experience in the hope that a fully trained team would be ready for the next season.

It was logical to approach successful cross-country runners to put together a group of ten potential ski candidates, including Paul, from which a team of four would be chosen based on their ability to master skiing in a short time. Cross-country skiing is hard work and holds none of the glory of downhill racing. No one in the 11th Hussars had had any experience of langlauf, so it was very much down to the Swedish trainer

---

[33] The German word 'langlauf' loosely translates as 'long run'. It is a sport something like cross-country running but on snow and, in the case of the biathlon, is on skis, carrying a rifle vertically on your back. Sometimes known as 'Nordic skiing', this is a normal sport in the winter Olympics, but, at that time, Britain was not yet providing a team. Hence, for the first year of their participation, the British made their selection from the experienced British Army teams. Paul didn't quite make it into the Olympic team.

to work a miracle. The ten novices spent six days a week slogging around a cunningly sited ski circuit through forests, down giddy gullies and up sharp inclines.

The trainer pushed them hard and within a couple of weeks the basics of the weird combination of running and skiing uphill and downhill on 2-inch-wide skis began to sink in. Some mastered the technique faster than others, which helped to make the selection of four from ten for the team, with four reserves. Their ski hut was shared with the 15th/19th Hussars, so a good cavalry spirit was generated. This helped the team unwind from their excursions on the slopes, which included the typical soldierly banter about each regiment's powers and their ability to stand up on the slopes.

The Army Championships started on 29 January 1964, just two months after the team's nervous and unsteady introduction to the ski slopes. Fortunately, two months of gym work beforehand had helped in preparing their fitness. In each of the main events – biathlon, 4x4 relay and the individual – the 11th Hussars did well enough, considering this was their first season. It all looked good for the next year. Paul's own experience was a personal success, achieving 52nd in the National Championship Individual, fourth in the 20 km patrol biathlon and ninth in the individual Princess Marina Cup race.

In the Princess Marina Cup, the regiment achieved a very creditable fifth place. This was all very encouraging for a first season in langlauf, again auguring well for the future. Paul was encouraged and spent a further two seasons with the team.

When not involved in major exercises or training, soldiers could apply for home leave: usually a two-week block each year, with short local leave in between. During his 1964 home leave, an army friend invited Paul to his home in Manchester. Knowing nothing of this major northern city, the opportunity to see the bright lights and get a taste of the mid-1960s northern pop scene appealed. His friend was a good host, showing Paul the delights of Manchester and introducing him to friends and family. During one party, he was introduced to a pretty, young Mancunian lass called Joy. Realising this was an early mutual attraction, he decided to maintain contact on his return to his regiment.

In the following year, 1965, Paul put himself forward for the canoeing team. This was a new sport for the regiment, so training, instruction and safety techniques had to be established. The Scots Greys, a heavy cavalry regiment, were happy to oblige and supplied a training officer, a young subaltern, Ranulph Fiennes.

Sir Ranulph Twistleton Wykeham Fiennes (Ran Fiennes) is a world-renowned explorer who served as an officer in the 2nd Dragoon Guards (the Royal Scots Greys) from 1963 to1965, after which he transferred to the SAS, captaining the Greys' canoe and langlauf ski teams. His many remarkable achievements are documented in his numerous books.[34]

Once they had mastered the basics, the team were able to practise on their own on the nearby River Aller. Not only did the newly formed team benefit from Ran Fiennes's instruction but they also went on to learn more by competing against him and the Scots Greys team both in canoeing competitions on the River Weser and in the British Skiing Competition in the Alps.

In 1965 Paul was still stationed at Hohne, a large garrison on the edge of the Heide (also known as Lüneburg Heath), many miles from a city. Celle, the nearest town, 15 miles away, was small, and Hannover, the nearest city, was 30 miles away. Few could afford a car on a soldier's pay, so city life with its varied attractions was a limited prospect. This all changed when the 11th Hussars were tasked to provide a relief squadron for the Queen's Own Hussars, the one armoured unit in Berlin.

At that time, in 1965, three prisoners remained in Berlin's Spandau Prison: Albert Speer and Baldur von Schirach, who were both released in 1966, and the infamous Rudolph Hess, who remained until 1987,

---

[34] Quite a few years after Paul's return to civilian life, he met Sir Ranulph Fiennes at a book-signing session at the Randolph Hotel, Oxford, in December 1987, where Ran signed Paul's copy of his book with the dedication 'To one of my pupils!! – Ran'.

when he committed suicide.[35] The Queen's Own Hussars were stationed in a camp adjoining the prison; the 11th Hussars would soon discover they were to be the relief squadron. The occupying powers in Berlin – France, USA, Britain and Russia – each took turn to guard this one remaining prisoner and it happened that it was the Russians' turn when the 11th Hussars were in Berlin. This was not a problem in itself until the first night-time 'call out'. This was a war practice emergency drill with kit packed in short order and stowed aboard each tank. The fifteen V12 Rolls Royce engines of the squadron roared into life and immediately caused panic in the prison. The Russian guards played their searchlights over the assembled tanks until they moved off into the Berlin night.

The Berlin Wall was a wall built by the East Germans in 1961, almost overnight, creating a bulwark between the 'socialist East and the fascist West' – at least that was the official reason given. It primarily served as a barrier to prevent mass defection to the West. Paul was stationed there at the end of 1964. There were only two access points for border crossings between East and West Berlin during this Cold War

FIGURE 3.5 Paul and friends in front of Brandenburg Gate and the Berlin Wall in 1965. An official army photograph. Paul Fischer Collection.

[35] After the death of Rudolph Hess, the prison was closed and demolished.

period – Checkpoint Charlie, being the most well known, most notorious and most used.[36]

Paul and his troop took full advantage of Berlin's nightlife, including travelling through the relatively new Berlin Wall into the East via Checkpoint Charlie. East Berlin was a surprise: there had been almost no development or change since the destruction from the Second World War. The only new buildings were angular concrete blocks of flats on the edge of the city and austere Russian war memorials that included sealed up T34 tanks set on plinths; it was rumoured that the original crews were still inside.

The change and excitement of Berlin was short-lived, as was the subsequent return to Hohne. Paul, now a firm member of the regiment's skiing team, was off to Bavaria for the BOAR and British championships once again. At that time, cross-country skiing was rare as a competitive sport, particularly in Britain, and so the army provided the ideal opportunity to select competitors for the British Olympic team.

When Paul had returned from Bavaria, he discovered that he was being moved from 'A' Squadron to the 'RECCE' (reconnaissance) troop. This was the cavalry regiment's elite troop, which used lighter and faster armoured cars to provide the freedom to roam and reconnoitre. Their role was to be the eyes and ears of the regiment, both on exercises and as part of regular border patrols between East and West Germany.

This was when the Cold War was at its height and the patrols were a serious business, with troops on either side glaring at each other through binoculars across the River Elbe, the natural and effective border. This border was made even more effective by the destruction of all the River Elbe's bridges during the Second World War, some parts of which still stretched out from the western bank.

The move to the RECCE troop was to become Paul's last year within

---

[36] Checkpoint Charlie later became an iconic symbol of the division of political ideologies: capitalism and communism. The wall was momentously pulled down in a historic action of the people in November 1989. It remains as a tourist attraction and now includes a small museum.

the regiment. Further delights and diversion came in the shape of a recruiting tour of southern England, travelling and displaying a Centurion tank and a Ferret scout armoured car. The cherry-coloured trousers of the regiment impressed the girls and the Centurion tank caught the attention of the boys.

Travel to the Norwegian mountains and fiords came about through volunteering for Outward Bound. It was not so much sport, but it was a character-building challenge nevertheless. Outward Bound, army style, is more extreme than its civilian counterpart. It is reliant on personal motivation and endurance but without the usual military discipline and orders to fall back on – an individual challenge. No rank was displayed, as dress was casual, usually in the form of jeans, climbing boots and whatever else was needed.

The motto of the course was 'Mind over matter'. Soldiers being soldiers, many changed it to 'We don't mind, so you don't matter!' But they understood perfectly well what was required.

Though no military discipline was imposed, personal and group discipline was expected, and as they were divided into three teams, the importance of that regime became obvious. Swearing, smoking, poor personal hygiene, a dirty kitchen or tented area brought down a quick response in the form of strange penalties: swearing was punished with twenty-five press-ups in the freezing stream, and poor hygiene by having to carry two sandbags up and down a hill, with one bag under each arm, repeated ten times. Each miscreant was encouraged to complete the task with the ultimate sanction of being returned to their regiment – failed!

This was all part of the training, along with climbing, orienteering, long treks over the mountains, swimming in the fiord, three-day-route marches and finally being dumped, literally, on a small barren rock of an island by a landing craft. Just to add to the fun, the ten members of Paul's team were dumped half a mile off the shore, which meant they had to swim to the island, wearing only shorts, a shirt and plimsolls; thus, anyone who had secreted matches and cigarettes about their person would find them ruined.

For the three-day duration on the island, a bare rock in the North Sea, fires could not be lit and clothing was limited. There was nothing to make a shelter with and nothing to eat, which induced strange dreams when they finally managed to sleep. The island had large rocks and Paul suggested they build something like a small cairn, which they could then fill with dried grass, similar to shelters made by mice. They built the cairn and filled it with the collected dry grass, but when they crawled inside, looking forward to some rest and warmth, they soon discovered that the blades of dried grass were so spikey that it was almost like sleeping on a bed of nails – in short, unsustainable.

So this 'clever' idea was quickly discarded and they reverted to plan B, which was to use the secreted matches that were still in good and dry condition. Using driftwood found on the beach, they could light a fire, which would keep burning the whole night through and provide them with the opportunity to sleep. They also spent some of the day sleeping, as the days were quite warm, fortunately.

They became aware of Norwegian fishing boats passing by and managed, with a combination of gestures and shouts to the Norwegian fishermen, to request some fish, which they kindly provided by coming close to the steep cliffs and throwing them ashore. Having acquired the fish, they excitedly put them near the fire, but of course didn't know they should gut them first; in any case, they had no knives. This was one of the many lessons they learnt for life on their three-day stay. The fish exploded and decorated a nearby rock and splattered like pebble dash. They were, however, in their desperation, able to pick off tiny pieces to eat. They were beyond desperate!

Although they were stranded on this small island, they were being observed from a nearby island by the training staff, using binoculars. Both the fire and the fish escapades were not treated as the required survival initiative. The next day, the team were swooped upon by the permanent staff, who came ashore and punished them for their use of matches to light the fire and for not catching their own fish (they had been given fishing line, but of course didn't manage to catch any fish, and were nervous, as they had been warned not to eat any brightly coloured fish, as they were poisonous). This brought down the wrath of the permanent staff, who were not at all impressed by this idea of initiative. As punishment, their shirts were taken away and they were left with just their shorts on!

They all survived! There were no major arguments but a lot of tough talking, as there was no leader and they had to work out their strengths and work together as a team. The whole exercise proved a fascinating test, exposing individual weaknesses but also bringing forth previously unknown strengths, which of course was the purpose of the exercise. Outward Bound was called the 'survival test', and though three days may seem short, in such extreme conditions the human frailties thus exposed provided valuable self-understanding and occasional surprises. During the last evening at the end of the month's Outward Bound course, the training staff took each member of the teams to one side, giving them a full report on their achievements and discussing what had been learnt.

The return to regimental routine after the Outward Bound course did not last long. Paul was posted on secondment back to the UK to join HQ Army Aviation at Netheravon on Salisbury Plain. At that time, the Army Air Corps, still in its infancy, comprised personnel from other units. In the case of HQ Army Aviation, apart from the commanding officer (CO) and second-in-command, who were from the Royal Artillery, the remainder were personnel from the Royal Armoured Corps.

Netheravon was a First World War grass airfield comprising a hotchpotch of First World War buildings and two later period aircraft hangars. It was shared with 2 Wing AAC, the Army Parachute Association and the Cheshire Infantry Regiment. As for aircraft, 2 Wing used Westland Scout and Bell Sioux helicopters. The CO, John Moss, used Austers and Beavers fixed-wing aircraft and the Army Parachute Association used the de Havilland Rapide.

Appropriately, Airfield Camp, Netheravon, in Wiltshire, was originally a cavalry training school, which became a training camp for the RFC (Royal Flying Corps) in its infancy and later for the RAF (Royal Air

Force). The airfield remained a grass strip proving, ultimately, ideal for the AAC (Army Air Corps) and helicopters. Various units of the AAC took up residence there in the early 1960s, including HQ Army Aviation, 3 Division. These units were made up of a mixture of personnel, including many from cavalry and artillery regiments. The airfield finally closed in 2012 for military use but is still in use by civilians.

HQ Army Aviation, 3 Division was a small unit consisting of only fifteen personnel working in an administrative role, so life was definitely slower and rather limited when compared with the demands of a tank regiment. Paul found this rather boring. During the summer months, there were opportunities for cricket and also sailing on the Solent. Come the winter, there was the new experience of hockey.

Through correspondence, Paul's friendship with Joy had been slowly blossoming. Joy was working in Manchester as a telephonist at the Singer sewing machine company. Telephonists had to manage complicated switchboards in those days and there would be a whole wall full of jack sockets with multiple cables lying in wait to connect calls. Several telephonists would be working alongside each other operating this bird's nest of cables, creating an atmosphere of non-stop chatter. Manchester was a busy city with a healthy nightlife, so there was much to write to Paul about.

In the early days, Paul's correspondence to Joy was full of army activities and sporting challenges. At some stage much later, Paul's thoughts and correspondence began to include instrument making. They continued to write to each other through to Paul's return to the UK and posting to the Army Air Corps at Netheravon. Thus, there were some new compensations for being based at this location, situated only about 60 miles from Paul's Oxford home and 150 miles from his girlfriend, Joy, in Manchester. As there were no motorways at that time, the journey could take many hours. Leaving Manchester at 10 pm on a Sunday evening could mean only just arriving in time at Netheravon for the first parade on Monday morning at 7.30 am – but the risk was worth it!

FIGURE 3.6 Paul's Austin Metropolitan, with Joy sitting in the passenger seat.
Photograph by Paul Fischer.

At that time, Paul had an Austin Metropolitan, which was a soft-top car for when the weather was good. Paul recalls visiting the John Rylands Library in Manchester to see the architecture and wonderful mahogany furniture; at other times, they would also drive out into the beautiful Peak District, exploring a part of the countryside that was not known to him. He found that the northern country people were open and welcoming, in contrast to Oxford, where rather formal social mores were observed.

Throughout Paul's time in the army, instrument making and its pleasures had remained in his heart, but trying to discuss it with his colleagues usually brought a blank response. When he was instructed to present a lecture on any subject, during his time stationed in Hohne, Germany, he chose a subject he knew well – harpsichord making – although he realised his audience of soldiers would not understand a word of it. Nevertheless, he himself began to understand what would be required in confidence and mental preparation to speak in front of an audience. The lesson was: know your subject! – then life is so much easier.

Paul was now thinking more of his future life after the British Army and two issues took precedence: marriage and a career. The first just needed a decision, but when? The second required him to return to school to sharpen up his rusty woodworking skills.

The first was resolved during Joy's holiday in Oxford, when the answer to the popped question was yes. The wedding was planned for the following year, 1967, to take place in Manchester.

In those days, getting married still required permission from the commanding officer (CO). Paul was marched into the CO's office following a request for an interview. After some preliminaries and polite conversation, permission was granted by Colonel John Moss. That permission was comparatively easier to arrange than the papal dispensation they needed to apply for. Joy is Catholic and went to a strict convent school, with all that that entails. In the 1960s Catholics were allowed to marry Protestants but had to write to the Pope in Rome for permission, which required Paul to present his baptismal certificate and agree that any children they had, had to be brought up Catholic – and he himself had to have six lessons in Catholicism.

Their plan was for Joy to move to Oxford and live with Paul's widowed father. As Paul was still stationed at Netheravon for a further eighteen months, this allowed him to travel home at weekends. In his father's usual sensible and generous way, he suggested they live rent free for the remainder of Paul's service life and hopefully then be in a position to buy their own home by the time Paul left the army.

The issue of a future career was resolved easily by applying to the local school in Amesbury, Wiltshire, to do evening woodwork classes. The purpose of this was to refresh Paul's skills and knowledge. Surprisingly, he found himself teaching during the lecturer's many absences due to ill health. This gained him a fulsome reference on completion of the course, as well as getting him back up to speed with woodworking.

It was Paul's wish and hope to return to instrument making, though

53

harpsichord making would have meant returning to the nineteenth-century 'bubble' from which he had escaped, and he was not keen to go back to the old routine. When soldiers are nearing the completion of their service, they are allowed to seek civilian work experience for one month before their demobilisation. Paul took this opportunity to find a job restoring antiques in Oxford, which was appropriate to his considerable skills. Not only did this work suit him, but also, in just that one month, he learnt much from temporary employment with Fred Kane, a very experienced craftsman.

Paul worked for Kane's Antique Restoration, which had its workshop in Oxford. It was a family business, with Fred Kane's daughter and son-in-law also involved. Interestingly, the workshop was in the style of Goble's and operated much in the same way. Paul took his tool chest from the Goble days to work at Kane's and was given his own workbench. There were four of them in the workshop where the antiques were restored. This was Paul's introduction to restoring antique furniture, which involved a familiar but different approach. The work wasn't always confined to the workshop and Paul found himself at Oxford's famous Bodleian Library creating bookcases in a style to match the existing cases; the originals were probably made in teak or mahogany. Another out-of-workshop assignment was building bookcases to line the walls of the library in the house of the former secretary to Sir Winston Churchill in Watlington, Oxfordshire. He was only with Fred Kane for one month but managed to finish a number of projects. His work can still be seen on the doors for St Mary's Church on High Street, Oxford; he built a new doorframe for the external door and converted the glazed area above into openable doors, all in oak to match the existing ancient door.

During his apprenticeship with Robert Goble, French polishing had been undertaken by a dedicated French polisher. Paul's introduction to this specialist craft came during his short period with Fred Kane, as antique restoration demanded a finish to match the original – an even more refined art than simple French polishing. Paul's training as an instrument maker proved more than adequate for the work required in antique restoration. Fred and Paul got along very well and, in fact, he would have liked Paul to stay on working; however, he understood Paul's wish to return to instrument making.

In late December 1968, with all his kit returned to the stores, including the famous Cherry Pickers uniform, Paul said his last goodbyes to his army pals and headed home to Oxford. This was the first Christmas he had spent at home in five years and was the first he and Joy would spend together as a married couple.

Despite his preparations for civilian life in his last months as a soldier, future work prospects remained a blank. With his wish to return to instrument making, fate was to come to his aid before the year's end. But for the moment he could relax and enjoy a home Christmas with his wife and family. The future could wait until 2 January 1969.

CHAPTER 4

Paul's Surprise Return to Instrument Making:

David Rubio at Duns Tew

When Paul's time in the army was drawing to a close, he knew deep down that he wanted to return to instrument making. Now, more than ever, he appreciated the words of wisdom from his father, who had impressed on him the importance of being trained in a civilian profession. Having fulfilled his boyhood desire to join the forces, and having apprenticed as a harpsichord maker, the way forward was very clear. Here there was an immediate option for him for future employment; however, much more than this, Paul's heart had been captured by instrument making and he knew this was what he wanted and needed to do to find happiness.

At that time, there were a limited number of instrument makers working by hand in Britain. It had only been by a combination of chance and initiative that, prior to his time in the army, Paul had learnt the skills of an instrument maker under the tutelage of one of Britain's leading instrument makers, Robert Goble. The chances of another such fortunate happenstance seemed remote, but once again fortune smiled upon him when an opportunity presented itself in the first week of 1969. Second-hand information came his way via a friend that a violin maker based in North Oxfordshire was looking for an assistant.

The information was not complete: there was no name or address given, just a general location. So without hesitation, or consideration that perhaps a Sunday might not be an appropriate day for an uninvited visit, Paul and Joy set off to try to find this man. They duly arrived in the village of Middle Barton, 15 miles north of Oxford, and stopped at the first pub they found to enquire about the elusive violin maker. The landlord knew nothing about him, but an eavesdropping customer did and directed them to a large thatched house opposite the church in the nearby village of Duns Tew, where he thought they might find him.

They set off northwards for roughly 3 miles and arrived in the centre of Duns Tew. After parking in front of the church, they crossed the road to the thatched house directly opposite. Paul nervously knocked on the stout, heavily carved, oak stable door. After a short while, the top half of the door opened and a slight woman in her mid thirties, speaking with a Midwest American accent, asked what they wanted. Apologising for the uninvited interruption – and on a Sunday morning! – they explained who they were and whom they were seeking. They were delighted to discover they had found the right house and that David, her husband, was an instrument maker – but not of violins. A few minutes later David himself appeared, in dressing gown and pyjamas, adding to his visitors' embarrassment. After Paul explained who he was and why they were there, they were invited in. Around the farmhouse's big kitchen table, the full story began to unfold and the atmosphere quickly became more relaxed. Their discussion continued over many cups of fresh coffee.

It transpired that David Rubio – they had finally learnt his full name – made classical guitars and lutes and his clients included luminaries such as Julian Bream. Guitars, lutes … this was what Paul had longed for – the opportunity to gain experience making other musical instruments. Paul and David shared their stories of instrument making: Paul, a fully trained harpsichord maker, and Rubio, a self-taught maker of guitars and lutes.

Rubio was pleasantly surprised to find that his self-invited guest was already qualified and more than willing to adapt his proven skills to other plucked instruments. As David confessed that he had always wanted to make harpsichords, Rubio's wife, Nest, chipped in, saying, 'When can you start?' The excitement of this meeting was obvious to all, and Nest, with an American 'can do' attitude, tried to get Paul to start the following

FIGURE 4.1 Rubio's home and workshops, The Ridge House, Duns Tew, in 2016. The building on the left was used for the small fretted instruments and the building in the foreground on the right was used for harpsichord making.
Photograph by Paul Fischer.

week. Paul's other commitments made this impractical, but a start date of mid February 1969 was agreed upon there and then.

The timing of this meeting was perfect for both of them. By coincidence, David Rubio had been putting out feelers through Jan Balkwell of COSIRA (Council for Small Industries in Rural Areas) to find a trained musical instrument maker to join his workshop. Jan had contacted Paul's old tutor from college, thinking he might know of someone suitable. Thus, through community gossip, a hint of the information had reached Paul, simply that a 'violin maker' of name unknown and at an unknown place in Oxfordshire was looking for a trained instrument maker! This was, after all, decades before the existence of computers or Internet search engines, where 'word of mouth' was an invaluable form of communication.

Before leaving Duns Tew, Paul and Joy were taken into the workshop/studio to see where the instruments were made and where he would be working. The workshop/studio was an extension of the house and could be accessed through an internal door, as well as one leading in from the garden. Beyond the wide gravelled drive was a storage barn, not in robust condition but soon to be transformed in a style to match the house, with a thatched roof. This workshop would be used much later on, specifically for the creation of harpsichords, with an adjoining smaller room – a quiet room – created for voicing and tuning the instruments.

During the tour of the large workshop, Paul's surprise and delight could not be hidden: this was an opportunity to work with another fine maker and with such superbly equipped facilities. A grin remained on his face throughout the tour as Paul gazed in amazement at all the new equipment: powerful lights, central heating and air-conditioning. Beneath his feet he could feel the spring of the wooden floor. Above was a vast space rising up into a vaulted ceiling, half of which was a mezzanine floor, which was accessed by a large central wooden staircase. This provided the ideal wood store, with the rising heat to season the rare and delicate tonewoods stored above, and added to the already heady smell of the cedar-panelled walls. This was a craftsman's delight and Paul's enthusiasm to begin making beautiful instruments in such ideal conditions could hardly be contained; but it had to be – at least for another month.

At this point he also discovered that, apart from Rubio himself, a young American by the name of Tom Hom would be working in the luxurious workshop with them. Tom had come over from New York with his young family and would remain until the spring, converting his considerable skills as a picture framer and gilder to those of a luthier. During his work as a gilder, Tom had suffered an accident – acid had affected his breathing – so he changed plans and chose to retrain as a guitar maker.

All that remained now was to stay patient for one more month – a month during which there was much to do. Starting this new job overlapped with the expected birth of Paul and Joy's first child, due around 20 February 1969; also, they were looking for a house of their own. Having taken full advantage of his father's generous offer of free accommodation during what was left of his army service, they had accumulated a healthy sum. This allowed them to get a mortgage without too much trouble.

The needs of their firstborn took priority, but not too far behind was the search for a house or, as it turned out, a cottage. During their quest for the 'violin maker', they had made enquiries at a public house in the nearby village of Middle Barton, and it was there that they eventually found a cottage. The age of restoration had not quite arrived, so older and period properties usually required much work and imagination to bring them up to twentieth-century standards while still holding on to their old-world charm and period features. Exposed beams, inglenook fireplaces and polished wooden floors were things that were to return to fashion from the 1970s onwards but were not so well considered at that time.

Despite the considerable work required, the price was well within their budget at £3,600 and they were prepared and patient enough to put the work in. It was also close to the workshop in Duns Tew. The cottage, though small, with just two bedrooms, would suit their immediate needs and was at a price they could manage on a single salary, as was the norm in the 1960s and early 1970s. Although a mortgage was applied for and approved, several months passed before all was complete, and this meant that for the first few months Paul would commute the 15 miles from his father's house in Oxford to work with David and Tom.

Just as a whole new world had opened up for him when he'd started with Robert Goble making Early Music instruments, working with David Rubio presented an amazing opportunity that appealed both to Paul's passion for craft and his experience in instrument making. That he would once again be working within an idyllic rural setting suited his temperament and personality. On 19 February 1969 Paul set forth to Duns Tew to continue his life making exotic and mostly Early Music instruments – the modern classical guitar being the only exception.

The first morning in this new and stimulating environment was spent familiarising himself with all the new equipment in the workshop. These included a planer, a thicknesser, a circular and band saw, and benches with vices (both normal woodworking vices and those specifically designed to hold the smaller and more delicate fretted variety of instruments). It was a veritable craftsman's playground, with a range of new woods to delight the eye and excite the senses, with the heady aroma of such exotic woods as ebony, Brazilian and Indian rosewoods, mahogany and cedar (both western red and Brazilian cedar, which were also used in cigar boxes), with beautiful, rippled maple providing a British contribution to the range of tonewoods. These carefully selected specimens were neatly stored horizontally and 'sticked' (thin sticks used to separate each piece so that warm air could pass between and season them naturally) in the atrium above the workshop, and so providing an uncluttered and spacious working area below. Though it was mid February, the workshop was comfortably warm, as was the reception Paul received from both David and Tom.

This first afternoon was spent setting out his work area, filling the racks provided for his tools. Usually, a craftsman's bench would have a tray set in the back for storing tools, but Rubio's benches were in a completely new style – these were brand new and made of hard-wearing beech. The work surfaces were completely flat, providing a larger work area, without the tray and the clutter of tools, and so were ideal for the fine work he was about to embark upon. Paul had brought with him his handmade tool chest, which contained all the tools he had acquired during his apprenticeship with Robert Goble. In this new workspace, Paul could have all his instrument-making tools regimentally lined up – with the shortest on the left and the tallest on the right – neatly on wall racks above the bench until they were needed. Paul becomes very emotional when talking about his bench:

> You must treat the top of your bench as if it were a sheet of glass, remaining perfectly flat without any blemishes. The golden rule is that you should never saw or chop directly onto the bench surface. You have a chopping board especially for this purpose.

This workshop layout was a revelation to Paul and he assumed that David had developed this system from his early days of working as an instrument maker in Greenwich Village, New York. Paul later added to this comfortable and efficient new system by designing a metal, wheeled trolley, much like those used by surgeons and dentists at the time, for the tools in use. He had two trollies built: one for David and one for himself.

While it was a pleasant but unproductive first day, at least as regards instrument making, day two was different. Paul's first task was to prepare the materials for a classical guitar, a flamenco guitar and a Renaissance lute. It was straightforward work for him but more care was required when reducing the precious maple, rosewood and cypress to thin dimensions he had not experienced before: 1.5 mm thick for the maple; 2.5 mm thick for the rosewood; and 2 mm thick for the cypress – all achieved by hand using a smoothing plane. This was delicate work indeed; guitars and lutes were so lightly constructed that it would take time for him to adjust to the vast difference between the larger keyboard instruments he was familiar with and the lighter fretted, plucked instruments.

Within a few weeks his understanding and confidence grew in the clever design of what at first appeared to be light and delicate but was in fact very strong and perfectly suited to withstand the tension of the over-100-pound pull for the guitar. There was an even greater tension on the lute, with its fourteen or more strings.

David was very patient as he guided Paul for several hours each day through the intricacies of the guitar and lute, new and such different instruments to the ones he was accustomed to. Not only were the dimensions on a much smaller scale, but the woods themselves were nearly all new to him. He began to understand, for the first time, the critical importance of selecting each species for its unique acoustic properties with the aid of what became known as 'The Bible' – a hard-covered notebook with the order of construction for guitar and lutes and all the measurements and drawings from David's New York days (Figure 4.2).

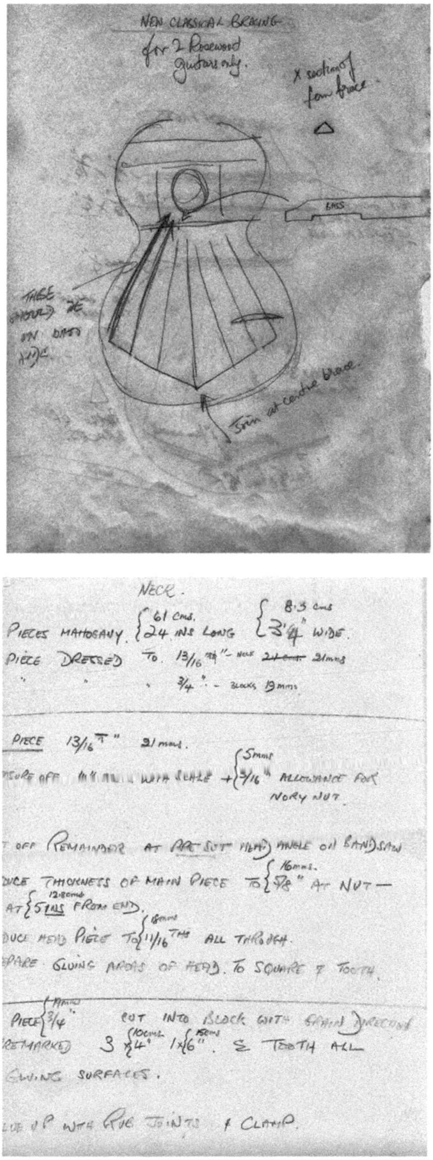

FIGURE 4.2 David Rubio's notes for the guitar's structure. These two pages are from what Paul refers to as 'The Bible'. The notebook was started by David Rubio during his New York days and was then passed on to Paul when he started working at Duns Tew; he then used it to write in his own construction details. When Paul Fischer left Duns Tew to set up his own workshop, David Rubio passed The Bible on to him. Photograph by Paul Fischer.

With David Rubio's guidance to the construction of lutes and guitars, combined with his previous training and experience, Paul was working on his own within a matter of weeks. David's own 'training' in instrument making was not something he discussed. As far as Paul knew, David had barely begun building guitars on his own in New York only five years earlier. There was mention of his visits to makers in Spain to observe the way things were done, but of course that is quite different from the gradual and necessary process of learning any craft. Even if an artisan had wished to impart all his knowledge to someone, there is no short, quick way to do this.

Sharing the workshop with Tom Hom added to the general conversation, with tales of his own life in New York and his work as a gilder. Prior to his accident, he was doing gilding work for Sotheby's, but he was only at Duns Tew for a few months before returning to the USA in April 1969.

Nest, David Rubio's wife, would enter the workshop each morning with a welcome cup of coffee, and she, like David, enjoyed talking. Sitting by Paul's bench, she would comment on the techniques Paul used, as they were 'so different' from David's woodworking style. These were woodworking skills Paul had learnt from Robert Goble, who had in turn learnt them from Dolmetsch, as well as from Goble's own father. With David's hunger for learning, through observation he soon adopted these also: for example, the use of a very simple tool called a cabinet scraper, which, if sharpened carefully, was an incredibly useful piece of equipment, particularly for instrument making.

Guitar makers don't need a vast range of tools, but as Paul was making a variety of different instruments – guitars, lutes and soon, once more, harpsichords – he had a large selection mounted on his wall rack. For guitar making, one needs a collection of planes, generally of the smaller variety, including smoothing planes, the block plane, down to tiny thumb planes. Then one needs a good set of bevel-edged chisels (the best ones Paul found were from Switzerland or Japan), a selection of cabinet scrapers, spoke shaves, small hammers, small bead saws, various punches, very precise steel rules, a vernier gauge, a micrometre, a scalpel and sharpening stones. When discussing these tools, Paul describes them as tools for engineering in wood; this refers to the delicate tolerances used in instrument making. For lute making, the necessary tools are quite similar but with the addition of half-round and hollow scrapers.

David was a forward-looking man, so everything in the workshop was modern and state of the art; however, he did have one particular antique tool in his toolkit: a Norris jackplane. This was rarely used at Duns Tew, it being too large for the small instrument being created. Norris used to make the finest planes, and Paul was always searching for them.

Throughout the workshop, photographs of instruments adorned the walls. Renaissance and Baroque lutes and guitars; they all bore the one name – José Rubio – written below each. The name was confusing; Rubio was Paul's new employer's surname, but why 'José'?

While Paul was absorbing the routine of Rubio's workshop, the vital guitar-making details and developing his own theories of acoustics, the stories kept coming – interrupting work but fascinating to hear, nonetheless. They finally included the full tale of 'José Rubio'. David told colourful stories of his early life travelling with the gypsies in Spain and learning the flamenco guitar.[37] During his travels, and in order to make a living, he began trading in the special woods used in guitar making. On his visits to the guitar makers in Madrid and Granada, he also absorbed some of the details of the art of instrument making. It was at this time that, being of Northern European origin, he acquired the soubriquet '*el*

---

[37] Many years later, Paul came to know one of David Rubio's early flamenco guitar role models and teachers, Bill Glover, who introduced himself at Paul's display during one of the annual Art in Action exhibitions at Waterperry House in Oxfordshire. As he later wrote to Paul in a letter of 14 February 2006 (note, Spink was David Rubio's family name): '… David Spink … turned up every night with a guitar and a notebook. He took free guitar lessons and was trying to steal the job I very badly needed. If I put down my instrument, he would immediately play the next piece of my limited repertory.'

At that time, the Spanish flamenco guitarist Pepe Martínez was a regular visitor to London, where he would perform, and eventually David Rubio followed him back to Spain in order to study with him more intensely.

Rubio' ('the blond one'). This was a reference to his pale complexion and not the colour of his beard, as is sometimes said. For the ten years Paul worked alongside Rubio, his beard remained a true, natural black colour.

Once David had gained a thorough grounding in playing flamenco guitar, he joined one of the leading flamenco dance troops – Rafael de Córdova Spanish Ballet Company – and left Spain for a tour of the USA with them.[38] It was during that tour that he decided to start making guitars. He set up a small workshop in a garret in Greenwich Village, New York, working with tools he had purchased from Woolworths (or so David claimed). His improvised bench was a chest of drawers (not quite the style of workshop Paul had envisaged for New York) and at first built flamenco guitars but then later began making classical guitars as well.

It was in the mid-1960s, during a New York concert commitment, that Julian Bream needed a small adjustment to his guitar. Bream was playing an instrument by the celebrated French luthier Robert Bouchet (1898–1986) and was advised to go and see 'The English Guitar Maker', who was then working in Greenwich Village, and it was this meeting with Julian Bream that inspired Rubio to begin making classical guitars. As Rubio later recounted to Paul, Bream had said, 'If you can make flamenco guitars as good as this, you should be able to make classical guitars.' Sometime after this, Rubio also began making his first lutes, and Julian Bream ordered lutes as well as guitars from him. It was common

FIGURE 4.3 David Rubio, the flamenco guitarist, on the cover of *BMG* magazine in October 1970. Photograph by *BMG* magazine.

---

[38] Despite this impressive background in performance, David never played a guitar or any flamenco in front of Paul in the workshop.

practice for David Rubio, and then later for Paul, to allow their visiting clients to choose the wood for their instrument, and thus Rubio still had the offcut piece from the soundboard signed by Julian Bream '7 February 1965'.

Years later, in discussing the first lute David Rubio had made for Julian Bream in New York in 1965, he recalled his dissatisfaction at copying the 'Bream lute'.[39] Rubio's New York and initially the Duns Tew lutes contain many of these modern compromises, which were expected by guitar/lute players at that time. Fortunately, within a matter of a year or two, by 1971–1972, Paul and David were only creating authentic copies of historical lutes. Paul's first lutes were made using the existing moulds David had built in New York. The makers whom David had copied and admired for these moulds were German lute makers, some of whom had worked in Italy, such as Laux Maler (1485–1552), who worked in Bologna, Michielle Harton (Michael Hartung) (c.1591–c.1627), who worked in Padua, Joachim Tielke (1641–1719) and Johann Christian Hoffmann (1653–1719). Paul and David also made new moulds based on fresh research at the Victoria and Albert Museum in London and the German National Museum in Nuremberg.

David Rubio was aware of the dangers of trying to produce a 'copy' of an instrument from an earlier age; he preferred to call his instruments 're-creations'. One of Rubio's concerns, when taking measurements from original instruments, was the dehydration of the wood in a historical lute; Rubio believed that the instrument might have lost up to about half its original weight over time. While Paul feels that David's estimate of about half of its original weight is a little extreme, this issue was often discussed by them during this period, when Paul and David were aiming to create more authentic early instruments. However, they were only too aware of another serious consideration that needed to be applied: throughout the

---

[39] This instrument is what Paul and David would refer to as a 'theorbette' in their discussions, as it enabled them to draw the distinction between the Baroque lute with its short neck extension and the much larger theorbo of the period.

intervening centuries, many of these relatively delicate instruments had undergone restoration or repair and the resulting alterations in the fine dimensions of the original instrument – even by a few thousandths of an inch – made critical differences.

In New York, David Rubio was receiving orders from Rey de la Torre, Charlie Byrd[40] and Nato Lima of the Brazilian guitar duo Los Indios Tabajaras. Paul remembers well the records by Los Indios Tabajaras, which David Rubio had in his collection and would play often on the workshop's record player.[41]

These were the heady days of David Rubio's time in New York. Another fascinating part of the story is his connection to Irving Sloane, the author of *Classical Guitar Construction: Diagrams, Photographs and Step-by-Step Instructions*, first published in New York in 1966. In his Acknowledgements, Irving Sloane writes, 'I have benefited from the valuable experience of José Rubio [David Rubio], a luthier with an impressive and well-deserved reputation.'[42] Some sections of Sloane's book, including many instructional photographs, are of David Rubio working. Although they are all shots of hands at work (no head shots), Paul certainly recognises those hands and tools as belonging to David

---

[40] Those early 'clients' stayed in contact with David Rubio after he moved back to England; for example, Paul made a guitar for Charlie Byrd during his time at Duns Tew. An order came through from Rey de la Torre; it arrived on Paul's bench but for some unknown reason the order was not fulfilled. Paul also remembers making a guitar for Konrad Ragossnig (but not a lute; that was made by David Rubio).

[41] The question arises of whether it was possible that David fulfilled all of the orders he had received deposits for in New York. When Paul first started at Duns Tew, he remembers that the instrument numbers started at number 170; that was in February 1969. If that number were accurate, then David would have made a substantial number of instruments over the very few years since he first set up the workshop in New York. When Paul Fischer joined the workshop at Duns Tew in 1969, they were together making around forty instruments per year. Rubio's guitar from 1966 New York is number 74; another guitar from 1967 is number 117.

[42] Irving Sloane, *Classical Guitar Construction: Diagrams, Photographs, and Step-by-Step Instructions* (New York: Dutton, 1966).

Rubio. For many years, Sloane's *Classical Guitar Construction* remained one of the few published books providing detailed instructions and thus was a seminal textbook for guitar makers in the 1960s and 1970s.[43]

David Rubio kept in touch with many of his old New York contacts. Thus, when Paul started at Duns Tew, David would buy materials from Juan Orozco, particularly rosewood, and varnish from H. Behlen & Bros, who were in Christopher Street, Greenwich Village. David and Paul also continued ordering their strings from the United States, from La Bella and Augustine. Orozco had a factory in New York, and as the manager of Rubio's workshop, Paul carried on buying wood from him.

David Rubio's preferred guitar soundboard design was mostly with seven fan braces, but when Paul was with him, they occasionally did nine braces. David and Paul did small experiments for about three years and then standardised the design. In short, they returned to the same design Rubio had followed for the Julian Bream guitars. This was mainly a Torres design, always with the addition of a nodal bar, which is a small horizontal bar bridging over the two outside treble fan braces directly in line with the bridge saddle.

The two braces above the soundhole were quite standard and very necessary; both are Torres in style. It was discovered that if the upper of the two braces fell between two of the frets from above, the notes would be almost dead with no sustain; however, when this upper brace was placed directly beneath a fret, the notes would then come alive and resonate fully.

These small changes would make a considerable difference; quite a few of their guitars had nine fan braces, but they did also make a few with five fan braces, following the style of the Spanish luthier Paulino Bernabé. In the end, they discovered that all these changes in bracing

---

[43] Irving Sloane remained in contact with David Rubio after he had returned to England. Paul remembers his visits to Duns Tew. Later, when he became interested in manufacturing high-quality machine heads, he would visit Paul at his Chipping Norton studio for consultation and discussion.

made little or no major difference and, therefore, they settled on seven braces. On occasion, Paul and David also took two or three of the bass braces up higher into the upper bout to see what the effect would be but, again, they found no major differences, so they reverted to the standard setting of bracing.

David Rubio had two styles of rosette during his New York days and would use them equally at that time. In Duns Tew, both he and Paul continued to use both designs until the workforce for guitar making increased. Those artisans would use the design, which Nest referred to as 'hearts and flowers'; Rubio used to call the other rosette design 'vine'. Following Rubio's usual style of thorough organisation, when Paul started working in Duns Tew they still had a good supply of these rosettes from his New York days. Interestingly, when this supply ran out, David Rubio had his vine-style rosettes made in Japan, as the demand for guitars was so high and they needed many and quickly. This change in production can be seen in the design, which remained the same but with very slightly larger detailing. The hearts and flowers design, however, gradually drifted out of use.

In the Duns Tew workshop, David Rubio had the half-profile wooden patterns of the bodies of guitars such as Santos Hernández (1874–1943), Francisco Simplicio (1874–1932) and Robert Bouchet (1898–1986), which had been made by David Rubio while he was in New York. He would lay the guitar on its back, on a sheet of Mylar, which is a special type of plastic, then gently draw around the body of the guitar onto the Mylar, carefully marking the centre line of the back. From this, one could make a half template in any material you wished, although David's preference was for wood.[44] Paul still has the template for a Baroque guitar made by David in New York, dated December 1966 (although David captioned the photograph in Figure 4.4 '1965'); although David insisted on calling it a Baroque guitar, it can clearly be seen to have the size and

---

[44] Paul continued this standard practice of making templates but would use a more stable material, such as clear Perspex, which would not warp with heat.

shape of a modern guitar. The feature defining this as a Baroque guitar is the fact that it had ten strings with Baroque tuning, but only in single courses rather than the standard double course. David was just starting to learn about instruments of an earlier age, having only recently moved on from making flamenco guitars. Even the first lutes made at Duns Tew were called 'Bream models' because they had metal frets and used guitar gauge strings by La Bella; these instruments were being made for classical guitarists so that they could play with their nails. This was a clear indication that he was still feeling his way with Early Music instruments, but David learnt quickly and was always seeking to improve.

FIGURE 4.4 A sequence of three photos showing the 'modern' so-called Baroque instrument made by David Rubio in New York. Paul notes that the body shape is in a distinctively Rubio style. Photograph by David Rubio.

In the Oxford days, they had the advantage of being near the Ashmolean Museum, with the beautiful Stradivari and Voboam guitars, which were part of the Hill Collection. Messrs W.E. Hill and sons were a family of violin makers who had put together a wonderful collection of bowed and plucked instruments that had been bequeathed to the Ashmolean Museum in the 1930s and 1940s. Paul had been trained in technical drawing and, as they were not on display at that time, it was his responsibility to search the vaults of the museum and thereby create all the drawings for these rare masterpieces. He was allowed to make measurements and drawings of the rare Stradivari guitar and spent many happy hours in the basement of the Ashmolean. Sadly, this is something less likely to be allowed today, because there is a reluctance for these delicate instruments to be handled too frequently. These days, most museums make their own drawings and sell them on a commercial basis. Paul was also able to make drawings of the Gasparo de Salo cittern and a Voboam Baroque guitar – the plans for the Voboam guitar being later used to construct a guitar for the guitarist John Williams during his short flirtation with playing on an early period instrument.

At the same time Paul expanded the range of plucked early instruments offered by Rubio's studios, authenticity became increasingly important and expected: for example, the metal frets on lutes and Baroque guitars were replaced by more authentic gut-tied frets and they were even experimenting with gut strings made by Ephraim Segerman, who used a combination of materials, which gave good results.

David was bursting with interesting stories, which Paul never tired of hearing. One of the many stories he remembers well from the daily sessions on his bench with Rubio was his meeting with the doyen of the classical guitar, Andrés Segovia. As Rubio told it, Segovia had made it obvious during their conversations together that it was generally believed that only Spaniards could make fine guitars – though it was accepted that the German maker Hermann Hauser had made instruments for the maestro.

With that experience and other indicators, Rubio realised that his real name of David Joseph Cohen might prove a handicap in the world of the Spanish (classical) guitar.[45] In his New York days, he Hispanicised his second given name to José and substituted his soubriquet Rubio for his

---

[45] When David Rubio's mother remarried, he adopted the surname of his stepfather, Cohen.

family name, and so became José Rubio. He hoped this would bypass the prejudices evident from his meeting with Segovia, among others. On his return to England in 1967, he began using his first given name, hence David Rubio.

Initially, David Rubio took up the offer of Julian Bream to set up his instrument-making workshop in a converted barn on Bream's property in Wiltshire, providing him and Nest with accommodation by means of a nearby bungalow. David had been wanting to move back to England and this provided the perfect catalyst. As so often happens in excited artistic discussions, both parties viewed the situation from their own angle and didn't imagine that the other party might have been thinking differently: Julian Bream thought he was entitled to choose from whichever instrument David produced in his workshop but, on the other hand, David Rubio had a healthy and growing client list and he felt obliged to be fair to all his clients, who had paid deposits on their instruments.

The outcome of this was that David and Nest were soon searching for a place of their own. David contacted COSIRA (the Council for Small

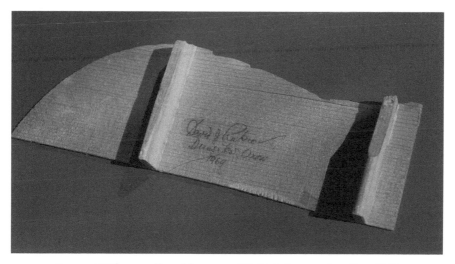

FIGURE 4.5 The soundboard from one of Rubio's Bream guitars from 1969.
Photograph: Paul Fischer Collection.

Industries in Rural Areas), and Jan Balkwell, who was responsible for southern England, found the premises for David in Duns Tew, Oxfordshire, which was almost derelict when they first moved there.[46]

During Paul's early months at Duns Tew, David would enter the workshop each morning via an internal door, rakishly attired in Savile Row trousers, burgundy velvet waistcoat, spotted bow tie and smoking a cigarette in a holder. Unusual dress perhaps, however this, coupled with David wearing full suit plus a bowler hat when going to concerts in his New York days, earned him the moniker 'Gentleman Guitar Maker'. Making less of a splash but still curious, he did eventually change to wearing the more conventional and practical uniform – a craftsman's apron – but the cigarette and holder remained.[47]

PEPE MARTINEZ—see page 143

FIGURE 4.6 Pepe Martínez featured on the January 1972 cover of *BMG* magazine playing his Fischer flamenco guitar. Photograph: BMG magazine.

By May 1969, Paul's first six months at Rubio's had passed and he had completed a number of guitars and lutes. The very first guitar Paul made was a flamenco guitar for the 15-year-old British virtuoso flamenco guitarist Ian Davies (1954–2003), soon to be internationally recognised.

The flamenco guitarist Pepe Martínez used to visit the Duns Tew workshop often and would always play. Flamenco guitars are similar to classical guitars but with the back and sides made of cypress (*Cupressus*), although the modern trend is to use

---

[46] It was also Jan Balkwell who was indirectly responsible for Paul's first journey of initiative to drive north to the village to meet the mystery musical instrument maker.

[47] This stylish dressing clearly appealed to his wife, Nest; so much so, that when Paul and Joy's smiley little boy, Scott, was about two years old, Nest bought him a black velvet suit.

Indian rosewood (*Dalbergia latifolia*), as found on classical guitars. The instrument is much lighter than the classical guitar and has a *golpeador* – the tap plate for the percussive strokes required in flamenco. The subtle differences between flamenco and classical guitars include lower action, lighter soundboard bracing and thickness, and the occasional use of traditional wooden tuning pegs instead of machine heads. The flamenco guitarist Juan Martín also chose the rosewood (*Dalbergia nigra*) style of flamenco guitar, which Paul made for him in 1972. This is a guitar that Juan has used throughout his career, notably in his solo recitals at Wigmore Hall, and which he still has in his collection.

FIGURE 4.7 A flamenco guitar by Paul Fischer, belonging to flamenco guitarist Juan Martín,[48] constructed in a traditional style with a cypress body and built many years later in his own workshop with, of course, his own maker's distinctive peg headstock
Photograph from Paul Fischer Collection.

Luthiers also choose specific woods for each component of the instrument; thus, a single instrument uses a range of tonewoods. Not *all* woods are tonewoods. Some examples of the tonewoods used for musical instruments include maples, rosewoods, cedars and spruce.

---

[48] Juan Martín used the guitar on several tracks on his *Serenade* recording with the Royal Philharmonic Orchestra including *Cavatina*, the Chopin *Prelude*, *Les Sylphides* and *Romance Anónimo*, and also featured on the cover of his *Solos Flamencos* books.

However, oak, beech and elm, for example, are not tonewoods, so careful selection of the most appropriate species has been determined by experience over centuries. The acoustic response of a musical instrument refers to the amplification of the energy produced by a vibrating string and the supporting material (usually wood) used in the instrument's construction.

FIGURE 4.8 Paul working on his first lute at David Rubio's studio in 1969. Although the photograph shows David working on the same instrument, this was only for publicity purposes, when *The Banbury Guardian* came to write an article.
Printed with permission of *The Banbury Guardian.*

At this time, in late 1969, David received a commission for a full-size replica theorbo, a new instrument for him, which thus required research and the preparation of drawings (with the so-called Baroque guitar and early lutes, which were modern interpretations of these instruments, Rubio had made only a theorbette during his time in New York). Apart from pictures in books, there was little information available, so to get a real feel for the instrument, including its weight, proportions and style, it became important to visit the Early Music instrument collection at the Victoria and Albert Museum (V&A) in London. These were early days in the rebirth of Early Music and its instruments. Research was vital, and museums were the obvious source for material and example instruments. However, many did not allow the actual handling of their exhibits and unlike Paul's good fortune and experiences of his regular visits to the vaults of the Ashmolean Museum, on his visit to the V&A it was a matter of learning as much as possible staring through the glass of a sealed case. However, this did produce a considerable amount of information, with the remainder coming from the few periodicals covering the subject at that time.

The other approach to the making of these rare ancient instruments, for which there was little or no access to extant examples or detailed information, was to try to make one, solving the construction problems as and when they occurred. This could be frustrating but was nevertheless quite an exciting learning process. The making of this first theorbo fell to Paul, as he had the wider experience of instrument construction. It was assumed that he would be able to solve the jointing problems of the multi-cranked neck on his own!

Thus, the first theorbo Paul created was based on an instrument in the V&A, which had been made in 1637 by the great Italian maker Matteo Sellas. This original instrument had the bowl (the back) made with ribs of ivory, and the highly decorated back of the neck was veneered with ivory and ebony. Out of respect for elephants and their unethical killing for tusks, the body (bowl) of Paul's lute was similar in construction but used maple wood instead of ivory. The body of the instrument was similar to the normal lutes Paul had already made and posed no great problem. The complicated cranked neck (offset from the centre line, for the correct positioning of the bass strings) was a different matter entirely, and with its 'swan head' upper peg box and seven double courses of strings, it proved a considerable challenge. Because David Rubio at this time was devoting his energies to the making of bowed instruments of a similar period (viols and the like), this challenge fell to Paul. Nevertheless, even his first theorbo was a success.

In the early 1970s he went to the concert of the famous Brazilian duo, the Abreu brothers, at the Purcell Room in London. Afterwards Paul of course went backstage to the green room to chat to them, innocently enquiring which guitars they were playing. They looked a bit surprised by the question, and Sérgio said, 'Yours, of course!' The pair of Rubio guitars had been made by Paul Fischer under the Rubio label. Paul attended many of their concerts in England, including those when Sérgio

SÉRGIO and EDUARDO ABREU

FIGURE 4.9 The Abreus with their Rubio/Paul Fischer
guitars.

began his solo career, and they would also always meet up when Paul
visited Brazil. After an incredibly successful career as a performer, Sérgio
Abreu decided to dedicate his life to guitar making, where he continues to
produce fine guitars in Rio de Janeiro.[49]

---

[49] Sérgio based his first guitar on the Rubio design. His workshop is a converted flat
and is full of dehumidifying machines, and he has to keep them on twenty-four hours
a day.

CHAPTER 5

Harpsichords at Duns Tew

With the theorbo finished and away at the client's premises, Rubio turned his attention to the making of the workshop's first harpsichord. Those first months had been filled with talk of harpsichords, until finally, with Paul on hand and his experience of making them, the temptation was too much to resist: the Hubbard harpsichord parts were retrieved from the loft. In the mezzanine, as well as storing the precious tonewoods, David had kept semi-prepared harpsichord components, which had been manufactured in the USA by the famous maker and pupil of Arnold Dolmetsch, Frank Hubbard. David had brought these components over with all his other equipment when he'd moved from New York to Julian Bream's workshop in Wiltshire: a keyboard, belly rail and wrest plank (the heavy board at the front of the harpsichord into which the tuning pins are fitted).

Paul's previous work with harpsichords would soon be required. The prepared Hubbard components were studied. The problem was, which model to follow? These Hubbard parts were replicas for a Flemish instrument, probably by Joannes 'Jan' Ruckers (1578–1642), but Rubio had different ideas, despite having little or no knowledge of harpsichord construction at that time. Paul was not able to help too much with these thoughts, as his own experience was with the Goble instruments, far removed from those of the seventeenth century. The age of 'authenticity' had begun, and gone was the time of the pianoesque and engineered harpsichords of Arnold Dolmetsch and Robert Goble, though Goble's son Andrea would join the new movement by the 1970s.

David had bought only three Hubbard parts – in other words, not the full kit – and, therefore, Paul had to make all the other components. The parts by Frank Hubbard were for a Flemish harpsichord, probably by

Ruckers, and the school of Flemish/French harpsichord making was very different in style to that found in Italy, which David eventually chose for the rest of the instrument. The structure of the carcass, or the skeleton, for the instrument was usually quite different, depending on which country the instrument had come from, partly because they used materials that were available in their own countries; for example, the body and soundboards of Italian harpsichords were made with cypress, whereas parts of English instruments could be made of oak, while in the Flemish instruments, we find poplar from the Ardennes.

After much discussion, David and Paul decided that it would be encased in English sycamore. This was an English compromise because cypress was not available in the large dimensions they required. In any case, sycamore is a very fine tonewood and is often used for violin making. Furthermore, David was familiar with it from making lutes and they also knew that with its tight grain it would take decorative paint very well. David came up with the idea of copying the casework of an Italian instrument, which was very lightly constructed (three-eighths of an inch sycamore), and incorporating the Hubbard parts, with a carcass (frame) to be built by Paul in the Italian style (in mahogany). Rubio was probably influenced in this unusual approach by the light and relatively delicate construction he was familiar with for the fretted instruments that were his stock in trade. Flemish and Italian harpsichords followed very different methods of construction from those of small, plucked, fretted instruments, so considerable skill and imagination were required – and perhaps a little luck.

Working through this seemingly crazy scheme produced a functioning but very unusual instrument. The internal mechanical components (the 'action') were Flemish in character and worked extremely well with the double manual keyboard using modern Delrin jacks and plectra. The Italian casework added Latin elegance, though the decoration was, again, in the Flemish style: the outside was a dramatic black with gilded moulding, and the inside was a luscious deep red colour, all of which was painted by David. Norman Goodwin, a neighbour who lived directly across the road, was a Royal Academician and created a painting in the Dutch/Flemish style, with lutes spread on Persian-style carpet, covering a table on the underside of the lid. It was an expensive addition but David never worried about expense.

FIGURE 5.1 Harpsichord number 1, created by Paul Fischer and David Rubio, with a lid painting by Norman Goodwin, RA. Ed Brewer gave a concert on the harpsichord in the church opposite the Rubio workshop; David Rubio is the central figure.
Photograph by John Marshall. Reproduced with permission.

Paul worked on this first Rubio harpsichord at Duns Tew at the same time as his guitar and lute making. At that time, there was one very large workshop, with just Paul and David working together. The harpsichord was created on a dedicated bench, as they had the luxury of having four or five benches in the same workshop. Paul had to explain the structure of the carcass of a harpsichord to David, but his experience was in the Goble hybrid, which was more in the style of those made by Dolmetsch. Of course, Goble followed his own style, which was more pianoesque, because the instruments had lead in the keys and the jacks, which made for a very heavy touch, and the case was much heavier in order to withstand the tension of the overwound strings – original harpsichords did not have wound strings.

One of the first people to play this harpsichord creation was the guitarist Julian Bream, who was a frequent visitor to Rubio's workshop, calling in for minor adjustments to a lute or guitar when travelling between recitals. This gave Paul the chance to become acquainted with the maestro. Bream had been trained on the piano, but the harpsichord is a different beast. This led to a hilarious moment when Julian tried to change the keyboard coupling mechanism with his right knee (rather than his hand). This is a manoeuvre usually achieved either by pressing a pedal or by pressing or pushing the upper manual forward, depending on the construction of the instrument. But it was a quirky design feature of this instrument to have a coupling lever set in the board at the front of the lower keyboard.

Harpsichord number 1 remained in the workshop for some weeks and was admired and even played in concert by the American harpsichordist Ed Brewer in the church opposite the workshop. Although this first harpsichord was a compromise – the Flemish-style double-manual action instrument resting in an Italian case – it was a success, if not exactly authentic. The Open University was the delighted recipient of Rubio harpsichord number 1 at a ceremony in 1970 attended by all involved in its creation.

Local and national press were beginning to take an interest in the unusual craft of handmade musical instruments and particularly those of an earlier age. The revival of performing on early instruments with performers such as the Early Music wind instrumentalist David Munrow and Julian Bream did much to inspire this, not only through their playing but also, for example, through programmes such as David Munrow with his *Pied Piper* series on BBC Television, which in turn encouraged the press and general media to seek out new stories about the exciting Early Music revival movement.

Radio, television and press started to pay frequent visits to the studio workshop in Duns Tew, adding to the interest and enquiries for instruments. The main source of these came from aficionados seeking copies of seventeenth- and eighteenth-century harpsichords (for example, those of Pascal Taskin, Blanchet and the Ruckers families). Performers wanted authentic copies, except where the use of modern materials improved stability and reliability.

The fact that they received a lot of publicity in the early days of Duns Tew impressed and confounded Paul. At the end of 1969, David took Paul to the Hop Cross Holt, a hotel nearby, for a Christmas drink. Paul, in his naivety, asked David why the press kept calling in. David smiled and said, 'You have to realise that I am a show-off.'

The Daily Telegraph visited them and this produced a great response, as did articles in magazines such as *Guitar International*. Paul remembers well the drama of the BBC television camera crews, with their cameras positioned on the top of an estate car, filming all the way from Oxford to Duns Tew. The American harpsichordist, who was living in Oxford at the time, played the role of a prospective customer and the process was filmed. By the time Radio Oxford came to visit, even David was becoming less enamoured of the attention, so he asked Paul to respond to the more local media attention, which was a new and good experience for him.

They always kept working when the press and clients visited the three workshops; David would leave Paul to escort visitors between workshops, so it really didn't stop them working, but the interesting questions and feedback did inspire. The atmosphere was always productive – even when the country was forced into a three-day week by Prime Minister Edward Heath battling against the miners. Although for most of the country the power went off in 1974, David managed to get special dispensation (this is because he told the authorities he was exporting most of what he produced, which got them partly around the regulations, but not totally). They didn't always have the electricity to use the machines but that didn't matter; they all had the necessary skills and sufficient light – even using little campers' gas lamps – so they continued working a full week.

David Rubio's reputation within the field of instrument making rapidly blossomed. Demand for early instruments was soon to follow. This caused a problem, albeit a good one: how were only two artists/craftsmen to meet the growing demand? Clearly, they could not do this without getting more staff with the right skills and also the right temperament. Rubio had often expressed a wish to create a community of highly skilled makers working on a complete range of early instruments, something along the lines of Arnold Dolmetsch's workshop in Haslemere, Surrey. It was not an idea he broadcast widely but it took the form of casual remarks made when leaning on the end of Paul's bench.

In 1970–1971 Rubio took the bold decision to take on more staff and accommodate them and the production of harpsichords in the humble barn in the garden. First he had to embark on remedial and sensitive work to convert the barn into a modern workshop housed within its aged Cotswold stone skin beneath a mantel of Norfolk reed thatch matching the existing house.

He also planned to increase the production of fretted instruments, with classical guitars and lutes continuing in the original workshop. The profile of the classical guitar was also burgeoning at this time, largely stimulated by the numerous recordings being produced by two popular UK-based classical guitarists: Julian Bream and John Williams. An undesirable consequence of this expansion was that his own time at the bench, doing the work he loved, would be reduced and interrupted by administrative work. This was partly mitigated by appointing Paul as the workshop manager, thus sharing the tedious jobs, as they saw it, of a rapidly (perhaps too rapidly) expanding business.

Finding more new staff with the required esoteric skills was not easy either. Where do you find such folk? Not only were the skills in short supply, but also the world of instrument makers was a small one. However, word got out and before long there was soon knocking at the door. One or two ex-Robert Goble personnel – and some not so ex – applied to join. Even this was not enough, and more staff were needed. Pattern makers and cabinetmakers were approached in the hope that their considerable woodworking skills could be adapted to the world of the luthier. Most of the employees had been trained with a full apprenticeship in harpsichord making. They also employed two highly skilled pattern makers, whose work was solely involved with the decorative finishing of harpsichords, including some of the gilding.

After the first harpsichord was completed, the next harpsichords could be made in a more organic way, completely from scratch. As they were employing ex-Goble staff, the design followed standard practice at that time, in which Paul was thoroughly knowledgeable. When building that harpsichord number 1, Paul had to create the coupling mechanisms for each key, which includes a device on every key, enabling the lower keyboard to be automatically coupled with the one above. This allows both keyboards on a double-manual harpsichord to be played just by using the lower manual. This coupling device is a five-part mechanism, which with a 66-key manual gives some idea of the painstaking labour required. This five-part mechanism was what he was trained to create at Gobles. After this first harpsichord, Paul wondered whether this work could not be modernised and made to work more efficiently, thus he designed a two-part mechanism made from Delrin – a non-static nylon. Oliver Brookes, who was an Early Music performer connected with David Munrow, was also involved in injection moulding and was then asked if he could produce these little devices Paul had designed. The result was pleasing and they discovered that they worked beautifully and reduced the work time on the keyboard considerably. From then on, all the harpsichords were fitted with this modern system.

One may ask whether Paul Fischer thought about patenting his design; however, at that time he was employed by David Rubio, and the law relating to patents meant that had he applied to patent the design, it would have to have been under the name of his employer, David Rubio. Therefore, Paul did not pursue it further.

By chance, Kazuo Sato, a young Japanese guitar maker, applied through an existing Rubio client, Shiro Arai, for a position. A godsend! Sato, an enthusiastic and trained guitar maker, was highly recommended; he joined the team and quickly learnt the skills needed to make lutes in addition to guitars.

FIGURE 5.2 Some of the authentic labels that David 'José' Rubio used; the first two were used in his New York days.
Photograph from Paul Fischer Collection.

As Rubio's instruments were becoming more sought after and valued, one of the things that concerned both David and Paul was the possible creation of 'fake' Rubio instruments. Therefore, they would put many more stamps and forms of identification, beyond the reach of forgers, such as an initialled stamp on the underside of the soundboards. Whenever makers were employed in the Rubio workshop, each maker would make the *complete* instrument – that was their responsibility. No one was officially employed as an apprentice, as all had been fully trained in their own right before joining Rubio's workshop. Kazuo Sato, for example, had trained with the luthier Kuniharu Nobe in Japan from 1965 to 1971. This, on the other hand, was sometimes restrictive for the individual maker because they were expected to follow the Rubio guidelines.

In around 1970–1971 David Rubio moved on and almost completely focused on making early bowed instruments such as the viola da gamba, and the Baroque violin and cello. These bowed instruments required the creation of yet another new workshop. This, Rubio did by converting one room of the main house. Thus, there were now three separate workshops: one for harpsichords, another for small plucked instruments and a third for bowed instruments. Rubio tried to split his time between the three and, at the same time, make the bowed instruments on his own. Paul did likewise, dividing his time between mundane administration and his own responsibilities for instrument making and teaching.

By the mid-1970s, the establishment included six staff: three dedicated to harpsichord making, one guitar and lute maker and one lute maker – of course, one of these six was Paul, who made all instruments. As well as this nucleus of six skilled craftsmen, there were others who worked alongside the instrument makers, some undertaking the polishing and decoration and others adapting their existing skills to the numerous other tasks required. One or two would leave, and new ones would arrive to keep up the numbers over the next few years. This was not always successful; some failed to show the passion and dedication needed and others failed to share the ideals that drove Rubio – needless to say, these craftsmen did not last long. However, new and enthusiastic makers and craftsmen did join the workshops, bringing fresh ideas from around the world. Along with Sato from Japan making guitars and lutes, there was Milan Misina from Yugoslavia making harpsichords, Christine Cooper from the USA voicing the harpsichords and Rubio's stepson, Reid Galbraith, also from the USA making lutes. At its peak, there were ten people – who shared the wide range of skills needed for the equally wide range of instruments – spread between the three workshops.

Towards the end of his time in America, David was using Landstorfer machine heads on the modern guitars. Initially, the Duns Tew studios used the Landstorfer machine heads and sometimes mass-produced machine heads by Fustero from Barcelona and Kolb from Germany. Gerald Crowson was one of the artisans who provided beautiful and very elegant Baroque and Renaissance lute pegs for their lutes.[50] In around 1971, on one of his visits to the Duns Tew studios to deliver a new consignment of lute pegs, David and Paul showed him a set of very elegant nineteenth-century machine heads, made by the English maker, Baker, in London. This was a finely hand-engraved machine head with a nineteenth-century style of gearing known as bevel gearing; these were often fitted to high quality guitars from that era, such as Panormos. Considering his excellent work on pegs, David took the opportunity to ask whether Crowson might be able to reproduce a machine head in the Baker style. Gerald's reply was that he couldn't, but he thought his cousin David Rodgers could! At the time, David Rodgers was an engineer working for Myford Lathes in Nottingham. Gerald suggested that he approach Rodgers about this idea. Paul and David provided him with the Baker machine head as an example. To their surprise and pleasure, David Rodgers responded very positively and the rest is history, for he went on to produce some of the finest machine heads in many styles, but all of the same quality. David Rodgers continued to develop and explore

---

[50] Gerald Crowson continued to make parts for David Rubio's instruments up until the end of the twentieth century.

and never failed to produce machine heads of the highest quality. Thus, David Rodgers started making machine heads because of David Rubio.

As the interest in Early Music gained many new converts, the search for fine examples of instruments from that golden age, and from which copies could be made, put more pressure on Rubio's talented workforce. This could only be mitigated by seeking the help of equally talented artisans from beyond The Ridge House workshops. In early 1973 two very gifted practitioners in the world of the crafts were Peter and Ann Mactaggart, whose talents extended way beyond just the world of craft. Many of the early instruments created at Duns Tew, particularly the early fretted variety, required fine inlay work; harpsichords of the period required fine

FIGURE 5.3 Rance machine heads.
Photograph by Paul Fischer.

artwork with painted soundboards, marbled casework and printed paper linings. The Mactaggarts came on board, adding examples of their many talents to the range of instruments that came from the Oxfordshire workshops. Peter Mactaggart produced much of the inlay work required for the back of the necks of lutes and on the viola da gambas and Ann Mactaggart painted some of the soundboards of the harpsichords. The Mactaggarts were two artisans whom Paul admired greatly because their work was of an incredibly high standard.

In the early days, another artisan who became involved with the creation of this fascinating range of instruments was the musician and wood carver Joe Skeaping, who carved the scrolls for the violins and viola da gambas, including the carved lion's head in the style of Jacob Stainer

(1617–1683), which Rubio was copying. David Rubio, with his methodical approach, had shelves of these lined up and ready for use in his own workshop. When Paul started making citterns, the talents of Joe were appreciated even more, as he carved the figures for the headstocks of the citterns.

Citterns have four or five courses (sometimes even six courses), with the courses either triple-stringed but more often double-stringed. One of David's favourite stories regarding citterns – to explain the built-in hook on the back of the peg head – was that they could then be hung on a barbershop's wall, and as the clients waited for their turn, they could strike up a tune. Citterns were a popular instrument throughout England and Europe. Shakespeare, in *Love's Labour's Lost*, had one of his characters call someone a 'cittern-head'. This was meant as an insult; although the heads of citterns could be beautiful, in many cases they were crudely fashioned and with quite ugly faces. Paul absolutely loved a cittern in the Ashmolean Museum – by Gasparo da Salo (1542–1609) of Brescia, Italy – and was inspired to copy this beautiful instrument.

FIGURE 5.4 Cittern made by Paul Fischer, based on an instrument by Gasparo da Salo in the Ashmolean Museum, Oxford. The photograph clearly shows the gilding on the head, which was applied in the Duns Tews workshop after carving. Photograph by John Marshall.

Paul was so taken with the design of the back of a Girolamo Brescia cittern (1574), in the Kunsthistorisches Museum in Vienna, that he used the decoration on a guitar magnum opus with that pattern on the back in highly figured maple, set in Brazilian rosewood – this was a purely decorative addition to the back of the instrument.

In the Rubio workshop, Paul was always working on a range of plucked instruments simultaneously. Pandoras were another early wire-strung instrument that Paul was commissioned to make at the Rubio workshops. Pandoras are much larger than the citterns; the pandora in Figure 5.5, which is hanging alongside two lutes, gives some idea of its proportions. Notice also in this photograph that the pandora is hanging behind a wall of 'go bars' that are holding down the braces of the harpsichord soundboard mid construction while the glue dries. This also gives some idea of the hub of activity in the Duns Tew workshops; if we looked at illustrations of luthier workshops from the fifteenth and sixteenth centuries, the view would be very similar. As Paul points out, the true definition of a luthier is a maker of stringed instruments, and is not usually dedicated to one single form of stringed instrument.

The commission for two pandoras was for the French ensemble Les Ménestriers, who had formed their Early Music group in 1969. On their visit to Duns Tew, they also gave a concert for the Duns Tew Music Society in the church opposite the workshops. Unlike the difficulties with the vihuela, outlined later, Paul had a picture of an extant pandora in the Conservatoire Royal, Brussels, in Anthony Baines's *Musical Instruments: European and American Musical Instruments*; Paul used this picture and his knowledge to create the pandora. Although the picture was a little crude, it helped enormously in reimagining its shape and proportions; once you know the scale length of an instrument, you can work out all the other proportions. Another instrument, which is quite similar to the pandora, is the orpharion (a wire-strung instrument invented in London in 1581 by John Rose), and this had a larger range of extant instruments, which Paul could use for reference. They copied many instruments by this renowned

FIGURE 5.5 A pandora hanging in the Duns Tew workshops, made by Paul Fischer.

maker, in addition to which, David Rubio also built copies of viols by John Rose.[51]

Just as Paul Fischer had built the first theorbo at the Duns Tew workshops, he was also tasked with the creation of vihuelas when they received the commissions in 1971–1972. In the early 1970s hardly any makers in the world were building vihuelas, as they were very new to the Early Music instrument revival scene and there was very little information to work with and few surviving authentic instruments to examine. These remarkable instruments existed in Spain (and South America) only during the sixteenth century. The Spanish guitarist and researcher Emilio Pujol was a champion of this instrument and repertoire and as early as the 1930s was performing on a vihuela – a primitive copy of one of the few surviving instruments. The extant instruments were often referred to as 'apprentice pieces', as they were extremely heavily constructed and Paul and David considered them unworkable for their realisation. Although David Rubio was involved in discussions about the vihuela, he had never made one, so the research was done by Paul and they were all created by Paul under the Rubio label.

Paul prepared the drawings, including those for eight-stringed vihuelas pitched at E, which were made for David Taplin, guitarist and lecturer at

---

[51] John Rose, father and son, were luthiers in Bridewell, London, in the late sixteenth to early seventeenth centuries.

the University of Huddersfield, and also for the Japanese lutenist Toyohiko Satoh, who was based in The Hague. The drawings Paul made were based on the illustrations in Luys Milan's *El Maestro*. From there he could calculate the proportions, and having already made lutes dating from a similar period, he could use his knowledge to recreate the vihuela. Paul also made six-stringed vihuelas for both David Taplin and Toyohiko Satoh, which were pitched at G. This ordering of two different-sized vihuelas was an indication of the experimentation in the early revival of vihuelas both on the part of the players and the makers. Most instruments existed in 'families' of different-sized instruments, in much the same way as the modern bowed instruments: for example, double bass, cello, viola and violin are of the same family but of different sizes. Later, orders for vihuelas were most often for a single instrument and usually of six double courses.

After these initial instruments were made, word quickly got around and more orders began arriving. Apart from talking things through with Paul, David Rubio was never involved in the construction of vihuelas or the early plucked instruments such as pandoras and citterns.

It was a time of much experimenting in the building of reproductions of early instruments, and thus Paul was happy to accommodate Toyohiko Satoh's request for an eight-stringed vihuela, even though

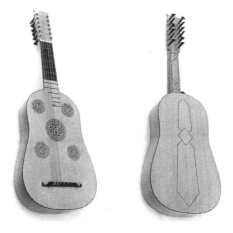

FIGURE 5.6 Vihuela made by Paul Fischer during this period at Duns Tew. Photograph from Paul Fischer Collection.

these didn't appear in any of the publications at the time. Paul simply upscaled the six-stringed version. Toyohiko Satoh was immersed in the Early Music revival and studied with the lutenist Eugen Müller-Dombois at the Schola Cantorum Basiliensis in Basel, who was also a client of the Rubio studio. He subsequently went on to have a high-profile career performing in ensemble with Early Music luminaries such as Gustav Leonhardt and Nikolaus Harnoncourt. These were incredibly exciting times for an instrument maker with a sense of adventure and an interest in experimentation, which Paul revelled in.

David Rubio was a rare figure and an inspirational one, and Paul was never able to understand how anyone could fail to be drawn into this magical world of creating and crafting beautiful instruments in idyllic surroundings under the influence of such a dynamic figure. It also provided the opportunity to meet many of the world's leading exponents of Early Music and the classical guitar, including Julian Bream, John Williams, Konrad Ragossnig, Gustav Leonhardt, Oliver Brooks, David Munrow, Igor Kipnis, Sigiswald Kuijken, Anthony Pleeth, and many others, who would all visit the workshops.

Rubio saw an opportunity with so many renowned international and British artists visiting and sometimes staying overnight. He appealed to their generosity and asked if they might perform at the newly created Duns Tew Music Society. Rubio was a leading light in this society and had spotted that the church across the road from the workshops would make an ideal venue, and also its proximity would be a boon when carrying a heavy

FIGURE 5.7 Blanchet harpsichord by David Rubio, 1974. Photograph by John Marshall. Printed with permission.

harpsichord to the concert venue.[52] Furthermore, the acoustics of the church were ideally suited to Early Music and acoustic instruments.

It turned out, to Rubio's surprise, that permission was needed from the Bishop of Oxford to perform classical music in the church. What is more, a prayer had to be said before each performance and no applause was permitted between pieces. The convenience of Duns Tew church and the quality of the available artists meant that the authority of the bishop was readily granted and the conditions agreed to. As a result, a small rural church in North Oxfordshire enabled local residents to enjoy performances by international luminaries including David Munrow and the Early Music Consort and the Consort of Musicke; Colin Tilney and Gustav Leonhardt, harpsichord; Pepe Martínez, flamenco guitar; Konrad Ragossnig on the lute and guitar; Marisa Robles, harp; and many others.

The inaugural concert featured a quartet of four students from the Royal College of Music: John Mills, guitar; Martin Loveday, violin; Michael Ponder, viola; and Julian Lloyd-Webber, cello – all of whom went on to have extensive solo careers in their own right. These concerts continued and the residents of North Oxfordshire benefited from the generosity and virtuosity of world-class musicians brought together by Rubio for many years – all because of Rubio and his gifted craftsmen's work and their 'to die for' client list.

The workforce needed to be fully committed, both those already on board and those yet to be recruited to support the expansion. David had no expectation that, making beautiful instruments and support from world leading artists, this commitment would not be forthcoming. There was a wonderful working environment complete with air conditioning and a full order book, something that had been achieved in just three years since Paul joined the nascent business back in 1969.

---

[52] Although the weight of a harpsichord varies greatly according to its structural design, suffice to say that lifting one is an acknowledged difficult process requiring a number of able bodies; a rough estimate of their weight could be 150 kg. The Dolmetsch and early Goble harpsichords were considerably heavier than the replica models.

Rubio's grand scheme required suitably skilled craftsmen (in those days they were almost exclusively male) to be recruited. Easier said than done in the rarefied and specialist world of musical instrument makers. New workers were found; some were instrument makers but others had to be acquired from related trades such as cabinetmaking and pattern making.

This community of highly skilled makers, much in the mould of Dolmetsch, came together under Rubio and Paul's direction and assistance. Rubio had prepared the ground well within his means; however, he was a newcomer to managing a larger business.

The fretted instruments, including the classical and flamenco guitars, Baroque guitars, lutes, citterns and pandoras, were made in the original workshop. One of the new workshops was given over to harpsichord construction and a third workshop was used for bowed instruments, both Baroque and, later, modern violins.

This new arrangement of workshops started well and was conducted with a light touch by Rubio and Paul. They needed to do little more than a daily visit to each workshop and occasionally distribute lists of instruments to be made and check on the availability of the materials to construct them.

Rubio was already well established in the guitar world and that of the lute. With the promise of increased production from his new workshops, he then set about marketing the Early Music instruments in much the same way as he had done for the guitars. His method was the personal touch. He went to many concerts and made a point of building relationships with the artists and performers in the classical and Early Music genres.

As in his New York days, he dressed conservatively and spoke well and with authority, despite being relatively new to the Early Music world. He was able to do this because he did his homework efficiently and was thoroughly prepared. He was also quick to take advantage of music fairs, in particular the first of the annual international exhibitions of Early Music in London, which was held at the Royal College of Music in 1973

– a prestigious venue. This event was well attended and included several members of the academic staff. Because harpsichords needed three people to transport them, Paul took the opportunity to attend and made contacts for himself, which were useful when he became an independent maker just two years later.

The rapid growth of the business, the expense of restoring the early seventeenth-century farmhouse, converting and equipping the outbuildings to modern standards and acquiring new stocks of expensive tonewoods, all loaded the business with upfront costs. David Rubio was nothing if not bold, and although he attacked the new projects with flair, enthusiasm and confidence, this did nothing to reduce the costs!

On the surface, all was now going well, with a waiting list for some instruments of four years or more. The order books were full and production was well in hand. So it came as a surprise when one week Rubio, diffidently and with a little embarrassment, came to Paul and asked if he could lend him some money for a week to pay the salary bill. Paul was able to manage this – just – using all his reserves, and Rubio, true to his word as ever, paid Paul back at the end of the week. Paul was curious as to how this had come about but his faith in Rubio was unshaken.

Things carried on as before until a few months later, having first sounded out Paul's views and gained his full support, Rubio called the staff together for a pep talk. It was felt that one or two members were not as helpful or productive as the others and were not always reporting shortages of materials in a timely manner. Indeed, in one instance someone was working on a home project during work time.

Some of this might have seemed a little petty but finances were very much on a short lead and Rubio's health was beginning to suffer as well. He had a back problem, which was now plaguing him twenty-four hours a day, despite the use of a special corset, but he didn't mention this to anyone in the workshops, except, of course, Paul. Firm measures were needed to ensure that all understood the essential commitments required for the business to carry on. The pep talk seemed to go well and have the desired effect. Once his staff understood the perilous cash flow situation – the enemy of many growing ventures – and hopefully after putting in more effort, this should have been sufficient to get Rubio through this difficult period.

Although things improved a little, it was clear they could not carry on with the less-productive members and still keep things afloat. Rubio came up with an innovative solution, which in those days was not common: to offer his employees the opportunity to become self-employed suppliers rather than keep them on his payroll. Although he would continue to provide them with work from the order book on that basis, they would need to establish their own workshops. They accepted this offer rather than becoming unemployed, and this new and interesting scheme became the pilot for the way the business would evolve later.

Having made the step of reducing the number of artisans in his workshops, it was at this time that Rubio could follow the next step in his plan, which was to return to working completely on his own again. For many artists/craftsmen this is the most personally satisfying way of being creative. The drive to create does not always sit well with the demands of running a business and his thoughts were moving increasingly in this direction.

This seed germinated, and within a year a fully costed and thought-through plan was realised. The plan was to wind down the business over a four-year period, at the end of which all committed orders, many with paid deposits, would be completed and everyone involved would make the transition to self-employment or seek work elsewhere. This complicated plan, fortunately, was accepted by all concerned; it allowed Rubio to complete his orders and make the transition back to independence. It also provided a potentially rewarding future for his loyal staff.

Of the rest of the staff, one also stayed on as a subcontractor in Rubio's workshop, helping to complete the instruments on the waiting list. The harpsichord voicer, Andrew Douglas, would be kept on, as he was nearing retirement. He had been the voicer for Robert Goble's instruments, which is where Paul had originally met him. The others became self-employed and established their own workshops but largely worked on instruments for Rubio.

Rubio's agreement with Paul was slightly different. Although he would continue to work at The Ridge House, he would begin renting the workshop space from Rubio. Another spin-off of the change was that Paul would become a maker in his own right, so when completing Rubio's orders, he would now get to sign the work as his own. Therefore, rather than placing the David Rubio label inside the instrument, with his initials 'P. F.' written on, Paul would now use the Paul Fischer label and signature inside his instruments. Part of this understanding was that at the end of the four years Paul would have to find a workshop of his own, involving the costly purchase of materials, premises and equipment. Still, this was a great opportunity and one not to be missed.

Paul's friendship with Rubio remained solid, despite the major change in plans and location on Rubio's part. Paul still speaks about David Rubio with the loyalty of a true friend.

CHAPTER 6

Independence at
The Ridge House

From 1 January 1975 a new arrangement was agreed between David Rubio and Paul Fischer. As part of Rubio's plan to wind down the Oxfordshire workshops, in preparation for his move to Cambridge, Paul began to rent his workshop space at The Ridge House from David and was now working as an independent luthier under his own Paul Fischer label.

At this time, and for the same reasons as Rubio (that there was some prejudice against non-Spanish makers but some acceptance of German makers), Paul decided on a name change. He only needed to add a 'c' to modify his surname from the English form of Fisher to the German spelling of Fischer. This Paul did in 1975 from the moment he started making under his own label. In some respects, this was the perfect form of transition period because his status changed completely in the Rubio workshops; however, his physical workspace did not, so there was no loss in time with regard to productivity.

Rubio's stock of wood for the workshop was now surplus, as his workshop would not be making the same number of instruments. This meant that Paul could purchase Rubio's well-seasoned wood, which gave him a boost at this stage of early independence; it was a perfect arrangement and helped both of them.

For the first year, as Paul had inherited some of David's waiting list, he continued to make the guitars using Rubio's pattern, as guitarists assumed he would do. However, even at that time he was already developing new designs. Rubio's was a fine and respected design but one that said nothing of Paul's own long experience as a maker – which

included creating harpsichords, lutes, vihuelas, pandoras and citterns –
over a period of many years both before and during his time with Rubio.

Although Paul's catalogue of work was already rather extensive, he still
had to build a reputation as an independent maker and naturally wanted
to express that experience through instruments of his own, but that
would have to wait a while. Paul could not ignore Rubio's reputation,
even though he was well aware of the critical opinions through
comments, which some musicians shared with him at concerts and when
he was alone in the workshop. This came as quite a surprise to Paul but
he sifted through these, retaining any useful feedback, which he kept in
mind as he was developing his own design. These views ultimately
influenced his vision and his fresh ideas for the modern classical guitar.

Using this new spelling of his surname, Paul Fischer became more
established and started exhibiting his instruments. Initially, this was at the
Early Music Exhibition at the Royal College of Music (RCM), Art in
Action in Waterperry Park, near Oxford, and the International Music
Fair in Frankfurt. At the RCM event, as well as his vihuela and Baroque
guitar, he was able to take a liberty and exhibit two modern concert
guitars, bracketing the display of early instruments (see Figure 6.1).

FIGURE 6.1 Paul Fischer at the Royal College of Music in 1978.

Considerable experience was thereby gained from these forays into the public arena. In the Arts and Crafts world the practitioner is viewed as closely as the work itself. The potential client wants to know about their background, training, experience and philosophy, preferring to discover it from the makers themselves. It is the person, not just the product, that matters. For Paul, being a part of this Arts and Crafts world was what made it so rewarding and fulfilling.

Another significant influence on Paul's instrument building came when he was still at Rubio's. Bernard Richardson,[53] then a physics PhD student, paid a visit to The Ridge House. His first contact was with David Rubio, but he received only a lukewarm reception for his work on acoustics. Speaking later with Paul on that visit, Bernard found someone who was curious and interested in learning more about the physics of the instruments.

Bernard was a musician and a guitar maker in addition to being a physicist and that added considerably to his understanding of the traditional approach to instrument making. Paul was hooked and continued to take a keen interest in Bernard's work, visiting the laboratory at the University of Cardiff and lending instruments to support the research. Eventually, they would give lectures on the acoustics of the instrument together in the UK and separately abroad. It may have been a chance meeting but the knowledge gleaned from it would be combined with Paul's own experience and studies in the 1980s and then incorporated in new designs.

---

[53] At the time of writing, Dr Bernard Richardson is Director of Undergraduate Studies at the School of Physics and Astronomy, University of Cardiff. He is a lecturer in physics at the University of Cardiff. His primary research area is the acoustics of musical instruments, especially the guitar and the violin.

FIGURE 6.2 The laboratory of Bernard Richardson, with the laser interferometry in use.
Photograph by Paul Fischer.

FIGURE 6.3 Laser interferometry pictures of a Paul Fischer classical guitar back (left) and soundboard (right) vibrating, the Taut system, no. 1.
Photograph by Paul Fischer.

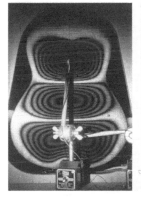

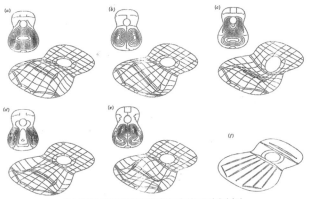

FIGURE 6.4 Vibrational modes of classical guitar soundboard by Dr Bernard Richardson.
Photograph by Paul Fischer.

Fig. 4 Modes of vibration of a guitar soundboard (schematic and contour plots) calculated by finite-element analysis[3]: (a)-(d) first four modes; (e) higher mode involving twisting of the bridge; (f) strutting pattern on the underside of the plate.

Up until the very end of the nineteenth century the guitar was generally considered a parlour or salon instrument rather than something for use in concerts; this popularity laid the foundations for its universal appeal as a classical instrument, which flourished during the twentieth century. With a move into the concert hall, and later the early recording studios, not to mention being used in trios and quartets, and even concertos, the instrument's limitations came to the fore. The classical guitar lacked volume and punch, or more precisely, a penetrating voice; this was something it had not needed in the drawing room or parlour. Even the smaller violin could easily overpower the plucked guitar.

A number of changes took place to compensate and correct this volume deficiency: the introduction of nylon strings in the 1940s, a change in right-hand technique of using the fingernails to pluck the strings instead of the flesh, and an increase in the body size of the guitar all helped. However, guitarists still needed – and demanded – more. On this often-debated issue, guitar makers and guitarists usually fall into one of two separate schools of thought:

1. those who feel that all they want is a more powerful sound, even at the expense of the warm, subtle and natural tones of the traditional instrument; and
2. those who prefer to retain all the warmth and beautiful tonality and are willing to accept the consequent loss of volume to achieve this.

This is a never-ending point of discussion among players and makers. Paul's approach was to keep the beauty but increase the projection and focus of sound rather than the overall power, thus gaining something closer to the clarity of the violin. His analogy was to make an instrument with a focused beam of sound, more like a torchlight rather than a non-directional lamp. By increasing the body size of the guitar, earlier experiments had shown that only the lower frequencies would be amplified, at the expense of the higher ones; this reduces the beauty and balance of the sound.

Dr Bernard Richardson's work was invaluable in helping Paul develop new designs for the instrument; Richardson's research was published later in his article, 'Good Vibrations' (1990). In parallel with this acoustic research, Paul was also pursuing further studies into period instruments. In particular, this took him to the Conservatoire Royal de Musique in Brussels, which had a fine collection of Early Music instruments. Notably, it had a Baroque guitar made by Giorgio Jungmann in 1633 – one of the many German instrument makers resident in Italy during this period. This was an instrument of special interest because of its form and elegance. Paul had made several copies of the Ashmolean Museum's Stradivari guitar, and thus the Italian school of lutherie was one he already knew and respected.

On this trip to Brussels, Paul was able to visit Kazuo Sato, who had worked at the Rubio workshops a few years earlier but was now independently making guitars just outside Brussels. They also went together to visit an old Rubio friend, the viol player Sigiswald Kuijen, and then on to the Royal Conservatoire to examine their Early Music instruments, which at that time were kept in their basement. That collection of instruments is now housed in the Museum of Musical Instruments in central Brussels.

His continuing journey into Early Music instrument research also took Paul to Nuremberg and the darker recesses of the Germanisches Nationalmuseum – he was interested in researching instruments from the sixteenth century through to the nineteenth century. This was part of his continuing interest in the evolution of the classical guitar. As in Brussels, there was an excellent collection of instruments, with the added bonus of X-ray plates of specific examples; also, one could request X-rays of particular instruments, which proved invaluable for the finer details this revealed. This gave new insights into the internal construction of these instruments, which even included the direction of the grain in the wood. This was vital in understanding the work of these early masters.

In addition to the harpsichords he had made earlier in his career, at Goble's as well as at Rubio's, Paul had made most of the other early plucked instruments during his time at The Ridge House. Whenever an order came in for early plucked instruments, it was assumed that Paul would undertake the necessary research and create a modern reproduction of the required instrument to be used in public performance. His interest in these early instruments continued throughout his working life.

Through the latter half of the 1970s the modern classical guitar came to form the bulk of Paul's production and he acquired many new clients in his own right. These included many leading lights, such as the Austrian guitarist and lutenist Konrad Rogossnig; the Greek guitarist Dimitris Fampas; the Finnish guitarist Jukka Savijoki; and the flamenco guitarists Pepe Martínez and Juan Martín.

By the end of the 1970s the modern classical guitar had become the bedrock and bulk of Paul's work. This was more a reflection of the demand rather than an artistic choice but it gave Paul the security to move to his own new premises. The enthusiasm of the 1960s and 1970s for ordering early instruments was quite unlike the demand patterns observed for modern instruments.

Musicians would cross the world in order to discuss and debate their choice of instrument and seek advice from the maker. It was a time when both makers and players were feeling their way in this new age of Early Music. In reality, they were learning from each other. This did not apply, of course, to the well-established instruments such as the classical guitar. The world of master-made instruments has always been one of close cooperation between the two – maker and performer – joined in music, so that the client is in fact ultimately receiving a bespoke instrument.

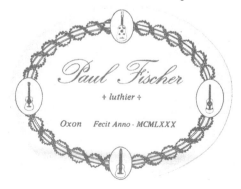

FIGURE 6.5 Paul's second label, dating from 1980. It was customary for the maker add the final Roman numeral by hand as required to MCMLXXX (198x).

Before his final departure from Duns Tew, Rubio passed on the 'Joseph Steinman' business to Paul; this cost the princely sum of £1, for which he received a business registration certificate and a pack of Steinman labels. This business had been created earlier, when trading in Rubio instruments had been restricted by sole agency agreements. It had been set up to take advantage of a strong demand in Japan for instruments as a new brand, Steinman guitars – most of the Steinmans were in fact being made by Kazuo Sato when he worked at The Ridge House.

FIGURE 6.6 The 'Joseph Steinman Lutherie' label.

As well as having a new name, the materials used for these guitars were very different; they were always made with Indian rosewood and had a new body shape, head design and rosette. Although the quality of the instruments was just as high as the Rubio-labelled instruments, as were the materials used, being an unknown brand meant their sale price was slightly lower. The Steinman guitars were an instant success and more than once caused a chuckle when Japanese guitarists told stories about the Steinman guitars they had played at home being 'as good as a Rubio'. This Steinman brand had lapsed with the reorganisation of the Rubio studios in 1974–1975; however, it would be resurrected later by Paul, but for very different reasons.

The resurgence of Early Music, with its serious research into both performance and authenticity of instrument making, came at a time of increasing interest in the classical guitar – an instrument not so restrained by tradition. The way was open for the curious and creative maker, encouraged increasingly by players, after a slow start to explore improvements. John Williams was one such player, who transitioned in the mid-1980s, moving from the more traditional style of instrument by the Spanish maker Ignacio Fleta (1897–1977) to the radically new style of construction made by the Australian guitar maker, Greg Smallman. Here was a well-established and internally recognised artist who was prepared to try something fresh, and in doing so, John Williams gave confidence to guitar makers who were at the threshold of exploring innovative ideas for themselves. Paul, who had already done preliminary work, now felt more confident to go forward with the work he had begun, following his first meeting with the physicist Dr Bernard Richardson. John Williams broke the anxiety of players who were hesitant to step out of the expected Torres-style instrument in their professional careers. This was a major step forward in the evolution of guitar history.

Rubio had planned to move to the other university city of Cambridge. As a result, at the same time as bringing the Duns Tew studios and workshops to a close, Rubio was paying regular visits to Cambridge to supervise the creation of his new workshop/home in the centre of the city.[54] In August 1979 Paul began working on and in his own newly established workshop in the Cotswolds (in a style emulating Rubio's Duns Tew workshops). Rubio left Duns Tew completely in September 1979 and from then on was in Cambridge; thus, 1975–1979 became a gentle wind down from a wonderful, if short, period of creativity in the inspiring atmosphere of the Duns Tew workshops and the Early Music revival.

The start of Paul's career in Early Music had begun in the middle of the twentieth century – a time well before the onset and fresh enthusiasm for Early Music in the 1970s. Rubio and his team of talented artisans

---

[54] The University of Cambridge colleges still have Rubio harpsichords. For example, Churchill College's purpose-built music centre with a recording studio has a French, two-manual harpsichord made for the College by David Rubio in 1983; Clare Chapel has a fine two-manual Rubio harpsichord used regularly for early liturgical repertoire and in performances at Clare; and Robinson College Chapel also has a Rubio harpsichord.

were caught by the mood of the moment; or at least some were, but not all. A plan that was full of promise, built on Rubio's passion and vision, could still fail before reaching full maturity. Sadly, although the required commitment by all was not forthcoming, for those who shared Rubio's vision, the healthy order book and individual reputations would form the springboard for their own future careers. Eventually, the whole scheme collapsed because some of the artisans/craftspeople failed to appreciate the enormity of what they were experiencing and had achieved and its future potential for instrument making. Oxford was governed by a car factory, and the minds of the young people, alive with a spirit of rebellion, began to quote the words of the unionists, despite the communal nature of their small workshops.

Paul and David were both moving forward when the time came to part ways. Rubio was a man who was constantly learning and continually excited by what was happening around him. Having started making guitars and lutes, he was then driven to build harpsichords and early bowed instruments. The move to violins was next, where he copied historical instruments, refining the details of all he could learn from extant instruments, down to the pozzolana volcanic ash (pumice) used on the wood before varnishing – by mixing pumice with slaked lime, one could apply it as a thin coat on the surface of spruce. David would argue that this benefited the acoustic properties of the wood; it also toughened the outer surface and prevented the oil varnish from soaking into the grain of the wood, which could otherwise have deadened the sound. Thus, pozzolana was used as a 'primer' for the wood. This was for violin making; Paul and David did not use pozzolana in their guitar making.

Although David Rubio began his initial research into violin making as early as 1971–1972, while he was still in Duns Tews, he had already begun relatively simple experiments using terpene resin for varnishing violins. It was his belief that these were the very ingredients for creating the varnish used by the great Italian maker Antonio Stradivari in the seventeenth and early eighteenth century. Paul remembers well the early work, which was relatively crude, first using utensils extracted from

Rubio's own kitchen, with the heat source provided by a small camping gas stove. He used a thermometer to control the temperature of what was considered a volatile mixture – that is, terpene resin and linseed oil. All this took place outside in the garden for safety, in case, as Rubio believed, the concoction overheated and went out of control, which was a possibility even after the heat source had been removed.

Another of Rubio's theories was that the final colour of the varnish was determined by removal from the heat at just the right temperature. The colour of the varnish is an important issue for all violin makers, and Rubio, at that stage, believed that the colour he wished to create was achieved by heating to a precise temperature –using a process called polymerisation. This was only an experiment and his ideas later developed quite differently. Before applying the varnish to the surface of wood, a thin film of a mixture of pumice and slake lime would be applied, and again Rubio's theory was that this acted as a primer and in the process laid down a thin, hard film to prevent deep penetration of the oil varnish to be applied later.

By around 1975 David had managed to create a varnish, which he was happy enough to use on his violins at that stage. Once he was installed in Cambridge, he began serious research with Emeritus Professor Jim Woodhouse, taking his earlier experiments to a new level, resulting in new discoveries. It must be remembered that those initial experiments undertaken during his time in Duns Tew were early indeed and based largely on Rubio's theories as told to Paul. The varnish was used only for violins and not for guitars at that stage; it may have also been used at a much later date on the guitars, after Rubio had moved to Cambridge. Paul was not involved with the Cambridge scientists whom Rubio consulted and worked with in the laboratories of the Organic Chemistry Department and in the Department of Engineering, both part of the University of Cambridge; they eventually published papers on their work.

During their time together, Paul Fischer and David Rubio were ideal working partners: both had a wealth of life experience under their belts, a love of their craft and the drive to learn and improve their creations. They understood and respected and admired each other; that is a rare experience in a working life and is certainly cherished by Paul to this day. They may have gone their separate ways, with Rubio setting up his life and workshop in Cambridge and Paul setting up his workshop in Chipping Norton in the Cotswolds, and they continued on different instrument-making paths, but they remained lifelong friends until Rubio's death in 2000.

Departure from The Ridge House took place in summer 1979. Paul loaded the last few things into his car and then went to thank David Rubio and his wife, Nest, for their kindness and the amazing opportunity to work alongside such an inspiring figure. Rubio had been both generous and encouraging; the years spent at The Ridge House had not been without difficulties but both Rubio and Paul had the same drive for creativity. What is more, they had not let others with different agendas deflect them from their goals.

The experience, both in making instruments and as a manager, gave Paul the confidence he would need to establish his own business. However, there were by then two small children to consider and the music world does not always follow conventional and smooth business paths. The initial reaction of Paul's wife, Joy, was a cautious one and Paul needed to provide a convincing case for self-employment as an independent luthier. His long experience meant he was fully familiar with all the facets of creating musical instruments and sustaining a viable business; he had a comprehensive appreciation of the difficulties and pitfalls that might lie ahead. Although Joy could only guess at what would be involved, her enthusiastic support was forthcoming and a new chapter was to be written.

CHAPTER 7

Chipping Norton:

Paul Establishes His Own Workshop

The love of a craftsman for this work is the essential difference between lifeless commercial product and the vital work of art.[55]

Hugh Baillie Scott (1865–1945)

Paul left The Ridge House in summer 1979 and began working exclusively from his own workshop/home set in the gently rolling hills of the Cotswolds, where he would build his own independent reputation as a maker. He and Joy had moved to their house in the Cotswold market town of Chipping Norton a few years earlier. A positive outcome of the gentle winding down of Rubio's venture at Duns Tew was that it provided Paul with vital security while he worked on the elements needed to build up his own business, which was still in its infancy.

Despite its small size, Chipping Norton has always had a nucleus of talented and creative people, such as the Reverend Edward Stone (1702–1768), who moved to Chipping Norton in 1745 when he became chaplain at Bruern Abbey. One day, as he was walking by the little river at the edge of the town and was feeling unwell with 'agues', he decided to begin experimenting with drying willow bark and discovered its efficacy for the treatment of fever; he had accidentally discovered a source of

---

[55] The architect Mackay Hugh Baillie Scott (1865–1945) was born in Ramsgate but settled on the Isle of Man in 1889. Blackwell, an Arts and Crafts house he designed with Thomas Hayton Mawson in Bowness-on-Windemere in the Lake District, is still open to the public. The quote is from M. H. Baillie Scott, 'The Fireplace of a Suburban House', *The Studio*, 6/32 (November 1895); for a digitised version, see www.isle-of-man.com/manxnotebook/people/archtcts/bs95.htm.

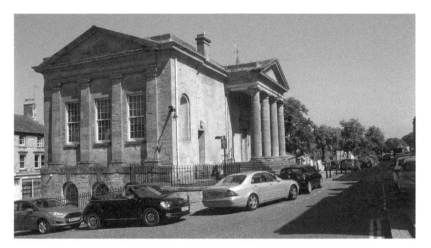

FIGURE 7.1 The Town Hall, Chipping Norton.
Photograph by Paul Fischer.

salicylate, the precursor of aspirin. A blue plaque marks his home in Chipping Norton, near the Town Hall.

Chipping Norton is still a small market town with a population of just over 6,500; it is a work-a-day town, particularly compared to the many neighbouring showcase locations, such as Chipping Camden, which is where many of those working in the Arts and Crafts first settled at the beginning of the twentieth century, encouraged by Charles R. Ashbee, the silversmith and architect; he set up the School of Arts and Crafts in Chipping Camden.

The areas surrounding Chipping Norton are largely agricultural, raising sheep and producing wool for export throughout the world; the soil is rather stony and unproductive, so historically the wealth of the region came from the wool industry. The grand church, which is a scaled-down copy of Canterbury Cathedral, was built with the proceeds of the successful wool industry.

Because of its situation, Chipping Norton benefits from having many of the shops and facilities of a much larger town. It is situated halfway between Oxford and Stratford-upon-Avon. The main road from Oxford to London, in Shakespeare's time, ran through Chipping Norton. It has excellent communication links, including nearby railways connections and access to the motorway network, no more than half an hour away. This provided viable travel to various airports, which was useful for the export of instruments, for visiting overseas clients and for Paul's travels to give lectures, attend music festivals and international music fairs, and for his trips to purchase wood.

Their house, which had been built from local stone in the seventeenth century, had naturally acquired some additions in the intervening years, including a shopfront and an external storeroom. Spanish luthiers often have their workshop accessible from a shopfront, which is open to the public, and this approach appealed to Paul. Although his early experiments of working in this manner – in the shop – caused considerable curiosity locally, it left him feeling more like an exhibit in a zoo. Thus, he gave up on the idea and focused his energies on converting the stone storeroom into a purpose-built workshop, with all the benefits of home and work co-location, *à la* Rubio.

Paul drew up the plans for the workshop himself; it was to be constructed/modified in the local Cotswold limestone so it matched the existing seventeenth-century house. Unfortunately, the local authority insisted it should be made of weathered stone, something not easy to obtain. A delay seemed inevitable and was a fly in the ointment of the new business. The local builder, who was to do the work, came to the rescue, as he knew that the nearby, famous Witney Blanket Mill was to be demolished. Its well-weathered stone would fit the bill and was soon to be available.

The work began on the carefully designed bespoke luthier's workshop. It was made to modern specifications and despite its outer weathered appearance was centrally heated, humidity controlled, had storage space in two lofts and had soundproofed walls and floor. The soundproof flooring had a double benefit, as it not only kept the noise down but also provided a soft surface underfoot that was kind to the legs that were on duty most of the working day.

FIGURE 7.2 Paul Fischer's Chipping Norton house and workshop (to right) exterior.
Photograph by Paul Fischer.

Expensive woods had to be obtained, as well as new tools, equipment, jigs, moulds, varnish and the hundred and one other things needed to make a viable instrument-making business. Of these, the most costly investment was the wood. Brazilian rosewood, ebony and mahogany are all exotic, tropical woods requiring careful selection, preferably at source. Some woods were easier to acquire than others; European spruce was only a short trip away to Switzerland, where you could select wood grown from the same region and at the same altitude as that selected by the great violin and guitar maker Antonio Stradivari. This is important because high altitude trees grow at a slower pace, which means that the annual growth rings are much closer together and produce finer material for instruments' soundboards. Southern Germany was another suitable source for spruce. Other woods required long-haul journeys: for example, to Brazil. This often meant flying out of London Heathrow on a Friday evening and returning on Monday morning after a short, tiring, but productive two-day visit to choose the best rosewood and mahogany in São Paulo, Brazil. Although this was quite an exhausting schedule, it reduced the time Paul was away from his workshop and meant he was working with the highest possible quality of woods for his instruments.

While it was possible to purchase woods through a dealer, experience quickly taught Paul that if he selected his own wood, he could guarantee its quality and make sure he would be able to make use of every piece he'd bought. Paul learnt so much from choosing all of his woods at source – not only the process of selecting the woods, but also understanding the different requirements for business negotiations when dealing with other cultures. Over the years, he established an international range of contacts – some of whom had developed into friends – who were to remain fruitful for many years. This became even more important for certain species, as their over-exploitation resulted in them being in short supply, and consequently there was reduction in quality and availability.

In order to establish his own workshop, Paul needed funding. Some of it was found in the form of a loan from his father and also from the redemption of an insurance endowment policy, which was not a huge sum but it was still a help. The Craft's Council also provided a 'setting up' grant, which they offered to those working individually in the Arts and Crafts. He received further support from the regional arts association, Southern Arts. With all of this, there was enough capital to get started. A healthy order book and hard work would cover the monthly costs of running the business and the home, provide the funds to keep building up the wood pile and, albeit slowly, repay his father's loan with interest. This would make good the transition from Rubio's business to Paul's own.

FIGURE 7.3 Paul Fischer in his Chipping Norton workshop. The guitar neck is being held in a special instrument maker's vice while he accurately measures the string spacing on the bridge using a vernier gauge.
Photograph by *The Oxford Times*. Used with permission.

Once the workshop facilities and materials were in stock, Paul was ready to focus once again on instrument making. Along with the new clients, there were also new orders from players for whom he had made instruments under the Rubio banner. Quality and production would be maintained and he could ease himself into marketing with the buffer of the waiting list he had already established.

By the time of the move, most of the new workshop was in place. The finishing touches that remained could, and would, be done by Paul. The designed layout was such that the main source of light came from the south-west, with added illumination provided by natural-light electric bulbs. By October 1979 all was ready to go.

The majority of Paul's commissioned work was for modern, six-stringed classical guitars. However, at about that time, a new enthusiastic group of guitarists could see fresh opportunities for playing chamber and ensemble music. The guitarist and composer Gilbert Biberian was one of the first in Britain, if not *the* first, to form a guitar ensemble – the Omega Players, in 1969, with composers such as Elisabeth Lutyens, Reginald Smith Brindle, David Bedford and John Lambert writing for the ensemble. These ensembles consisted mainly of six-stringed classical instruments but sometimes added percussion and brass. This stimulated a pioneering enthusiasm not only for new works and arrangements but also for the commissioning of new instruments such as the eight-stringed guitar and the smaller requinto guitar.

A few years after the Omega Players was established, the Omega Guitar Quartet came into existence. Initially, the Omega Guitar Quartet used four standard guitars; however, in Gilbert Biberian's compositions, he began to explore mixing different-sized guitars, including a requinto and an eight-stringed guitar, both designed by Paul Fischer, which, at that time, were relatively new in the modern guitar world. These were new instruments to Paul and provided a welcome challenge and the opportunity for further research. The requinto guitar is a smaller, higher-pitched version of the standard instrument, typically with a 56 cm scale length. The requinto guitar made for the Omega Guitar Quartet had an extended fingerboard with two extra frets for the first and second strings. This needed careful consideration in the making of the instrument; extra support is required beneath the extended fingerboard, otherwise the added notes will not sustain.

FIGURE 7.4 The requinto guitar made by Paul Fischer for the Omega Guitar Quartet. Note the extended fingerboard with two extra frets for the first and second strings. Photograph by John Marshall.

The introduction of different-sized guitars to the guitar quartet was an attempt towards expanding the range and combination of instruments, as found in the bowed string family in a traditional string quartet – that is, two violins, viola and cello.

Eight-stringed classical guitars usually have the two additional strings extending both the lower and higher range of the instrument – that is, one in the bass register and one in the treble register. The eighth string would be a low B and the first string would be a high D; thus, moving from the lowest to the highest, the strings would be: B E A D G B E D. One exception to this would be the tuning Paul Galbraith uses on his eight-stringed Brahms guitar, where he tunes the eighth and first string to an A: A E A D G B E A. These are also known as extended-range guitars and usually have the same body size as a six-stringed classical guitar, but their necks are wider and the headstock with the added tuning machines are longer to accommodate the extra strings. Paul was always grateful for David Rodgers' creations on these extended-range guitars, as he would happily make any combination of machine head required, and the result would be elegantly engineered.

A more unusual request for an 'instrument' came from Forbes Henderson, who was a young, promising guitarist. He was one of the guitarists chosen for the Julian Bream television masterclasses, which were filmed by the BBC at Bream's home in Semley, Wiltshire, at the end of the 1970s. When Sérgio Abreu was teaching at Dartington Summer School in the UK, filling in for Julian Bream who was unwell, Forbes Henderson drove him there. Forbes requested that Paul design and build him a small-bodied practice guitar for use in the passenger seat of a car, which he could play as Sérgio drove![56] It was an urgent request from Forbes, leaving Paul only three days to create it. Apart from using this as a practice guitar, Forbes also used it, albeit amplified, with the group called Incantation when they performed on BBC television.

Forbes Henderson was not only playing this practice guitar created by Paul; when he gave a Wigmore Hall recital in London, on 23 February 1979, he was performing on a Paul Fischer concert guitar. As one reviewer wrote, he was 'displaying the best side of his playing, further enhanced by the impressive sounds drawn from his Paul Fisher [*sic*] guitar'.[57]

Paul had attended the First Segovia International Guitar Competition on 9–13 October 1981 at Leeds Castle in Kent. Andrés Segovia was the head of the jury, and the other jury members were the Spanish composer Anton García Abril, the Spanish violinist Agustín Leon-Ara, Gordon Crosskey, the British composer Stephen Dodgson, Luis Galve, John

---

[56] Sérgio Abreu had built his own practice guitar from a block of wood, but it was only for exercising the right hand, interestingly, and thus had six strings mounted over the piece of wood with the right tension so that he could work on his right hand. Paul's practice guitar had a focus on both hands and was a much more developed idea.

[57] Hugh de Camillis, 'Guitar Concert Reviews', *Guitar*, 34, April 1979. Forbes Henderson had made his Wigmore Hall debut in 1976. He played the Fischer guitar for a few years.

Manduell and the Polish composer Alexander Tansman, with thirty-four competitors from sixteen countries, such as Stefano Grondona, Paul Gregory, Cheryl Grice, Eliot Fisk, Charles Ramirez, Helen Kalamuniak and Forbes Henderson. The competition was filmed by the BBC.

***

The workshop in Chipping Norton had been running for nearly one year when Paul and Joy decided to make a second attempt at opening up the shop, which already had a shopfront; but this time, instead of following the Spanish luthier's approach, it would be a regular music shop. The new purpose-built workshop was at the side with its own entrance, but was also connected to both the house and the shop.

The shopfront had been created in the mid nineteenth century. At that time, it was run as a general store, and, in fact, the shop had only closed shortly before Paul and Joy bought the property. The shop front itself had been modified sometime during the twentieth century, with very ugly plate glass set in rotten wooden frames. Regardless of their condition, Paul wanted the whole façade completely changed to be in keeping with the period of the house, with smaller windowpanes that included hand-blown bull's eyes panes, costing £20 per pane in the 1980s. None have ever been broken because they are so strong. Paul took out the old sheets of glass and used them as secondary glazing, set behind the period frontage for security as well as soundproofing.

They didn't need to apply for a shop licence, as the original licence was still valid. There had been an old storeroom attached to the house, which was accessed through an internal door; at some time, this had been bricked up. Paul removed the bricks, reopened the doorway and installed a fireproof door to give direct but safe access to the workshop. The storeroom was then converted, largely built with golden Cotswold weathered limestone rescued from the demolition of the Witney Blanket Mill in Witney. Paul created three lofts for storage of the precious woods, which allowed him to walk through from one loft to the next. The materials within the shop were also rescued items, including a nineteenth-century display cabinet from a haberdashery shop. One of the walls within the shop features the original, large inglenook fireplace, which is about 8 feet wide and 3 feet deep; the ceiling has the original exposed beams.

They named the shop the West End Studio, making reference to both the studio workshop and the shop itself where a whole range of small instruments could be displayed, such as recorders, flutes, clarinets, violins, nineteenth-century guitars and Neapolitan mandolins. The selection of music included the tutors needed by the local schools and also accessories such as cello pegs, strings, machine heads, fine tuners for violins, metronomes and music stands. It mainly aimed to provide a music service for the local community, otherwise people would have had to travel far to purchase music-shop items. Joy managed the shop after sadly resigning from her work as assistant to the director of the Chipping Norton Theatre. As Joy explains:

Formerly a Salvation Army Citadel, the building became 'The Theatre' in 1975, co-founded by Tamara Malcolm with her then husband John, together with massive support, hard work and money from the community. I joined as assistant to the director in 1979 and stayed for a year. Working for the dynamic Tamara was enjoyable and interesting. I learnt a lot from her – mainly that it's okay to make a mistake as long as you try to rectify it!

As it was the early days of its life as a theatre, a lot of the time was spent on the sometimes tedious but vital work of fundraising and completing balance sheets and appealing to the generous theatregoers in the Cotswolds. Finding suitable productions that would work in a relatively small venue (200 plus seats with small stage) was also a challenge. Half the week was live theatre; the other half was cinema. In those early days Tamara would call upon her friends from the Royal Shakespeare Company, such as Dudley

Sutton and Melvyn Hayes, who both appeared in the now legendary pantos.

The West End Studio was often referred to as an Aladdin's cave because Paul used to go to auctions and buy second-hand instruments, which he would restore and then sell in the shop. Restoration work was something Paul relished when it came to restoring eighteenth- and nineteenth-century guitars such as Panormo, Preston or the French and German makers, or Austrian makers such as Stauffer. Occasionally, his training with Robert Goble was called upon by local musicians/friends for repairing their historical wooden recorders.

It is vital for the making of fine musical instruments that the right variety, quality and fully seasoned wood is used. Artificial seasoning can be achieved relatively quickly using a kiln. Most luthiers frown upon this method because the wood is considered to be seasoned too rapidly and, as a result, is prone to splitting because it is too dry and inflexible, which makes the wood inappropriate for instrument making. Wood that has been naturally dried over time – preferably air dried for many years – and has been properly sticked and stacked gives better results. Instrument makers also have to take into account the fact that many handmade instruments have to endure extreme changes in humidity and temperature, as international performers travel extensively on tour and many overseas clients live in very different and sometimes difficult climatic conditions: for example, compare the 40 per cent humidity of California, with the 90 per cent humidity of Singapore or Brazil.

All small instruments such as guitars, lutes and cellos can suffer from even the slightest change in humidity, as they are made using very thin woods in order to make them responsive to sound; however, it also makes them fragile and subject to expansion and contraction in different conditions, which can cause cracking or swelling of the wood.

Most violinists choose instruments that are old, and not just because they were made by acknowledged past masters. The ageing of the wood gives a particular resonance, lightness and brightness because the resin

FIGURE 7.5 This wood in Paul's storeroom for drying was sticked and stacked for many years before use. The fact that it was pre-cut into 4 mm thicknesses meant that it would dry quicker than normal. Note the dark hue of the end grain of the Brazilian rosewood on the middle shelf, which is almost black. This is in fact paraffin wax, into which every piece of wood is dipped on purchase to prevent the wood drying out too rapidly through the end grain and suffering splitting. Photograph by Richard Winslade.

content changes along with the cell structure of the wood itself over time. As a result, the wood sings with a freedom that is simply not possible with younger wood.

FIGURE 7.6 Paul checking the resonant dryness of the rosewood. This process of tapping of a piece of wood with the tip of your fingernail or knuckle became an automatic response when selecting new wood. It would give some indication in the form of a bell-like response to the natural dryness of the piece of wood, suggesting whether it was sufficiently seasoned for use. Photograph by Richard Winslade.

Funds permitting, luthiers like to buy stocks of wood well in advance so that they have control over the seasoning process and, eventually, have older wood to hand. With this in mind, and with Paul's increasing advance order list, it became important to secure more Brazilian rosewood. Initial enquiries to procure this rare and precious wood resulted in samples of poor quality. In addition, the wood purchased directly from Brazil would be priced in American dollars, with unpredictable and often dramatic changes in the exchange rate.

Being already familiar with the difficulty with the supply in the UK, Paul wondered if things would be the same in Brazil. If the supply of wood was really shrinking, then perhaps it was time to consider different species of wood. Indian rosewood was already commonly used on lower-priced instruments and was actually a fine alternative to Brazilian rosewood. However, Brazilian rosewood was, and is, held in high regard, and so it commanded a premium for the best guitars. Mahogany was another Brazilian wood whose supply was becoming a concern for instrument makers in general. Paul decided to make a trip to Brazil to explore possible new species, which seemed an expensive but a practical solution. The forests of Brazil held a vast range of beautiful, exotic woods, some of which might prove to be possible alternatives. He also wanted to understand the true supply situation of traditional rosewood and mahogany.

The results of such a research trip could also be of benefit to other makers; they were all in the same boat. Indeed, when two or more makers got together, wood was always the number one topic; there was almost a mantra: 'Where can we get good material?' English guitar makers were generally on good terms with each other and would offer help if required. They were few in number and the view was that 'the world is big enough for us all'. Perhaps that is not so true in the twenty-first century, but it was definitely the case then.

Chatting with a journalist friend, Diana Davenport, about his thoughts and reasons for wanting to visit Brazil prompted her to suggest that Paul should consider applying for a Winston Churchill Travelling Fellowship. During this conversation, she explained the history and philosophy of the Winston Churchill Trust that was set up in 1965 after the death of the great man.

In the meantime, soon after setting up the workshop in the Cotswolds, Paul received a letter from Japan. This was something that happened quite often, as he had many clients in the 'Land of the Rising Sun'. This letter was written in perfect English and turned out to be from a childhood friend, Alan Lewis. After university Alan had travelled to

Japan to teach English. He had also recently taken up the classical guitar, so he took the opportunity to visit the many specialist dealers in high-end instruments in Tokyo. The name 'Paul Fischer' came up quite often. He remembered that Paul had been an instrument maker, so he wrote to find out if he was one and the same person and, if so, to let him know that he was well known in Japan. Alan went on to say that he had now made a few guitars and wondered if they could meet up on his return to the UK. This would be a meeting of long-lost friends, so Paul was happy to oblige – there would be much to talk about. On his return to the UK, he paid a visit to Paul's Cotswold workshop, and Alan explained that he was at something of a crossroads in his life. He was not sure if he wanted to continue and expand on his venture into guitar making or, not at all related, follow a path to enlightenment through the Buddhism he had encountered in Japan.

However, inspired by his experiences in the heady atmosphere of Paul's workshop, Alan felt emboldened to ask if he might become a mature apprentice – with the caveat that it would help him decide where his path actually lay. At that time, Paul's teaching experience was relatively limited and the workshop was not set up for two people. Would it work? They would never know unless they tried, and the workshop could be rejigged for two workbenches, and, if necessary, another workshop could be set up below decks. It was decided to go ahead and the experimental arrangement was agreed with Alan to start in early 1982.

The first week's work consisted of moving things around, some to the new workshop, and making space for the new workbench with its related tool racks and vices. Alan had a limited amount of experience, but although he needed much hands-on teaching, he proved to be a quick learner. Within six months, due to the close proximity of their benches, direction and support was always available. After a year, Alan was well settled in. His work was of a good standard and, despite the confined working conditions, harmony reigned.

What had been an experimental scheme, especially with regard to Paul's untested teaching abilities, and possibly his patience, had worked out well and they benefited from each other's company. Alan never failed to deliver stimulating conversation.

Towards the end of the first year, Alan planned a holiday to revisit friends he had made in Japan. His Japanese, both written and spoken, was good. Paul saw an opportunity for Alan to do some work for him while enjoying his vacation. Paul had been selling his guitars for many years in Japan through local companies, which was the normal way of doing business there at that time. In return for a contribution to his travel costs, Alan agreed to do some marketing on Paul's behalf. This would be mutually beneficial, as in addition to helping the business in Japan, Alan would gain skills in marketing musical instruments.

Paul provided letters of introduction so Alan could make contact with existing clients, as well as seeking out new ones. After a while, a fulsome letter arrived from Alan in Japan, which covered the full story of his experiences and gave a detailed panorama of the classical guitar scene. The interest in Fischer guitars was good and there were also some useful comments and thoughts concerning specific design details. These would prove very helpful to Paul in developing and innovating his work, while keeping up the highest standards that the Japanese market demanded.

Alan's companionship, good humour and enthusiasm for instrument making made for a productive and harmonious working relationship and gave an indication of how, in the future, such training arrangements might work out.

The original agreement with Alan was for a two-year period, which was now nearing its end. As if by magic, and with almost no break from this first teaching experience, a new request for training arrived. This applicant was already trained to college level; he had completed a three-year instrument-making course at the London College of Furniture. This was the first college to offer such a course and had not been available to Paul when he'd set out in the world of lutherie.

Although still in its infancy, the London College of Furniture's course provided the ideal entry point for someone to then join Paul for a couple of years in what he called 'the finishing school approach'. Working with

Paul provided an excellent springboard for those wishing to establish themselves as independent instrument makers.

This new student's name was Christopher Dean and he came with both good results and references. Having a new and enthusiastic pupil at hand would make the challenge of the Winston Churchill Travelling Fellowship a little easier, and Paul's happy first experience of teaching made him confident that repeating the exercise would go well. Chris's obvious enthusiasm and confidence added to his technical suitability, so a start date in autumn 1983 was agreed to fit with Paul's return from Brazil.

The Winston Churchill Travelling Fellowships provide a unique opportunity for UK and Commonwealth citizens from all backgrounds to acquire innovative ideas and experiences overseas. In the process, they gain fresh perspectives in their own field of interest and return with enhanced expertise and are able to be more effective in their work and contribution to the community.

The first step towards getting this 'chance of a lifetime', the phrase used by the Winston Churchill Trust itself, was completing challenging and detailed application forms. Fortunately, Paul's ideas were considered worthwhile and so he was asked to attend the final interview stage of the process. The interview was before a panel of distinguished experts in areas relevant to the proposal, thus in Paul's case it included Sir David Wilcox of the Royal College of Music; General Lascelles, then the director general of the Winston Churchill Trust; Nick Danziger, a writer and traveller; and the chief executive and various board members of the Trust.

With that final hurdle cleared, it was time to make firm plans with contacts in Brazil – timber merchants and research establishments, particularly in São Paulo – and to include a proposed conference on the environment, focusing mainly on destruction of the rainforests at the Universidada Federal do Pará, Belém, in July 1983, which also had a small section for instrument makers.

CHAPTER 8

Brazil 1983: The Winston Churchill Fellowship

Paul's trip to Brazil started with a flight from London Heathrow to São Paulo, where he met up with Dr Eugênio Follmann, who was a dealer in wood, with extensive knowledge, specifically for wood used in creating musical instruments; Paul had already been doing business with him for a few years. Follmann was a great help in planning the trip and also as a host; he was Paul's guide from Bahia onwards, introducing him to all his contacts.

From São Paulo, Paul took another long flight on his own to Belém, in the state of Pará, to attend a conference at the Universidada Federal do Pará, in July 1983. The conference focused on the environment, mainly on the very serious destruction of the rainforests through burning and clearing for farming use, but it also had a small section for instrument makers. This was almost forty years ago and it is sad to reflect that over that long period of time, despite continuing local and global efforts, the situation has become increasingly worse.

None of the lectures were in English; however, Paul managed to receive a summarised translation from fellow instrument makers. Among the many other instrument makers, there was a harpsichord maker; surprisingly, however, there were no guitar makers. As the harpsichord maker spoke good English, he invited Paul to his house for dinner, where they continued their lively discussions on these period instruments.

In Belém Paul employed a guide who was excellent, knowledgeable and spoke good English, with a pleasant personality. Paul had brought with him some small silver medallions from the Winston Churchill

FIGURE 8.1 A timber yard on the banks of the Guamá River, Belém, with stocks of mahogany and Brazilian cedar stacked on the riverbank.
Photograph by Paul Fischer.

Memorial Trust to give as presents to those who helped him on his journey. The medallions had the face of Winston Churchill on one side and the logo of the Trust on the other. This guide was one of a number of recipients of a medallion on Paul's trip.

Belém, on the Guamá River, was the most important port for timber export in the state of Pará and the Amazonas. In the main dock area, Paul visited two large timber merchants who supplied mahogany (*Swietenia macrophylla*) and cedar (*Cedrela odorata*) to the USA and Europe. Their directors informed him that the supplies from that region of both of these woods would be exhausted within three years; they were preparing to switch to plywood production instead. This was bad news, as both mahogany and cedar are commonly used in guitar making.

After Paul had been in Belém for four days, he flew to Bahia. Travelling around Brazil was not a fast experience, even when flying, because of the vastness of the country. It wasn't a direct flight to Bahia: the aeroplane made stops in San Luis, Fortaleza and Recife before arriving in Ilhéus on the coast. With each steep landing in these small airports, the passengers would break out in spontaneous applause in appreciation of the very skilled pilots.

From Ilhéus, Paul then caught a bus inland to Itamaraju, which took around six hours. Itamaraju, in the state of Bahia, is where he planned to

FIGURE 8.2 A map showing Paul's journeys in Brazil.
Photograph from Paul Fischer Collection.

meet up with Dr Eugênio Follmann again so they could visit the forests and timber merchants of that region together. Follmann was a Hungarian who had worked for Steinway pianos in Braunweg, Germany, before emigrating to Brazil. He was very knowledgeable about woods, and specifically about Brazilian woods, used in musical instrument manufacture.

The whole region of Bahia was engaged in the timber trade: felling, converting and transporting timber to the ports and cities of the south. With no railway in this region, all felled timber had to be transported by the poorly maintained roads. It was not uncommon for whole sections of the road to be washed away by heavy rainfall; with so little forest remaining, the light soil was easily washed away, along with the road. Paul and Eugênio travelled the whole length of the state of Bahia, and the destruction of the forests and roads was the same throughout: vast areas of barren hillside with just solitary dead, burnt tree trunks remaining. It was a sad testimony to what had once been a flourishing rainforest before its fiery destruction to make way for cattle rearing. The few pockets of trees that did survive were on difficult, inaccessible terrain.

FIGURE 8.3 A desolate scene in what was once rainforest in the state of Bahia.
Photograph by Paul Fischer.

In all his travels, Paul saw no signs of replanting. This problem was made more severe and urgent because of the practice of burning indiscriminately, destroying also the future stock, as 70 per cent of the trees being burnt were immature. One of the methods of starting a burn-off in these very moist and lush, green timbered rainforests, which would not burn easily, was to stack a pile of old car tyres, cover them with old oil and then set fire to them. It was a heartbreaking experience to watch such beauty become a raging inferno. In addition, the fire-based clearing decimated the whole ecosystem needed for the rainforest's and the earth's survival – a literal scorched earth event. This practice seemed to be the rule throughout Brazil, not just in Bahia.

While he was in Bahia, Paul became aware of an established system, in theory at least, of cutting only mature trees, about 30 per cent of the total, then burning the remainder in order to clear land for cattle or sugar cane production. At that time, much of the forest was owned by peasant farmers who were supposed to replant three trees for every tree felled. In practice, partly because of the remoteness of these farms and poor communications with the outside world, this was seldom done. The peasant farmers were more concerned with eking out a basic living and trying to create some sort of regular income in their struggle to survive. Their circumstances were understandably difficult and this made them vulnerable to all sorts of exploitation. Paul asked one farmer how much they would get for selling a single tree; his reply was $4.

FIGURE 8.4 Young trees remaining in a rainforest following the removal of the more mature trees. Photograph by Paul Fischer.

For Paul, Bahia was important because it was generally believed that the finest rosewood was found in this state, as it has a much drier climate than the humid Amazonas region. Although Paul did purchase some rosewood from the Amazonas, it was incredibly hard, dense and brittle. What is more, in Bahia a number of other interesting species grew as well. When he visited local mills and timber merchants, it was made clear that rosewood had not passed their saws for some time. Any enquiries resulted in shaking heads and it was hard not to come to the conclusion that rosewood was already effectively extinct, for commercial purposes at least.

Many of the large sawmills were in the throes of closing down and even some of the smaller ones were short of work; this was a clear indication of how depleted the rainforest had become. The mills were mainly converting the more regular varieties of timber for domestic use – any tree at all would do. Suitability for purpose appeared not to be considered, Paul even saw Brazilian ebony being cut for railway sleepers! At least it would last well … but what a waste.

The mills themselves were particularly primitive and with very limited use of lifting gear. The logs were generally manhandled, even the largest ones of 4–5-feet in diameter. Logs were moved from truck to saw carriage using only crowbars and winches; this was a very dangerous procedure, which must have led to injuries of the workers. Saws were equally primitive, with unguarded, large driving belts and exposed blades. The most common type was the frame saw. Although these were of vintage manufacture and design, they did seem particularly well suited for cutting some of the extremely hard woods such as ironwood and pernambuco – some of these woods are so hard and dense that they do not float. With logs that do float, another form of transportation was to float them downstream on the main river systems available.

After nine days spent in the Itamaraju region, Paul and Eugênio moved on to Vitoria in the state of Espirito Santo to visit Atlantic Veneers, a veneer and plywood factory that also stocked domestic timber in log and plank form for domestic sale. Here he was shown six small logs of rosewood, each about 15 cubic feet, priced then at USD 8,000 (this would be enough to produce fifteen to twenty guitars). He also found three other interesting woods in the yard, all of promising colour, weight and tonal quality. Sadly, the company would only sell wood in large quantities, and that was not viable for an instrument maker's own use. The three woods were macacauba (*Platymiscium*), cardinal wood (*Brosimum paraenses*) and sabourana (*Swartzia laevicarpae*).

FIGURE 8.5 Travelling in the forest by taxi. Surprisingly, this was not unusual. Dr Eugênio Follmann is leaning on the back of the bulldozer with Nilson, his local timber agent.
Photograph by Paul Fischer.

Diary Extract Friday 15 July 1983

A most fascinating day, which began by arranging for a taxi to be with us for the whole day. The idea was to go to the forest where Eugenio wanted to see some logs he had been offered by Nilson, his local agent.

We first travelled 6 km on the main north–south tarmac road then turned inland westwards onto a hard dirt track and continued on this for another 15 km, turning off again onto an even rougher track for 10 km more in these conditions, to arrive at our destination. Already directly inland, we had travelled over 30 km. The whole scene was staggering for its beauty, as well as the shock. It was clear, as seen the previous day, that the whole area, as far as the eye could see – 20–30 km in all directions – had been cleared of trees. Only an occasional group remained, 150 to 200 acres, on the most difficult ridges. Most of these were youngish trees growing through a mass of undergrowth. Still remaining upright and dotted here and there were the charred trunks of once majestic trees – in nearly all cases absolutely straight and very tall at 50 to 60 feet and now dead but refusing to lie down. The reason for this rather weird landscape was agriculture. Over forty years ago, the large trees were felled and the remainder were burnt to make way for cattle grazing. Despite the many square miles cleaned for this purpose, I saw few cattle.

Along the whole of the 25 km track, timber was still being extracted where it passed through a forested area. Most of the remaining timber was what they called softwood for general use and not the exotic varieties sought by us.

We are now going to see six logs known only to the farmer/landowner living in this very remote area. Not rich farmers; in fact, they are extremely poor, despite owning large tracts of land. The timber remaining is not worth much. It is small and not worth cutting, at least not commercially.

They have so much timber (also coffee), they do not (or didn't) respect it and show little interest in its conservation. Some replanting does take place but, of course, you can't replace a rainforest. Something that had developed naturally over millennia cannot be easily reproduced.

We finished the journey through the forest on foot – too steep for the car. Our guide knew the exact location of the six logs we wished to see and led us through the forest, hacking a path with his 2-foot-long machete.[58] The undergrowth was dense and consisted mainly of young trees and creepers. The path led down a steep incline for about 1 km, wet and humid, water constantly dripping from above, also from my forehead.

We found the logs, being the remains of major felling many years previously.

---

[58] Even in the villages and towns it was not uncommon to see men walking through the streets with a 2-foot-long machete in hand.

Another log lay half a kilometre away and was still moving down the slope. I had the impression these logs had been left many years ago, when the demand for this wood was far less. The surrounding trees were only half their age.

Eugenio believes that to all intents and purposes rosewood is, commercially at least, extinct!

We hear stories of a rosewood tree here and there, a bit like the Yeti, but only found six small scorched logs, which we shipped back to Eugenio's yard in São Paulo. When we came to cut these logs into smaller sections, we discovered the centres were hollow and, despite being solid wood at each end, we found a small, crude, ancient hand axe in the hollow section [possibly 300–400 years old]. Much of my time in Bahia was equally exciting but the six small logs remained our only rosewood prize.

FIGURE 8.6 Paul Fischer with six small logs rescued from the rainforest, packed up for transport back to England. Photograph from Paul Fischer Collection.

The visit to Atlantic Veneers in Vitoria initially went well. After a fine lunch with the directors, they showed us gigantic raw logs in the yard and we watched their conversion on massive lathes, reducing a complete log into 4 mm laminations for veneers. Paul had never seen anything like this before in his life! A log would be boiled for six days in hot water to soften the timber, making the process of conversion very easy; this would avoid having the veneers split while they were being processed on the lathe. Though fascinating, it bore no relation to his own work as an instrument maker, particularly as he did not use plywood in his instruments. However, the variety of woods they were converting were of great interest, and before their conversion samples of the log could be made available for his research. Out of curiosity, he and Eugênio continued to follow the process through Atlantic's complex, thus observing the complete production of plywood.

They adjourned to the director's office to discuss Paul's interest in acquiring a variety of woods for instrument-making research. While talking further about his work and research, suddenly the whole atmosphere of the meeting changed dramatically; Paul drew the impression that they were only interested in orders for very large quantities of timber, but at that moment, fortunately, they allowed him to choose several interesting samples, and ones of a size he could carry with him. From that moment onwards, they were ushered off the company's premises with haste. Paul's impression of this rapid turn in mood was twofold: first, he would require only very small quantities of wood as far as they were concerned; and second, the word 'research' seemed to ring some alarm bells, as if their methods of operating were being scrutinised. The name Winston Churchill did not resonate with them. They arrived at the main gates rapidly and left by taxi, carrying Paul's wood samples.

From Vitoria, they caught a bus back to São Paulo, stopping at rest stations along the way, as it was a long journey of almost two days' duration, with a constant changing view of the eastern coastal route, which left a dramatic impression on Paul.

On their return to São Paulo, Paul and Eugênio spent a full day studying the 2,000 timber samples available at the Instituto de Pesquisas Tecnológicas (IPT), the Institute for Technological Research. Paul had contacted them before leaving England and had made arrangements to visit. The IPT is a public research institute linked to the Secretariat for

Economic Development of the State of São Paulo, and Paul found them to be very helpful and interested in his work. He was impressed with the level of organisation. The samples were each in sliding drawers within glass cabinets. Most of the process was left to Paul, as he was examining the samples as an instrument maker; however, Eugênio, as a timber merchant, was interested in Paul's comments for his own future reference.

At Atlantic Veneers Paul had collected three samples of new woods that he could use in his work. At the IPT he was able to narrow down the search to six further possible woods that would be suitable for making guitars. There were nine in total, and Paul found the Latin names of the three samples from Vitoria: *Caesalpinia ferraea*, *Swartzia fasciata*, *Astronium fraxinifolium*, *Coniorrhachis marginata*, *Diptadenie macrocarpa*, *Machaeriam villosar*, *Astronium macrocalyz*, *Dalbergia frutescens* and *Ferreira spectabilis*. Although most of these might prove suitable for making guitars, some were, or soon would become, as hard to acquire as rosewood itself; their close resemblance to rosewood made them sought after as substitutes and for use in furniture making and for veneer.

After the intense study in Belém, Bahia and at the IPT in São Paulo, Paul felt the need for some light relief; he accompanied Sérgio Abreu on his visit to the guitar factory of Tranquillo Giannini – at that time, Brazil's leading concert guitarist. Sérgio worked as a consultant for the firm, helping them to improve their instruments. As an organisation, Tranquillo Giannini were keen to fill the needs of the discerning concert artist and could not have chosen a better advisor. The visit to the research and development department stimulated much discussion, particularly on the subject of new woods. The company had experimented with a couple of new species but cracking of the wood had caused delays. The high humidity in Brazil is a problem and Paul was able to contribute something from his own experience and research on workshop humidity control.

With the knowledge gained in Belém, Bahia and at the IPT, Paul was confident in selecting a final set of seven of the nine wood species to make into guitars on his return to England. Although none of them had

FIGURE 8.7 From left: Paul Fischer, Sérgio Abreu, Shigemitsu Sugiyama and Henrique Pinto in São Paulo in Sugiyama's guitar making workshop.

the same rich colour and beautiful grain of true Brazilian rosewood, the weight, density, flexibility and tone matched sufficiently to offer a great chance of success.

The Churchill Fellowship encourages recipients to have a small holiday at the end of their research, thus Paul took the opportunity to meet up with two great guitarists in Rio de Janeiro: Turibio Santos and Sérgio Abreu. Together they paid a visit to the beautiful Botanical Gardens of Rio de Janeiro, and in this 'holiday' part of the trip, Paul examined the very mature trees, including a rosewood tree. What he found remarkable was the size of the leaves, which were tiny compared to the huge size of the tree. In contrast to European trees, Brazilian trees grow incredibly straight, offering a larger quantity of usable material.

Paul stayed with a friend of Sérgio Abreu in Copacabana, which was only a short walk to the Botanical Gardens, and he also visited the famous Copacabana Beach. Apart from the kindness of offering him a place to stay, Mario Passos, who was beginning to make guitars, also introduced him to many of his friends. What really impressed Paul, when listening to

Brazilian guitarists, was the combination of virtuosic skill and musical naturalness, particularly when he had the great pleasure of hearing Rafael Rebello (1962–1995) playing on a seven-stringed guitar. At that time, Paul was making seven-stringed guitars, and so he took a particular interest. Rebello, whose untimely death is still mourned today, was an outstanding musician. For a few years, Paul used to provide Mario with ebony, which he couldn't get in Brazil. Paul found Brazilians refreshing to be with, self-confident and at ease with themselves and, therefore, relaxed with others – in short, they were so un-English!

Paul also visited Sérgio Abreu's workshop in Copacabana. The first thing he noticed was the dehumidifier, which, Sérgio explained, ran for 24 hours a day; this was necessary to deal with Brazil's high humidity. As an example of the effects of this high humidity on the guitars, the machine heads could become green with the algae that might grow on them, and there would also be issues resulting from the wood swelling as it took in the moisture from the atmosphere, causing further problems. Of course, all things made from wood will expand and contract with changes in humidity and temperature. Furniture makers can create their work allowing for some expansion and contraction without serious damage to the piece of furniture. However, in the making of a musical instrument, such 'allowances' cannot be made in same way; the best luthiers can do is ensure that all the woods they use are extremely well seasoned.

The world-renowned classical guitarist, Turibio Santos, is also the director of the Villa-Lobos Museum in Rio de Janeiro, and, together with Sérgio, Paul paid a visit to the museum, which was an exciting experience, being able to view Villa-Lobos's original manuscripts and his musical instruments.

The primary reason for Paul's research was to explore other possible woods to use instead of the now-precious Brazilian rosewood. At that time, Brazilian rosewood had already become expensive, hard to find and sometimes of poor quality. Paul also needed to understand exactly what the position was for future supplies of the existing rosewood, mahogany and Brazilian cedar stocks.

Another part of the project for the Churchill Fellowship included making test instruments using the new, alternative wood species that would be obtained during his trip to Brazil. After his return to England Paul did indeed make seven classical guitars using the new species of wood, as well as an eighth classical guitar in Brazilian rosewood as the control instrument for the experiment. Each was made using the traditional spruce soundboard and with the same bracing pattern, but he used his experience and professional skills to adjust the thickness of the back and sides, which were made from the new woods, to achieve a similar sound from each instrument. His view was that between 20 and 25 per cent of the character of the sound came from the woods themselves, which were used in the back and sides of the guitar.

By October 1984 Paul had completed the eight classical guitars, and a blind testing was set up at the October Gallery in London. The gallery

FIGURE 8.8 Six of the guitars for 'blind testing' at the October Gallery, London.
Photograph by Paul Fischer.

was full with both makers and players. Paul opened the proceedings with a lecture outlining the purpose of his research in Brazil and the results of his work up to that time. A special guest at the event was the director general of the Winston Churchill Memorial Trust, Sir Richard Vickers. A review of the event was written by the editor of *Classical Guitar* magazine, Colin Cooper:

> More people packed the October Gallery to hear Paul Fischer's seven new guitars than normally attend a London guitar recital, which says something for the interest in guitar making and the materials used.
>
> The purpose was to discover if viable alternatives to rosewood could be found in the forests of Brazil. The nine samples brought back by Paul Fischer are described in his report to the Winston Churchill Trust (*Classical Guitar*, July/August 1984). Two were rejected and the remaining seven used to make guitars identical in every respect but the back and sides. ...
>
> John Mills contributed greatly to this enterprise by playing each of the seven instruments in turn, unidentified and far enough away for the panel of judges not to be influenced by the visual aspects. ...
>
> The proceedings concluded with an illuminating lecture by Dr Bernard Richardson, whose acoustic research into the guitar at University College, Cardiff, must be of interest to guitar makers everywhere ...
>
> Ancient craft it may be, but Paul Fischer and Bernard Richardson between them pointed it firmly towards the twenty-first century on this informative and entertaining occasion.[59]

John Mills performed on each of the instruments, seated on the far side of an open doorway to the audience, so that they could *hear* but not

---

[59] Colin Cooper, 'Paul Fischer's New Guitars', *Classical Guitar*, 5/3 (January 1985), 33–34.

see the back and sides of the instruments. This gave the audience the chance and challenge to take part in a serious examination comparing eight identical guitars with only the backs and sides made from different species of wood.

The judges were a panel of four, seated among the audience, assessing the guitars for projection, clarity, balance, sustain, response and tonal characteristics. Paul had even drawn up a table for grading these various aspects of the instruments. The clear winner was aruda de bolo (*Swartzia fasciato*, which looks very like Brazilian mahogany. Joint second were kingwood (*Dalbergia cearensis*) and brownheart (*Ferreira spectabilis*). Princewood (*Cordia trichotoma*) came in at a respectable third. Paul hoped that timber merchants and guitarists might keep their ears open and take the hint.

This was a serious experiment with serious intentions. It was looking a little way ahead at the time but, in fact, within seven years, in 1992, rosewood (*Dalbergia nigra*) was placed on the CITES Index, Appendix 1, of endangered species.[60] The fallout from that drastic decision has ricocheted throughout the world of lutherie ever since. The pointers towards this were there in that October Gallery event.

Paul's extensive travels through Brazil, though sometimes gruelling, brought forth an interesting and different impression of his abilities to cope with the extreme climate. In a letter from Dr Eugênio Follmann to the Winston Churchill Memorial Trust, he described in quaint English, and a little Latin, Paul's visit thus: 'the local people of the Amazon region were surprised by his unusual activity, rhythmus and he appeared to take a little walk round Trafalgar Square. [*sic*]' Follmann was surprised at the apparent ease with which Paul travelled through the difficult conditions in Brazil, showing little sign of strain – this was perhaps due to his strict military training.

---

[60] Appendix 1 is the highest category of endangered species on the CITES Index: the Convention on International Trade in Endangered Species of Wild Fauna and Flora (CITES). For more on this, see also www.cites.org/eng/app/index.php. The CITES Convention came into effect in 1975, in Washington, DC.

Paul's first public lecture was presented at the Clarendon Laboratories in Oxford, such as were made by all Churchill Fellows who had completed and received their Churchill Fellowships. The lecture was illustrated with many slides taken during his travels in Brazil. Paul's local branch, the Thameslea Churchill Fellows, were in attendance with members of their families; they would meet four times a year at various places throughout the southern region and on each occasion a new fellow would give a lecture on their Fellowship adventures and experiences. These meetings were occasionally attended by a senior figure from the Trust itself; more recently it would have been Jamie Balfour, the director general of the Winston Churchill Memorial Trust. Many had a military background; for example, Jamie Balfour was colonel of the Royal Green Jackets (now The Rifles), a unit made up of other regiments, including the Oxfordshire and Buckinghamshire Light Infantry. Over the following years, Paul was asked to repeat the lecture, as new Churchill Fellows joined the Trust.

As the future for the prized and historically desirable Brazilian rosewood looked bleak, instrument makers in general and classical guitar makers in particular would be forced to rethink their choice of wood. Paul's experience in Brazil was in line with a growing public awareness of, and pressure on, the supply of these precious woods, resulting in international concern for their sustainability. The full effect of

Figure 8.9 Paul receiving the Winston Churchill Medal from the Speaker of the House of Commons, Lord Tonypandy, in London, 1984.

this would not be felt for some years (merchants had stocks in hand), but the writing was clearly visible on the wall. While many makers were only just waking up to this crisis, players were even slower in taking heed of the impending shortage. At the time, East Indian rosewood (*Dalbergia latifolia*) was being used as an effective alternative. Today, in the early twenty-first century, that wood is also becoming impossible to obtain, thus making Paul's research from near to forty years ago increasingly valuable.

CHAPTER 9

New Classical Guitar Developments:

The Taut Bracing System

After Paul returned from his Winston Churchill Fellowship research in Brazil, Christopher Dean began his two-year placement in Paul's workshop, and thus worked with him on some of the experimental instruments, which was an ideal introduction to Paul's approach to construction. These became labelled as 'Fischer Lutherie' instruments and were the very instruments that were premièred at the October Gallery in London in October 1984. After this significant event, he could no longer ignore his client waiting list, so they made a start on this together. With so many new ideas buzzing in his head, following the instrument tests in London, Paul was itching to take things further in a steady and measured way.

Paul's waiting list had been established several years before the Brazil trip and was around three or four years' waiting time, thus his clients' expectations were for his earlier design of instruments. However, from the mid-1980s, working on some of the ideas gleaned from the research of Dr Bernard Richardson in combination with his own experience, Paul had developed three fresh designs of guitar to meet the ever-broadening tastes and requirements of guitarists, some of whom were willing to explore non-traditional approaches. Until then, Paul felt that the general expectation was for a Torres-style guitar, which was very limiting to the creative mind. In Paul's case, not only did he have ideas through building guitars but he was also inspired by his early training in making other plucked instruments, including harpsichords, lutes, citterns, vihuelas and pandoras. Of course, David Rubio's guitars were all fundamentally based on the Torres-style construction; however, in the 200 or so guitars Paul had made during his time with Rubio, they had explored many different variations on this model. Paul was now ready to take his explorations one step further by moving away from the Torres model.

Christopher Dean moved to Chipping Norton with his wife, and as Paul's workshop was close by, he found his new circumstances to his liking. His early tasks of working on the test instruments and exploring the fascinating new woods, which Paul had brought back from Brazil, proved to be an exciting introduction to working with an established maker. And the purpose-built studio/workshop provided all the necessary equipment, which eased his path from being a student to a journeyman. The company of this new assistant was proving to work well and his skills, commitment and enthusiasm were exactly what Paul had hoped for, and he realised that Christopher would soon be ready to set out on his own path.

During this period, Christopher had gained much from working in this multifaceted business with Paul. He gained not only in the craft and discipline of making, but also in marketing and contacts for both clients and materials. Consequently, he was able to make a fairly easy transition to independent working and later achieved success in his own right.

Time passed quickly and soon Christopher's two-year 'finishing school' experience, as it became known, was coming to an end. Not only did Paul provide help and guidance from his adjoining bench, but Christopher had also been introduced and schooled in lutherie at the sharp end, the finer details of the craft – that is, guitarist's expectations and foibles, suppliers of materials and special tools, costings, and the general but important elements of running a business as a solo, artisan craftsman.

The interest in guitar making was beginning to take off, largely due to the work of numerous colleges, which were now teaching the subject and producing a fair number of graduates, all looking to be independent makers. Paul's advice to Christopher was the same as to all the others who asked the question, how can I begin as a luthier?

It's tough and requires hard work for several years. If your craftwork is of a high standard and you can demonstrate your passion and commitment, you stand a good chance of succeeding. In the end, lutherie is a fine and rewarding profession through the beautiful instruments you create and, in the process, the music you provide for others. The struggles of the early years are worth enduring.

Despite having spent all those years working with David Rubio, it was only after establishing his Chipping Norton workshop, where he mostly worked alone, that Paul fully appreciated the benefits of having another maker working alongside him with whom ideas could be shared and discussed as they arose during their work. Thus, he was surprised by the unexpected feelings he experienced as he spent long days working in solitude – often for ten hours a day. It felt strange; it wasn't a matter of loneliness but just the result of the unusual state of not communicating with anyone for long periods, apart from client visits. This was something Paul could advise young makers on as well, consoling them that those feelings of the first few months would soon pass, as they had for him, to be followed by a lifetime of blissful work. Some of Paul's solitude was created by his advice to his own two young children not to disturb him in the workshop and to imagine he was still working at Duns Tew. A workshop can be a dangerous place, with sharp tools and machines. His own children heeded this warning without issue and he was only just one room away if he was needed.[61]

Of course, there were further keen students to follow on from Christopher Dean – though they were joining Paul as pupils rather than

---

[61] Interestingly, when Scott was deciding on his future career directions, Paul did suggest guitar making but it wasn't taken up by Scott. It was some years later, when Scott was able to articulate his feelings from his teenage years regarding this, that he told Paul he didn't believe he could manage the isolation and self-discipline required for the profession.

as assistants – and most were a pleasure to teach, despite their quite different personalities. One of these became a maker in his own right: Pepe Toldo, who set up his own workshop in Liechtenstein. Another, Matthew Brittan, did not plan to become a professional luthier but did make a fine guitar, so adding to his other talents from which the theatre world would benefit, particularly the Cheltenham Everyman Theatre.

By 1986, when Paul was mostly working on his own again, he focused on preparing the drawings for a new guitar design, consolidating his work on the Taut system to date. He had begun developing this system in the early 1980s, largely inspired by the work of the physicist Bernard Richardson, who summarises the aims and results of his investigation very well here:

A long-standing research programme at Cardiff University has established the low- and mid-frequency mechanics and acoustics of the classical guitar. Techniques such as holographic interferometry and finite-element analysis have yielded considerable information about the modal characteristics of the instrument and their relationship with the construction and materials of the instrument. Considerable work has also been undertaken to determine the sound-radiation fields associated with these modes, establishing those modes that make the greatest contribution to the radiated energy. Studies of string dynamics (including the interaction with the player's fingertip) show how readily the strings' energy is coupled to the body and sound field. Our measurements and models allow a relatively small number of measured parameters to be used to predict the sounds radiated by a guitar; these sounds can be used for psychoacoustical tests to gauge those modifications to the guitar's structure that are likely to produce perceptible differences in sound quality.[62]

---

[62] Bernard Richardson, 'Guitar Making – The Acoustician's Tale', Proceedings of the Second Vienna Talk, University of Music and Performing Arts Vienna, Austria (September 2010), 19–21.

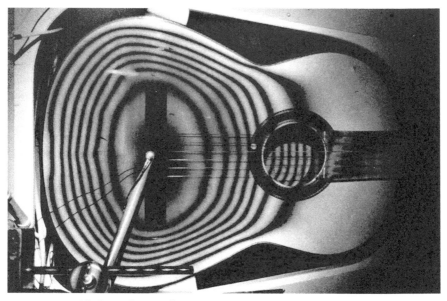

FIGURE 9.1 A holographic interferometry image showing how the soundboard on the classical guitar can vibrate. This photograph was taken in Richardson's laboratories at Cardiff University and is of a Paul Fischer fan-braced guitar. Photograph by Paul Fischer.

Paul returned to the draughtsman's drawing board in his workshop with a clean sheet of paper. He began working through the ideas first introduced to him by Bernard Richardson, to create something completely fresh with his classical guitar construction.

Later, practical work would show that Paul's Taut bracing style for the soundboard was a move in the right direction, as volume was vastly increased. However, in the process, the tone had become hard and thin, especially in the treble. Using his considerable experience, in conjunction with the feedback received, the project was to refine the Taut system. The problem was how to retain the wonderful warmth and richness of the traditional guitar while delivering the increased volume needed by the modern concert guitarist, performing in increasingly larger concert venues. Could it be done?

The first instruments built using Paul's Taut system demonstrated the accuracy of his theories, although refinements were still required. The early production consisted of eleven fine parallel braces, with four lateral braces bridging over each of the eleven verticals. This was discovered to be too rigid and the vertical braces were reduced to nine and splayed slightly to create a gentle fan pattern in the Taut bracing system no. 2.

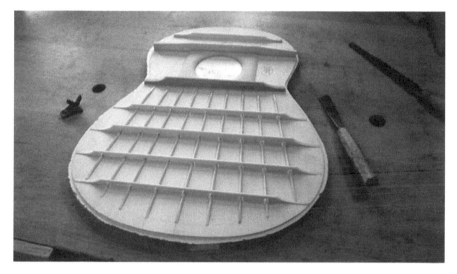

FIGURE 9.2 A Paul Fischer soundboard with the Taut bracing system no. 2.
Photograph by Paul Fischer.

Sitka spruce, which is light but extremely strong in comparison to European spruce, was used so that the dimensions of each brace could be reduced, thus lowering the mass and giving the soundboard slightly more flexibility in the extremities. To give an idea of its strength, Sitka spruce is used on the masts of sailing ships.

The Spanish maker Antonio de Torres (1817–1892) created a design of a 'modern' classical guitar during the nineteenth century, with seven fan braces and a slightly larger body than earlier instruments. This design has remained a template for classical guitar makers throughout the twentieth century and continues to be part of the discussion as regards soundboard bracing even today. Students usually begin their training as classical guitar makers by following the Torres design, which provides a model for them to follow and either develop or move away from in their future careers.

As mentioned, Richardson's work provided a better understanding of the physical principles at play in sound production for the guitar. Paul then needed to follow this up with work on the bench to refine the results. Some of his earlier work with lutes and harpsichords would be helpful here. They used very different bracing systems but both provided clues to soundboard efficiency.

Sound is produced when the surface of a vibrating string transfers energy to the soundboard, which in turn excites the surrounding air and then carries the sound to the listener's ear. In the case of the guitar, this begins with the soundboard (which is sometimes referred to as a plate). The sound reflected by the soundboard is further influenced by the body of the guitar and the types of wood used. The soundboard being the first and most important resonator is required to have great strength, stiffness and low density. Alpine spruce has been shown over many centuries to be the ideal and remains the most commonly used in quality instruments, though many other softwoods are also used today: for example, western red cedar and Engelmann spruce, to name just two. The bracing systems and dimensions of the soundboard remain broadly the same in each case, regardless of the wood used.

Paul's own approach was to create a soundboard of low mass, high strength and medium stiffness (for personal convenience, he uses the term 'weight', as it is by estimating the weight of the soundboard that he assesses mass). The reduction of weight can be achieved through making the soundboard thinner – within limits. Traditionally, this was between 2.2 and 2.5 mm, depending on the wood's natural qualities. In the Taut system, this thickness was reduced to 1.8 mm but was more than well supported by the lateral braces. Paul increased the more usual seven fan braces to eleven (which he later reduced to nine). With this increase in the number of braces and their relative position to each other, their dimensions were reduced to minimise mass. In both the soundboard and the braces, the mass of the material was lowered and the stiffness was increased.

These ten images show the input admittance and sound field measurements for a Paul Fischer Simplicio Taut system guitar (Figure 9.3). Each measurement is calibrated at a different Herz level, which refers to pitch level at a given frequency. In other words, image B(1-1)-1 Mode is a measurement of the vibrational response of the top of the guitar when the lowest string is plucked.

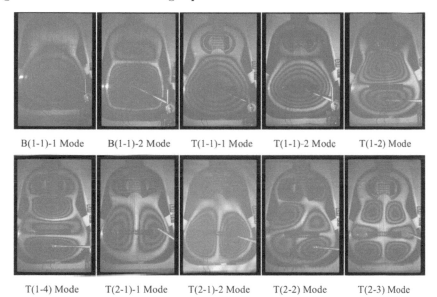

| B(1-1)-1 Mode | B(1-1)-2 Mode | T(1-1)-1 Mode | T(1-1)-2 Mode | T(1-2) Mode |

| T(1-4) Mode | T(2-1)-1 Mode | T(2-1)-2 Mode | T(2-2) Mode | T(2-3) Mode |

FIGURE 9.3 Holographic interferograms of selected modes on the guitar. (Input Admittance and Sound Field Measurements of Guitars: B. Richardson, T. Hill and S. Richardson.) This shows the vibration pattern on the soundboard of one of Paul's Taut system guitars. Photograph from Paul Fischer Collection.

Note that the vibrational patterns in the two T(2-1) Mode images indicate that the bridge is more flexible in the extremities than in the centre and Paul Fischer regarded this as not altogether desirable (see Figure 9.3). From that, he redesigned the bridge on all future instruments so that it would flex as one single unit.

Over the following twenty years subtle adjustments would take the Taut guitar from being loud but with a dry and brittle tone to being loud but with a warm and refined tone. This was the general direction of guitars in the latter part of the twentieth century. The success of the Taut instruments gained many converts among leading performers, as well as receiving positive and complimentary reviews.

***

After returning from Brazil, during the 1980s Paul was invited to join the advisory panels of the Crafts Council of Great Britain and the Southern Arts Association. These panels consisted of practitioners working in a broad range of crafts, including potters and ceramicists, glassmakers, clock makers, bookbinders and instrument makers of electric as well as acoustic instruments. The panels met quarterly at the Crafts Council headquarters in Islington, London.[63] One other instrument maker on the Crafts Council panel was the early instrument maker Norman Myall. The panel for the Southern Arts Association also met quarterly for the very same purpose but for crafts people working within the regions.[64] Apart from Paul, there was no overlap in the members of the panels of both of these institutions, despite their work being similar. The Crafts Council provided set-up grants for craftspeople establishing their own workshops. This added both to his knowledge and experience, so he could help fellow craftspeople progress in their respective careers.

Paul's guitar production was maintained in addition to these extra-curricular activities and now extended to seven–, eight–, ten– and

---

[63] The Crafts Council was a renaming of the earlier CAC (Crafts Advisory Council), whose objective is to advance and encourage the creation and conservation of works of fine craftsmanship and to foster, prioritise and increase the interest of the public in such works. The Crafts Council continues its work today, and since March/April 1973 has published a regular magazine called *Crafts*.

[64] The Southern Arts Association was one of twelve regional associations set up as intermediate organisations linked to the Arts Council. The aim of these associations was to encourage and support artists and craftspeople living and working within the twelve different regions throughout the UK. In 1990 these were replaced by ten Regional Arts Boards.

even eleven-stringed guitars, not to mention the eight-stringed Terz, alto and bass instruments.

At this stage of Paul's career, he was ever restless and his energy seemed to know no bounds. Towards the end of the 1980s he started work designing and making fibreglass instrument cases. These were carefully designed with the input of the flamenco guitarist Paco Peña, with the specific needs of air travel in mind. These cases were called, appropriately, Pegasus. Within a couple of years, it became clear this had been a step too far. Too much work had been taken on, and to rationalise his commitments, the Pegasus case business had to go. It was sold as a going concern and remains in business to this day.

In around 1986 Paul continued to buy some of his wood from Juan Orozco and made another one of his many trips to Brazil; Juan flew down from New York to meet Paul in São Paulo. Together they visited the Brazilian guitar manufacturer, Giannini, who was selling off a lot of their rosewood; the factory was located just outside of São Paulo. Juan was the intermediary and the quality of the wood was exceptional. This was an opportunity that could not be missed and Paul had to take out a bank loan to buy all he needed, as it was a lot of money, but a worthwhile investment

Much of the development work in guitar construction was maker led and demonstrated their appreciation of the instrument's struggles to meet the demands of the twentieth- and twenty-first-century guitarist – needs that had not been foreseen during the instrument's previous incarnations. Roughly every 100 years or so, from the fifteenth century onwards, the instrument has undergone a major change: from the small four-course (four pairs of strings) instrument in the fifteenth century to the highly decorated five-course instruments of the Baroque period, followed by the change to six strings in the seventeenth century. A larger body was created in the nineteenth century, with many changes to the internal bracing evolving into what would become the standard arrangement by the late twentieth century. As is normal with these things, the design was not set in stone and individual makers made slight alterations, but what is known as the Torres pattern became the standard model upon which most makers based their own designs.

Players were actively and frequently consulted but they usually had only a limited knowledge of the instrument's construction and the specialised skills needed to evolve it. Their input was mainly gained in terms of the assessment of a finished guitar. Nevertheless, this input was vital to improve the breed.

Paul passed many hours sharing ideas and thoughts on the changing world of classical guitar making and, with hindsight, he recognises that 'the latter part of the twentieth century was the most exciting time, so far, to be an instrument maker'. This was particularly true for the classical guitar, which was, and still is, going through a period of significant evolution. Many of these discussions took place at festivals; some courted controversy, but out of these lively exchanges came many fresh ideas and steps forward in guitar design. In particular, he benefited from the input of players; Paul was not one himself and their thoughts on tone production, technique and expression aided his understanding of what players needed from the instrument in order to improve it.

At that time, the guitar world held many festivals, summer schools and masterclasses throughout the year. There were also colleges and universities, as well as guitar societies, which were dotted throughout the UK; they met regularly and had enthusiastic memberships. Paul's interest in passing on the results of his research led him to begin lecturing. Once he'd started on this path, the invitations to present his work soon built up. His plan was to lecture on his research in acoustics, benefiting considerably from the work of Dr Bernard Richardson, together with what he had learnt in Brazil and its related experimental use of alternative woods. It was Paul's hope that this would encourage makers and players to consider instruments made from less-endangered species. He had already begun lecturing, even before his trip to Brazil, to local schools and music societies, including the Classical Guitar Society of Oxford University. However, after his return from Brazil, his lecturing developed on a much more technical level, as there was a marked increase in the number of instrument-making courses at colleges.

In 1985 Paul gave a lecture at the College of Music in Leeds, which was the year their instrument-making course was established. The guitar maker Peter Barton was teaching the course there; it was quite unusual for a music college to offer an instrument-making course at that time – or even today. His visit began with a lecture on guitar making as well as an introduction to acoustics, which was rarely discussed. This was something he would expand upon in future lectures as his experience regarding acoustics developed. Following his lectures, Paul would examine the students' work and offer guidance where necessary.

Peter Barton had trained under Roger Rose at the West Dean College of Arts and Conservation in Sussex. Roger Rose, in turn, had trained in the keyboard department at Arnold Dolmetsch's workshops in Haslemere, thus there was a lineage with a passing down of knowledge, which resonated with Paul. Sadly, Leeds College closed their guitar-making and violin-making departments in 2002.

One of the first colleges to teach instrument making for all instruments (except brass) was the London College of Furniture in the early 1970s, which was located on Commercial Road in the East End of London. In 1974 Herbert Schwarz began tutoring classical guitar construction there. He was originally from Czechia (at that time Czechoslovakia), where he had learnt guitar making.

Coincidentally, Herbert Schwarz of the London College of Furniture came from the same town as Manfred Gleissner, the timber merchant from whom Paul and many other instrument makers in the UK would buy their wood. As Paul was the manager of David Rubio's studio/workshop, he became acquainted with Manfred Gleissner even before he set up his own workshop.

Manfred Gleissner had a good knowledge of English, which made for a comfortable business relationship. Paul started attending the annual Frankfurt Musikmesse in 1979 and would combine these trips with a visit to Bubenreuth, where the Gleissner family have their timber business for musical instruments. These visits meant that Paul could hand pick his woods, which Manfred kindly allowed him to do. Afterwards they would pack all of the woods he had chosen and arrange for them to be collected on the same day and shipped back to England. While they were packing the wood, Manfred would often throw in extra pieces of spruce, free of charge, to be used for the bracing. The day would end with a fine dinner with Manfred and his wife, or a trip to the theatre together. On these trips, Paul often flew from Heathrow to Nuremberg, where he would catch the train to Bubenreuth to visit Gleissner. He would then travel by train from Nuremberg to Frankfurt to attend the International Frankfurt Music Fair (Musikmesse).

Luby is a town in the Czechia, in the Cheb district. It has had a tradition of instrument making for centuries. Luby was for a time known as Schönbach, but immediately after the end of the Second World War, in 1946, the borders between the two countries were moved back to their pre-1938 position. Many of the German-speaking instrument makers who were expelled in 1946 moved to Bubenreuth in Germany and so it became known as the village for instrument making and related industries.

Both Herbie Schwarz and the Gleissner family were originally from Schönbach in Sudetenland and had known each other well, as they had all lived in the same community of instrument makers. Hence, the village of Bubenreuth is now filled with generations of instrument makers; for example, Anton Hannabach, Musikinstrumenten- und Saitenfabrikation was established in Schönbach, and after the war the Hannabach family moved to Bubenreuth and nearby Egglkofen, where they continue to make guitars and strings. Kolb – the machine head maker – and bow makers for stringed instruments are also there. Paul says it is a very special place.

Paul was an assessor of the students' work at the London College of Furniture. Thus, he was invited to lecture at their open day on 14 May 1986, along with other leading figures of the guitar world, such as the guitarists John Mills and Cobie Smit, who played the students' guitars, and Bernard Richardson, who was also lecturing there. Terry Pamplin, who was an ex-Dolmetsch employee, was head of instrument making at London College of Furniture and Herbie Schwarz was the tutor for guitar making.

FIGURE 9.4 London College of Furniture Open Day, 14 May 1986.
Left to right: Lily Mairants, Terry Pamplin, Marian Romanillos, John Mills, José
Romanillos, Ivor Mairants, Paul Fischer and Herbert Schwarz.
Photograph © Colin Cooper.

Paul paid a few visits to Cardiff, sometimes working with Bernard Richardson in his laboratory at the University of Cardiff to see the equipment that was in use for holographic interferometry, from which he gained so much, and his curiosity was being stimulated continuously, with some questions being answered.

Paul's lectures at the music department of the University of Huddersfield followed a similar pattern to that at the College of Music in Leeds, but of course were more developed, as his work on new designs and acoustics were beginning to show results. Also, he was lecturing guitarists – not instrument makers. The guitar tutor at Huddersfield was David Taplin (1944–2013); he was a classical guitarist and an Early Music performer. Taplin had also been a customer from the early David Rubio days and remained a customer of Paul's when he set up his own workshop. David Taplin ordered many guitars from Paul, including a copy of the Stradivari guitar, held at the Ashmolean in Oxford, as well as two vihuelas: one six-stringed and one eight-stringed.

In his lectures, Paul believed that guitarists would benefit from understanding more about their instrument and its construction and the materials used; it would help them explore their instruments more effectively. He gave lectures annually at Huddersfield for a number of years.

Roy Courtnall Summerfield started the guitar-making course at Newark and Sherwood College, Nottinghamshire, in 1984. There had already been musical instrument technology courses there for a number of years.[65] The tutors on the guitar course have included Tony Johnson, Adrian Lucas, Mal Brady and Jamie Swannell. The guitar maker James Lister started teaching at Newark and Sherwood College much later, in 2005, and is still teaching there today. In the meantime, the college had changed its name from Newark and Sherwood College to Newark and Lincoln College. Paul began giving lectures there when James Lister became head of the guitar-making department. It was almost a full-day visit to Newark and Lincoln College each time, beginning as usual with a lecture, followed by the rest of the day in workshops looking at the students' work and offering advice.[66] Many of these students would follow this up later with a visit to Paul's own workshop in Chipping Norton.

---

[65] At Newark Technical College, the school of Musical Instrument Crafts was founded in 1972 under Principal Eric Ashton. It comprised originally of courses in 'violin repairs and construction' led by Maurice Bouette; 'piano maintenance, repairs and tuning' led by David Taylor' and a 'general instrument repairs', that included brass instrument repairs, by Louis Rousseau. The courses were validated by City and Guilds under the title of 'Musical Instrument Technology'. In 1977 Newark School of Violin Making (NSVM, as it has become known) moved into its current home in Kirk Gate. The new school site was opened by Yehudi Menuhin on 11 April 1978. In 1989 the Glasgow School of Luthiery, offering training for instrument makers and repairers, was established within Glasgow Clyde College.

[66] By coincidence, Paul's son, Scott, later studied a music industry management course at Newark and found himself with a placement with Virgin Studios' mobile recording studio, travelling around the country recording live concerts of artists such as Pearl Jam. This was at the start of the 1990s, and unfortunately the whole industry was going through a revolutionary change, which resulted in many job losses. Scott decided to go travelling and working as a teacher of English as a foreign language in Thailand, Corfu and Slovakia.

A real benefit of these talks was not just passing on the fruits of his work to others but also the continual learning gained from talking and listening to those in the audience. Although this was a time-consuming and expensive exercise, it delivered significant benefits from the information, new friends, clients and the experience gained.

On other occasions, he would visit Cardiff on the invitation of John Mills to lecture to groups of his students at the Royal Welsh College of Music and Drama. These meetings and lectures also took place in many of the other leading institutions, such as the Royal Academy of Music in London, and then overseas at the University of Cleveland, Ohio, in the USA, and the annual Singapore International Guitar Festival.

Another annual foray, which only required a short flight to Germany, was to the Frankfurt Musikmesse – a large international event held each springtime. Paul first started visiting the Frankfurt Musikmesse in his final years with David Rubio. As mentioned, he would combine his trips with a visit to timber merchants in Bubenreuth. At the Musikmesse itself, Paul had the opportunity to meet up with some of his regular customers, such as Sho Kido, president of Rokkomann; Shiro Arai of Aria Guitars; Thomas Liauw of Tomas Music Consultants from Singapore; and the Fana Corporation from Tuyko. Paul would also meet up with Nicoli Alessi, a maker of fine-quality machine heads from Italy, and the timber merchant Manfred Gleissner. A visitor to the stand of Michael Macmeeken, the Chanterelle music publisher, was a given because it was a meeting point for many important visitors, such as George Varney, creator of the Dynarette cushion; Maurice Summerfield of *Classical Guitar* magazine; and many guitarists as well. As one wandered through the enormous halls of the exhibition, one would also inevitably bump into many people from Britain, such as Juan Teijeiro and Pam Hoffman from the London Guitar Studio, Michael Doughty of Stentor Music and Barry Mason from London Spanish Guitar Centre.

For the first three days it was a trade-only event, and this increased the possibility of having non-stop meetings. There were also guitar makers from all over the world, so there was a lot of opportunity for discussion and viewing other makers' work – guitar makers such as Amalia and José Ramírez, Paulino Bernabé, Manuel and Pablo Contreras, Hermann Hauser III, Masaki Sakurai, Yuichi Imai, Stephan Schlemper, and many more. Paul would meet up with Gernot Wagner – whose workshop is in Frankfurt – both at the Musikmesse and at his workshop each year.

世界の名工達集う
The World's Greatest Guitar Craftsmen Gather.

FIGURE 9.5 As the caption below this photograph stated when it was published – 'The World's Greatest Guitar Craftsmen Gather' – the German maker Hermann Hauser III, Paul Fischer and the Spanish maker Pablo Contreras together at the Frankfurt International Musikmesse. **Photograph by Sho Kido, president of Rokkomann.**

Shiro Arai was a very important figure in the Japanese and international guitar-making scene; he was often affectionately referred to as 'Mr Guitar'. He had been an early and strong supporter of David Rubio in his New York beginnings and continued to purchase guitars from David Rubio on an annual basis when he set up his workshop in Duns Tew. Equally, once Paul Fischer had established his own workshop, Shiro Arai also became a regular client of his for another forty years. He was an uncomplicated man to do business with and showed much understanding and knowledge of the developments in classical guitar making outside of Japan.

Paul found himself in the vanguard of the classical guitar movement and became a pioneering spirit through the late twentieth century into the new millennium. His Damascene moment had come after his meeting with Dr Richardson and they stayed in touch for over fifteen years. They both contributed to the advancement of the instrument, working in parallel – Paul making and Richardson researching the science of guitar acoustics. Richardson's scientific work was often at the back of Paul's mind when trying new ideas and techniques. Tradition can be the enemy of innovation and although his apprenticeship had been steeped in it, he was keen to explore.

***

Paul's work at the Crafts Council and its younger brother, The Southern Arts Association, brought other opportunities. Their work was to support artists and craft workers, and Paul's involvement on their advisory panels meant he had the daunting task of selecting deserving and appropriate recipients for financial support for tools, equipment, exhibitions, and so forth, from what were relatively limited funds. There were too many young, and not so young, talented and gifted makers and craft workers to choose from. Paul himself had benefited from their largesse in his early days, so was keen to give something back by donating his time.

In 1987 Paul applied for a commissioning grant to support a relatively new guitarist/composer called Nicholas Hooper, who had studied with John Williams at the Royal College of Music in London. The concept was to write a work based on the theme of 'creating a musical instrument' – a rare subject perhaps, but one with many creative possibilities to musically explore the stages of an instrument's construction.

The themes of Nicholas Hooper's four-movement composition, *Song of the Four Trees*, ran from the selection of beautiful, seasoned tropical hardwoods through to the painstaking and artistic creation of the instrument itself, which is brought to life finally in the expressive hands of the musician – 'Let the wood speak a phrase Paul would often use when teaching.

Often the enthusiasm of a student aiming for perfection would get the better of them and they would overwork the wood. Paul's response was always to say, 'Let the wood speak. Do not spoil the beauty of what nature has created by overworking it!'

Nicholas Hooper premièred the *Song of the Four Trees* on 14 July 1988 during the Cheltenham Festival of Music – renowned for its championing of contemporary music. Each movement was followed by a talk from Paul explaining the point reached in the instrument's construction. In the first movement, 'The Forest', four themes are presented, each of them reflecting the four major woods used in the creation of a guitar: spruce (a theme in harmonics), rosewood, ebony and mahogany (with grand chords). The second movement, 'The Creation', is a light allegretto developing the 'spruce' and 'mahogany' themes. The third movement is lyrical, as it describes the transition from the hands of the maker to those of the player. In the final movement, 'Celebration', Nicholas Hooper reflects the joy and excitement of music making on this sonorous instrument, taking full advantage of its and his expressive abilities. After the initial lecture-introduction to each movement, Nicholas Hooper played the whole piece through once more, complete.

The première was scheduled to coincide with an exhibition of musical instruments by Midlands- and South Wales-based makers at the Pittville Pump Rooms Museum. It was a fascinating and unique occasion, showcasing both Paul and Nicholas's new work.

Nicholas and Paul toured this successful Cheltenham Festival programme in ten schools in Oxfordshire, again generously supported by the Southern Arts Association. They considered it an ideal concept, as it took the craft of instrument making and coupled it with a music performance on the creation straight into the classroom.

This enjoyable partnership was coming to an end, but before that a last and surprising invitation arrived, which again was education related. It was to repeat the first performance before craft teachers of Oxfordshire at Kelmscott Manor, the former home of William Morris, a founding father of the Arts and Crafts movement. It was planned by Mary Comino, who had responsibility for the Applied Arts collection at the Cheltenham Art Gallery, with a special interest in the work of the Arts and Crafts movement.

> Fischer talked about the timbers used in guitar making, their beauties and sound producing qualities, the construction and the finishing of the instrument. After this the whole work was performed once more without the talks demonstrating its strengths as a concert suite. Nicholas Hooper's clean and subtle playing successfully penetrated a somewhat reverberant acoustic and it is likely to be much played.[67]

Paul and Nicholas's experience of performing together meant they felt very much in their element in the ambience of Kelmscott Manor. They were scheduled at the culmination of what was a three-day event, where Paul gave an illustrated lecture of the Brazilian forests, or what was left of them. This was punctuated brilliantly by Nick playing his finely crafted guitar suite, *Song of the Four Trees*.

Nicholas Hooper is a remarkable person, and since that time, his career has moved from strength to strength; not only has he become a renowned British film and television composer, having scored work for BBC documentaries such as *Land of the Tiger* and *Andes to Amazon*, as well as providing music for films such as *Harry Potter and the Order of the Phoenix* and *Harry Potter and the Half-Blood Prince*, he is a crime novelist – and, yes, he is still playing the classical guitar.

---

[67] Colin Cooper, 'Classical Guitar News: Song of Four Guitars', *Classical Guitar*, 7/1 (September 1988), 6.

CHAPTER 10

The 1990s

The 1980s had been a busy and productive decade for Paul and Joy, without whose help and tireless support things would have ground to a halt. Two small children, Scott and Rachel, had to be taken care of, together with office work and general business management. These were necessary and important tasks, which largely fell into Joy's very capable hands – something for which Paul is eternally grateful. If he were to combine most of the major annual events he attended throughout the year, it would have added up to about a month a year out of the time available for vital production. As a solo maker, as with most others in the Arts and Crafts, the myriad of important tasks besides making had to be taken care of – replacing vital stocks of wood and other materials, dealing with correspondence, workshop maintenance, and so forth – all falling on the shoulders of one or two people.

Of course, there were always family trips in between Paul's heavy work schedule, including a trip to China that Paul and Joy had planned at the beginning of the 1990s. This was a trip they had long dreamed of; however, after the events of Tiananmen Square, Joy was less enthusiastic, and so Scott stepped in and travelled with Paul to China in her place.

At the beginning of the 1990s Paul's work at the Crafts Council was coming to an end. The Crafts Council's decision to withdraw financial support from instrument makers caused much surprise and hardship for those makers just leaving college. Their first step had often been an appeal to them for what was known as a 'start-up grant' – funds that would give them a kick start into independence in the form of money for purchasing tools and equipment. Paul himself had benefited from such a start-up grant for buying tools and equipment. Other benefits of support for exhibitions, travel, further study and bursaries came from regional arts.

The Crafts Council of Great Britain was challenged to explain why instrument making was suddenly no longer considered to be a craft or an art. The response was, 'It doesn't demonstrate originality.' This could be rationalised, perhaps, as musical instruments are essentially reproductions and evolutions of centuries of development from an original form, which is more clearly evident in the case of Early Music instruments. However, it is far less so for the modern classical guitar, which, as discussed earlier, had undergone major acoustic development since the last quarter of the twentieth century. This represents the originality of the art and the creativity of the modern maker. Understanding the materials used, the different species of woods and their properties and unique qualities, and exploring how to use these qualities to make fresh sounds is the artistic process – something not seemingly understood or appreciated by the decision makers within the Crafts Council. Sound cannot be seen but the creative results can certainly be heard.

In 1992 Paul was commissioned to make an instrument based on, but not a copy of, a guitar from 1930 by Francisco Simplicio (1874–1932) – an instrument Simplicio had made towards the end of his life. This was a welcome commission, as Paul had long admired the work of this Spanish maker and it fired his imagination. The response to that first instrument was such that two more commissions followed. All three of these initial Simplicio instruments were based on Simplicio's distinctive fan bracing style, extending into the upper bout area, which is usually where the soundhole is located on a Torres-style guitar. To explain more fully, Simplicio had divided the soundhole into two halves and placed them on either side of the upper fingerboard.

After making these first three instruments, Paul was inspired to create more Simplicio-style guitars, with the soundhole shaped and positioned as per Simplicio but using Paul's own Taut bracing pattern. He found that both Simplicio's extended fan bracing and his own Taut system bracing effectively increased the working soundboard area by 20 per cent. While on this path of exploration, he also decided to make some of these Simplicio-model guitars using well-understood, alternative tonewoods such as satin wood (as Simplicio himself had done) and bird's-eye maple (see Figure 10.1, a satin wood instrument).

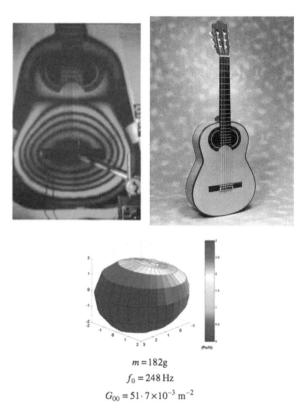

$$m = 182\text{g}$$
$$f_0 = 248\,\text{Hz}$$
$$G_{00} = 51 \cdot 7 \times 10^{-3}\,\text{m}^{-2}$$

FIGURE 10.1 shows the rich vibrational response of the sixth string on this guitar and is an indication of the bridge, in this case working as a single unit. From Bernard Richardson's measurements of the modes and radiation fields on this Paul Fischer Taut system Simplicio model (PF 952).[68]

---

[68] From Richardson paper 66. Bernard Richardson, 'Guitar Making – The Acoustician's Tale', *Proceedings of the Second Vienna Talk*, University of Music and Performing Arts Vienna, Austria (September 2010), 19–21. See Appendix for Bernard Richardson's contribution, which includes his recommended bibliography of up-to-date research.

The Taut system is often referred to as a 'grid' system, but with closer inspection the subtle details show it to be completely different and, in fact, it was designed in the early 1980s, before the so-called grid pattern came into use. The American guitar dealer Paul Heumiller describes Paul's Taut system guitar in these terms:

> The voice is simply astounding. It is as if each string is amplified, yet they are all in perfect balance ...
> It's clear that Fischer's bracing system really works.

In the world of Arts and Crafts, exhibitions are the established norm for presenting practitioners' work to the public and potential clients. A very unusual but fascinating event called Art in Action was held annually in the magnificent grounds of Waterperry House and Gardens, Oxfordshire. It brought together artists and craftspeople from all over the world who were both exhibiting and working 'live' in their exhibition spaces and it offered a rare opportunity for the public to glimpse into the world of gifted and talented people.

Art in Action began in 1976 and held its last event in July 2016, marking forty years of Art in Action. Paul first began demonstrating his instrument making there from the beginning of the 1980s and continued to demonstrate the art and craft of the luthier over many years during the forty-year history of this four-day event. The lute maker Michael Lowe was also a regular exhibitor, as was the wooden flute maker George Ormiston, and Andy Crawford, who was a maker of beautifully crafted boxes; he was also a flute player who was part of the Early Music scene, so he would play an impromptu concert together with Michael Lowe on the lute in their exhibition space. This was the full spirit of Art in Action. There were also more formal concerts given in the large house, featuring the instruments on display, performed on by many leading musicians.

The ethos of Art in Action was that visitors could see the artists at work and were encouraged to ask questions. The artists were meant to work as if in their own workshops, so Paul would transport a large part of his workshop to Art in Action. It offered an opportunity for him to improve his communications skills, which he considered to be a valuable opportunity for his quiet-spoken nature at that time. But he soon dropped his shyness and he recalls the great pleasure of explaining his work to the enthusiastic audience; they loved it and Paul felt encouraged. For Paul, this annual excursion into the public arena was as much a learning exercise for him as it was for the visitors.

FIGURE 10.2 At Art in Action, visitors trying out two very different styles of guitar built by Paul Fischer: on the left, a Simplicio-model guitar with twenty-two frets, and on the right, a copy of a nineteenth-century salon guitar by an unknown maker, which had a beautiful tone, as did Paul's copy. He chose to make the body out of an exquisite piece of Macassar ebony (rather than rosewood). Photograph by Paul Fischer.

From his first Art in Action in 1980, Paul grew to enjoy and benefit from the communication exercise, which helped him market his own work much more effectively. This was especially useful on the many overseas trips to fairs and conventions that came later. He remained a regular 'demonstrator' – the Art in Action terminology – for over twenty years, making many friends in the process while advancing public knowledge of the craft of the luthier.

Exhibitions were important for bringing a maker's work before the public but usually they were restricted to that function alone. Thus, in order to show their work to the most appropriate audience, contacting guitar societies and summer schools and offering to give talks on construction and acoustics, often demonstrating the latest developments, was necessary. Part of this exercise included allowing players to hear and play recently built instruments. Fortunately, makers were warmly welcomed to these events, livening up the festival programmes and fostering a closer interest in the luthier's art.

Although Paul was often away from his workshop when on such duties, the production of instruments remained constant; it had to be, as the order list continued to grow apace. From the start, the forward order book never dropped below a three-year wait and at one point reached a challenging six years! Surprising as these time-frames appear, makers can have even longer waiting lists; however, wisdom tells us that six years is about the maximum a maker could expect his clients to wait. Under such healthy conditions, the need for marketing was not that pressing; however, it was still important. The world of music is a very active one; attending guitar festivals and guitar society meetings not only offered opportunities to stay up to date with a new generation of players and the demands of their chosen repertoire, but they were also enjoyable occasions. Then, almost by a process of osmosis, an increased interest in the instruments would often surface during the leisure time at these events.

This happy and productive method of gentle marketing was all that was needed. This was doubtless the same for other makers, many of whom Paul came to know at festivals, exhibitions and guitar events. In general, makers are a friendly bunch and it was delightful to discuss common concerns and ideas. The hard-edged competition of a more commercial world did not seem to exist among these makers – or if it did, it didn't show. Evenings of shared conviviality could include makers from Spain, Japan, Germany, Italy, the USA, and elsewhere, all happy to discuss the events of the day and their own experiences of instrument making.

Musical instrument makers in general have no guild or institution of their own, as the jewellers, ceramicists and painters do in the UK, where many counties have their own guild – the Oxfordshire Guild of Craftsmen, the Sussex Guild of Craftsmen, etc. However, there are annual musical instrument fairs in various countries and continents. These include the large international show in Frankfurt – the largest such show in Europe – and more recently, the international music fair of Music China in Shanghai. These heavily commercial shows are not always ideal for exhibiting acoustic instruments in general, and the classical guitar in particular, owing to the intrusion of background noise. This is especially true when amplified electric instruments share the same exhibition space.

Before dropping their direct support for instrument makers towards the end of the 1980s, the Crafts Council of Great Britain held a summer exhibition that included the works of many of the UK's fine and growing band of instrument makers. At the time, it was a rare opportunity for their work to be displayed in London, and at the highest level. However, soon other such opportunities seemed to come along thick and fast: the Cheltenham summer exhibition; the Barbican musical instrument exhibition, and even requests for Paul's work to be sent to the USA for shows at the Sheehan Gallery in Washington and the Maryhill Museum of Art in Washington State.

At that time, the prestigious auction house of Bonhams of Knightsbridge had a dedicated musical instrument department, led by Peter Horner. In January 1992 they hosted 'Decorative Arts Today', a selling exhibition of contemporary work, which was an absolute pleasure to view. There were about 500 exhibits, including furniture, wall hangings, ceramics, glass, bookbinding and, of course, musical instruments. Three instrument makers were invited to exhibit their work there: Paul Fischer, Brian Cohen and Robert Deegan. The harpsichord maker Robert Deegan displayed a double manual harpsichord made in the style of a two-manual German harpsichord by Christian Zell of Hamburg in 1728. Brian Cohen, who makes a range of instruments, often with very elaborate ornamentation, exhibited a lute and a cello, as well as a guitar. Paul Fischer, as one of England's most established guitar makers, exhibited two guitars: one was a ten-stringed instrument and the second guitar was especially crafted for this exhibition and had an extra label on the inside saying 'Bonhams Exhibition'. The instrument has a spruce soundboard, but the body of this guitar was made of bird's-eye maple, giving a warmer, richer sound and with internal bracing to compensate for the use of a softer wood (maple). The choice of wood was part of Paul's research into finding substitute woods for guitar building. This bird's-eye maple guitar was a special instrument for another reason as well: the year 1992 marked Paul's twenty-fifth wedding anniversary, and to celebrate this he had written his wife's name, 'Joy', on the label of the guitar. Mark Ashford, a young graduate from the Royal Academy of Music, was invited by Paul to perform on this special instrument.[69]

For many decades guitarists in England had enjoyed numerous small guitar festivals, weekend masterclasses and summer schools at venues throughout the country. However, it was not until the 1990s that they had their own annual International Guitar Festival and Summer School held at the wonderful venue of West Dean College in West Sussex, which continues to this day. This was largely the brainchild of the lutenist and guitarist Barry Mason and the equally gifted mezzo-soprano Glenda Simpson; they were a perfect husband and wife team, performing and researching Early Music together, both with incredible drive and energy. It was generously supported by the guitarist, businessman and founder of the *Classical Guitar* magazine, Maurice Summerfield.

The first festival was held in high summer 1991 and offered masterclasses, recitals, private tuition with world-class guitarists, tutors and lecturers, including Leo Brouwer, John Mills, David Russell, Carlos Bonell and the flamenco guitarist Ian Davies. This all took place within the magnificent atmosphere of an English country mansion with superb

---

[69] Just before graduating from the Royal Academy of Music, London, in 1993, Mark Ashford won the BBC Radio 2 Young Musician Award.

facilities, including workshops for the practical classes. From the start, Paul supported the festival's high ideals, and as well as attending the annual open days, he presented masterclasses and lectures and exhibited his instruments there.

By the second West Dean Festival in August 1992, Paul was already heavily involved in the organisation of a 'Gallery of British Luthiers', aiming to promote the growing number of young colleagues producing fine quality classical guitars. He, more than anyone, understood the importance of support in the early years and it was a great opportunity to display the craftsmanship that was becoming an established field in classical guitar making in Britain.

Paul's lecture presented 'a review of the success of the luthier's craft in Great Britain during the last thirty years'. That lecture was in 1992 and was, therefore, looking back to the early 1960s in Britain and the developments since then. However, first he talked of the influence of two earlier important figures: Arnold Dolmetsch and Robert Goble. Although Goble was a keyboard instrument maker, he was very influential in handmade instrument making in Great Britain. Not only was Paul trained by Robert Goble, many others followed and, like Paul, often moved into making different instruments. The quality of Dolmetsch and Goble's craftsmanship was invaluable – not only offering a good grounding and a springboard for other branches of early plucked string instrument making, it was also a rare privilege to be guided in this extraordinary profession by such outstanding makers. David Rubio, like Arnold Dolmetsch and Robert Goble in each of their times, inspired a new generation of instrument makers, including modern classical guitar makers. Their influence, in turn, had a ripple effect way beyond their immediate circle. And yet, it is important to note that out of the many who began their training, a relatively small number were able to achieve success in their own right as instrument makers.

From the start of the early 1970s in Great Britain, classical guitar making in particular benefited from the establishment of luthier training within colleges, which had not been available during Paul's early beginnings. And from this, many new and talented makers would establish their own careers and, in the process, receive global recognition. Paul was happy to say that the British school of classical guitar making had come of age.

After many years of hard work, Barry and Glenda decided it was time to take a well-earned rest from the festival that took up about nine months of their time every year. Their activities covered planning, scouting for sponsors, and all the rest of the details needed to put on such an event. West Dean College was, and remains, a great support and has always extended a warm welcome to all attending the festival – a part of a comprehensive series covering the visual arts, crafts and music.

Barry and Glenda remained at the helm of the festival until the start of the new millennium, when John Mills, a brilliant guitarist and former pupil of John Williams, took over. This made for a smooth transition with the benefit of fresh enthusiasm. Their legacy was an established festival on the international calendar that attracted world-class artists to a celebrated venue. John was assisted by his wife, the guitarist Cobie Smit, and remained director until 2012, maintaining the high standards with the same faculty of world-class teachers.

John Mills is regarded as one of Britain's finest guitarists and is a performer of international repute. He began learning the guitar at age 9 and later studied with John Williams at the Royal College of Music, London. He had masterclasses with Andrés Segovia at Santiago de Compostela, Spain, and with Julian Bream. John Mills was appointed professor of guitar at the Royal Academy of Music, London, and later coordinator of guitar at the Welsh College of Music and Drama. He was director of the Guitar Festival of Great Britain, at West Dean, from 2001 to 2012.

Another important step in broadening Paul's experience of the international guitar-making scene came in the 1990s with Paul and Joy's first visit to Japan; the timing of this visit also coincided with Japan's own international music fair in Tokyo. From the beginning, Japan had been his most active market. Numerous guitar specialists sought out his guitars

FIGURE 10.3 West Dean director Barry Mason and Paul in 1993.
Photograph by Colin Cooper.

and the challenge of working with people from a very different culture added an extra stimulus. Paul was already personally acquainted with many of these clients, as they would meet in early spring each year at the Frankfurt Musikmesse. This annual opportunity to refresh contacts and talk over issues in general always proved useful. When the idea of visiting Japan was raised over sushi and sake on one of his Frankfurt trips, his hosts for the evening were only too keen to welcome Paul to their homeland. The marketing opportunities were already fermenting in these specialists' minds and the chance to show off the English guitar maker to their clients was a significant coup.

Few European makers ever visited Japan at that time. The very different culture could throw up challenges and there was a perception that English and other European languages were not widely spoken or used on signage, making travel a challenge. Japanese protocol was another consideration: it might be all too easy to cause offence. The food was also (in those days) unfamiliar. Undaunted by this, Paul and Joy planned their visit for spring 1993, cherry blossom time – a much-celebrated season, especially in Tokyo.

These Japanese clients made up 50 per cent of his annual order book. Some were based in Tokyo, with others in Nagasaki and Kobe, which would make for a good round trip. In each location, contacts and their local staff were very kind and willing to act as guides. This proved to be vital and saved Paul and Joy from many disasters, though after a very short time they began to feel confident enough to explore on their own. It was a challenging but very rewarding experience.

During their time in Tokyo, a long-standing associate and friend, Yoshi Hayashi, arranged a visit for them to Yokohama and the International Niibori Guitar Academy, which had been established in 1957. This academy teaches not only the solo six-stringed guitar, but also many sized instruments, from the contrabass guitar through to the very small soprano guitar, in order to make up a broad pitch range of instruments for their guitar orchestra. The Niibori Guitar Academy Orchestra has toured regularly throughout the world and has made many recordings.

The academy and orchestra were established by Dr Hiroki Niibori, who conducts the orchestra and made many of the arrangements for it. In 2007, to celebrate its fiftieth anniversary, the Niibori Guitar Music Academy held concerts on 22 and 23 September 2007 at the Takemitsu Hall, Tokyo Opera City Concert Hall. Then, later that year, the Niibori Guitar Philharmonic Orchestra performed at the Stadthalle Germering in Munich on Saturday, 17 November, and at the Musikverein, Vienna, on Monday, 19 November 2007.

Yoshi Hayashi has considerable

FIGURE 10.4 Bass, concert (prime) and alto guitars made by Paul Fischer. Photograph from Paul Fischer Collection.

FIGURE 10.5 Paul and Dr Niibori at his home viewing his private collection of guitars.
Photograph from Paul Fischer Collection.

experience in the world of the classical guitar and is also a fine player. His aid was vital for this first trip beyond central Tokyo. Arriving at the Niibori Guitar Academy, they were welcomed by members of the staff, who then introduced them to the senior tutors and finally the Niibori Guitar Academy's founder, Dr Hiroki Niibori. After these introductions they were treated to a performance by a chamber orchestra made up entirely of various-sized guitars: soprano, alto, concert (prime), cembalo and contrabass guitars – all just for Paul and Joy! There was a further surprise: a chair was placed in the centre of the stage and Paul was invited to a question-and-answer session focused on the English guitar scene and its leading players – with a special emphasis, on their part, on John Williams. This baptism by fire was followed by a tour of the Niibori Guitar Academy, ending with refreshments. They were invited to Dr Niibori's home to see his collection of instruments, which took up most of the afternoon, but the celebrations were not yet over.

An unforgettable dinner with the senior tutors had been planned for the evening in a seaside restaurant with views of Mount Fuji. The Niibori party had reserved the entire restaurant, where one wall was made of plate glass so diners could take in the magnificent view. The menu alternated between French and Japanese cuisine in each course, coupled with the appropriate wine, beginning with champagne, moving through to sake for the Japanese courses and ending the meal with a French brandy. Despite some linguistic difficulties and some unusual food (sea slug springs to mind), the evening was not just a great success but also an event that further cemented an already long-established friendship.

The Niibori Guitar Academy, while not unique, was one of the first to explore the use of the guitar in guitar orchestras and chamber ensembles, such as guitar quartets using instruments of various sizes. In the process, they expanded the instrument's repertoire. A consequence of their visit was that Paul would extend the range of instruments he created for Niibori to include alto and bass guitars.

Yoshi Hayashi, who arranged this visit, was the dynamic head of the Tokyo office of the Rokkomann Company of Kobe, with whom Paul had a long-standing business relationship. Their next trip was to Kobe, to the Rokkomann head office; the journey was made by Shinkansen, the famous and rapid bullet train. Here they met the president of the company, Mr Sho Kido, and stayed with him in his very traditional home, which was a special experience. Each of the rooms in the house was divided, in traditional manner, with paper covered sliding partitions and they slept on the traditional tatami on the floor.

Mr Kido was a dignified figure who followed Japanese tradition and each evening would dress in a kimono. He was a private man, and despite welcoming Paul and Joy into his home, he retained the quiet traditions of the evenings at home, and so arranged for a member of his staff to act as their chaperone in Kobe and Kyoto. However, buoyed up by having managed the Shinkansen on their own, they felt confident enough to go it alone after just one day. This plan first required the permission of Mr Kido, as he had provided a chaperone to be courteous and attentive, as little English was spoken in this part of Japan. This was duly obtained.

Some years later, on 17 January 1995, the Rokkomann head offices were damaged by a massive earthquake – the Great Hanshin earthquake destroyed much of Kobe and its effects were even felt in Tokyo, where Rokkomann's offices were also affected, though with only minor damage.

Paul and Joy returned to Tokyo after a week of enjoying Kobe and Kyoto, thus rounding off a delightful and productive trip. In Tokyo they again met up with colleagues and associates, such as Yoshi Hayashi.

CHAPTER 11

Lecturing and Masterclasses in the UK and Abroad

Paul's lectures regularly took him to the Royal Academy of Music, London, music colleges and summer schools in the UK, and then later to the USA, Europe and the Far East. It was a gradual process; he built on his initial experiences of giving talks to schools and music societies, and the success of the lectures at UK festivals, concerts and masterclasses led to invitations from abroad. The first invitation came from Professor Bernard Hebb in Zevenor, North Germany, in the 1980s. The lecture might have been a challenge, despite Paul's, albeit limited, German language skills from his time in the army. Fortunately, most of the audience's command of English was considerably better than his German, so the first speaking event went smoothly. A useful foundation for lecturing was the presentation Paul had made about his Churchill Fellowship at the Clarendon Laboratories in Oxford in 1984.[70]

In 1997 Paul received an invitation from a friend and client, the Venezuelan guitarist Rubén Riera, to give a lecture on acoustics as well as a guitar-making masterclass at the prestigious Festival Internacional de Agosta in Caracas. Ruben Riera, the son of the guitarist and composer Rodrigo Riera, was a long-standing client of Paul's and thus an admirer of his instruments; however, Paul was hesitant because of the possible

---

[70] Apart from Paul's extensive travelling for work, he and Joy travelled a lot with their children, Scott and Rachel, to balance out the intense demands and isolation required by a guitar maker's work. Of course, many overseas trips managed to include a little guitar work/socialising, such as the delivery of a Fischer guitar to the Greek guitarist Dimitris Fampas and a driving holiday visit to Pepe Toldo in Liechtenstein.

language difficulties, both for the lecture and also for the masterclass. Up until this time, all of his guitar-making masterclasses had been given in the UK, where his tools and equipment could be easily transported. Taking tools – especially sharp ones – by air might present airport security issues; however, it was pre-9/11 then, so things were slightly more relaxed. With the minimum of tools – packed carefully inside a drum, with the vellum then refitted – and three soundboards, he thought he could manage. Having sorted all this out and deciding that any risks had been mitigated, Paul wrote to Riera accepting the invitation.

The reason Paul placed his tools inside a drum was that part of the lecturing kit was a side drum. This was used to show how a thin, taut, membrane of vellum or wood could effectively and efficiently transmit the sound energy of a striking drumstick or plucked string to the surrounding air and on to the listener's ears. Tightening the drum skin demonstrates how membrane tautness changes the efficiency of the process; by analogy, this explains how the guitar soundboard works and the properties it needs. Paul has never seen anyone else using a drum in their guitar sound production lectures; however, he believes that it offers the ideal vehicle for demonstrating the changing results of tightening and loosening the tension of a membrane (a drum skin or a guitar soundboard) and the efficiency of a tighter membrane for changing the character of the sound produced by the guitar's soundboard.

The drum was an important piece of kit for Paul's lecture. Although it would fit in the baggage allowance, it could only do so at the expense of clothes and most of everything else. The answer was to remove the vellum skin from one face of the drum and then fill it with carefully folded clothes – with a sharp chisel placed inside his socks, hoping that the vellum would not be punctured – and then replace the vellum. This was not done to deceive any airport officials inspecting the luggage but to use the space efficiently to get everything in.

The Festival Internacional de Agosta featured masterclasses, lectures, recitals and evening concerts – all held in the hall adjoining the Hilton Hotel, which was hosting most of the visiting artists and a major sponsor of the event. To get to this concert hall from the hotel, it was necessary to cross a major highway via a bridge. It was a short journey, but only a safe one because armed police patrolled the bridge and the auditorium every day during performances. Initially, it was slightly unnerving, even for Paul with his military background, to have such a strong police presence, and they were armed with submachine guns, but the atmosphere at the festival itself was completely music focused and inspiring because of the enthusiasm, particularly of the Venezuelan students.

FIGURE 11.1 Programme for the Festival Internacional de Agosto 1997, Caracas, Venezuela.
Photograph from Paul Fischer Collection.

There were many Brazilian performers there, such as Everton Gloeden.

Paul's masterclasses were held in the workshops of a technical college some distance from the hotel. On meeting the fifteen enthusiastic

FIGURE 11.2 Paul teaching the preparation of a guitar soundboard at the Festival Internacional de Agosta in Caracas, Venezuela.

students, it became clear that all communications would have to be conducted through an interpreter, including the lecture itself. So began the intensive week's training, made up of eight-hour days, all translated into Spanish. In such a short space of time, Paul needed to focus on one aspect of guitar making, which was the production of the soundboard in various forms: fan bracing, Taut bracing and a combination of these styles.

The students and Paul quickly got the measure of one another and the atmosphere became more relaxed, so much so that by the second day some of the students extracted cuatros and bandola llaneras from beneath their benches and began to play them. Their singing voices and harmonies were a pleasure to hear, as well as their playing on these Venezuelan instruments dating back centuries.

Soon others joined in singing, until most of the class were involved in an impromptu concert. Paul's first thought was to call things to order — there was a lot of work to do in just one week — but the playing and singing was so good that it felt better to relax and enjoy their natural exuberance. These concerts became a daily event at his masterclasses and the enthusiasm for both music and work was infectious. This admirable combination of seriousness, pleasure and exuberance related to music making reminded Paul of the experiences he'd had on his visit to Brazil.

FIGURE 11.3 An impromptu concert, with a bandola llanera being played on the left (with a plectrum) and the cuatro on the right, during a break in Paul's guitar-making masterclass in Caracas. Photograph from Paul Fischer Collection.

When they were not playing, they were a keen and hardworking group. They appreciated the opportunity to have a leading European maker teach them; it was a rare chance, if only for a week, and they took full advantage of it. If in that brief time, they could grasp the importance and choice of wood for the soundboard, its cut, feel and bracing; they would have learnt much about the heart of the guitar.

They were shown three examples of completed soundboards, prepared by Paul before departure and very carefully transported across the Atlantic. The three examples were: the traditional Torres, the modern Taut, and a modified Torres pattern. The students could choose one or more to explore during that week. The differences between the three patterns, their benefits and limitations were fully explained to them. Despite the ad hoc concerts, they worked hard and most students completed their assignments in a fun and productive week. Unsurprisingly, it all ended with a party shared with all the festival participants, including the young and patient lady interpreter.

There were concerts given by Everton Gloeden and Henrique Cazes from Brazil, Carmen Teller and El Cuarteto from Venezuela and the Orquesta Sinfonica Gran Mariscal de Ayacucho, also from Venezuela. It was a week of teaching, music spontaneous and otherwise – culminating in a party at the home of the CEO of Mavesa, a major sponsor of the festival, along with support from the British Council and Iberian Airways. It was an unforgettable experience.

A few years later Ruben lost his first Paul Fischer guitar and his house in a landslide in Venezuela. The British guitarist, David Caswell, who has maintained a close relationship and respect for Latin American composers and performers, raised the matter with Paul at West Dean, telling him the tragic news. Ruben was in a desperate situation and David had offered to help Ruben purchase a new Fischer guitar; Paul offered to help as well. In short order a new guitar was produced to the delight of Ruben.

***

Many of the international festivals included concerts by the world's leading artists; they offered a veritable who's who of the international guitar world. Some of those whom Paul met included the Assad Brothers, John Williams, David Russell, Manuel Barrueco, the LA Guitar Quartet, Paul Galbraith and Liona Boyd. And, of course, there were not only players but also makers of international repute attending these events, such as Dominique Field, José Ramírez II, Hermann Hauser III, Kohno, Paulino Bernabé, Gernot Wagner, and many more.

One of the foremost is the annual festival of the Guitar Foundation of America's (GFA) International Convention and Competition. Paul's American representative, Armin Kelly, suggested a visit. So, together with Joy, Paul visited GFA International Convention and Competition in Charleston in 1999 – 'Guitar stuff', as Joy called it, and it would be possible to include many days for them both to sample and enjoy the delights of Charleston and South Carolina.

The GFA Convention is actually a moveable feast held in a different location each year, not just within the USA –San Antonio, Texas, Montreal, San Francisco and Los Angeles – but also in Canada and Mexico too. As already stated, Paul gained many benefits from trips to exhibitions and he regretted having left it so late to take advantage of this particular one; it would have come in handy earlier in his career.

This convention, together with its international competition, is one of the most prestigious in the world – typically attracting fifty to sixty major concert artists and scholars from around the world in addition to the usual teaching and masterclass sessions. The so-called vendors' section also brought in makers, dealers in strings and wood and a host of music publishers. This made for a much bigger and commercial attachment than was the case for UK events, where there were limited opportunities for makers to show off their work. In the UK, makers seemed to be tolerated rather than welcomed – though this has changed over time. America did these things on a grander scale and it was of great benefit to meet other makers and fine players.

Paul's first visit to the GFA Convention was in 1999 and there were about forty stands in the vendors' area; by his visit in 2008 there were eighty stands. Each time he attended a GFA Convention, Paul was visiting in support of his representative, Armin Kelly of Guitars International, Cleveland, Ohio. Armin Kelly is an inspirational figure and it was always a pleasure to be with him; Armin involved each supporting maker with his staff and other visiting makers. He is a man of high ideals and integrity who represents only a select group of internationally renowned makers. As a representative of the English school of guitar making, Paul's annual attendance at the GFA Convention provided him with the opportunity to meet with members of this select group, including Gernot Wagner and Bernhard Kresse from Germany; Enrico Bottelli and Andrea Tacchi from Italy; and Greg Byers and Manuel Velazquez from the USA. There were many others.

An invitation in 2000 caught Paul's interest and allowed him to meet up again with his old friend and long-standing client Thomas Liauw (see Appendix I). He was, and remains, the organiser of the prestigious International Guitar Festival of Singapore and, since 2005, this included an International Guitar Competition. Liauw is energetic and always bubbling with ideas and his great enthusiasm for the classical guitar. This invitation was for Paul to present a lecture on his recent exploratory work and give a practical class. He would be joining a galaxy of distinguished luminaries, including from Argentina, Jorge Morel; Italy, Flavio Cucchi; and the Japanese maestro Kazuhito Yamashita. He would also meet

FIGURE 11.4 Enrico Botteli, Greg Byers and Paul at the GFA Convention, Charleston, South Carolina, in 1999.

another long-standing client – the orchestra's conductor Kazuyuki Terada – and other members of the Niibori Guitar Academy, both in person and in concert – people for whom he had made many instruments over the previous twenty years, including alto and prime guitars.

It was a fascinating and productive annual event. Five years later, in 2005, Paul was again invited to give a lecture and offer consultancy to guitarists regarding their instruments; he was also a member of the jury for the Singapore International Guitar Competition. This festival featured Oscar Ghiglia, the flamenco guitarist Juan Martin and the Brazilian guitarist and composer Marco Pereira. This festival remains a prestigious and important event in the classical guitar calendar, offering a broad and exciting programme to a mainly Far Eastern and Australasian audience.

Paul's lecture at the Stetson International Guitar Workshop on Monday, 9 June 2003, was on 'Understanding Instruments and Other Developments of the Guitar'. Stephen Robinson was the artistic director.

The twentieth century had placed demands on the classical guitar, which is an acoustic instrument; this stimulated a mood of curiosity and innovation, so that by the end of the twentieth century the guitar was in a very different place to where it had been fifty years before. That said, the traditional instrument, recognisable to Torres, was not forgotten, and both the traditional and more modern designs of instruments still coexist happily, supporting different schools of thought.

During Paul's first visit to the Frankfurt Musikmesse in 1980, he became acquainted with Siegfried Hogenmüller, a larger-than-life mover and shaker in the European classical guitar world. Neither a maker nor a player, Hogi, as many know him, appeared to have many contacts throughout the guitar world. As a result of this large group of friends and associates, combined with his ebullient nature – he was quite the raconteur – he had the knack of bringing together a somewhat disparate band of artisans. By the turn of the millennium, this talent would be put to good use by establishing an annual seminar timed to coincide with the annual Musikmesse in Frankfurt, which would already be bringing many potentially interested aficionados and experts to town. Hogi used his influence and contacts to spread the word and the first seminar took place in springtime 2000, at Rückersbach, 30 km south-east of Frankfurt, in the wooded hills of Hahnenkamm. There, nestling in the woods, was a modern purpose-built conference centre with accommodation, restaurant and bar facilities – a convenient and ideal location.

Aided by his encyclopaedic knowledge of the guitar world, Hogi planned each event thoroughly, always introducing a fresh subject or issue for examination. Likewise, many of the contributors were drawn from a wide range of countries, mainly within Europe, each with different interests and involvement in the classical guitar. This created a rare opportunity for both players and makers to come together and discuss and debate something which was much appreciated and needed by all. Naturally, many friendships were established and it also helped to welcome a new generation of young makers into the fold. These newcomers

FIGURE 11.5 Paul lecturing at Rückersbach, Germany. He began this lecture with an explanation of the comparative energy radiated from a conventional guitar and from one created with the Taut system.
Photograph by Claus Nürnberger.

not only learnt from the experience of established makers but also contributed their own fresh ideas. Lively debates took place, both in the lecture hall and later in the bar. Many enthusiastic young student makers from the Markneukirchen School would also attend these seminars.

Markneukirchen was another German town with a long tradition in instrument making; it is in the old German Democratic Republic. Once the wall dividing East and West Germany was removed in November 1989, these makers were even more inspired to engage with others, and they also shared their historically valuable knowledge. These students impressed Paul greatly with their thorough approach to researching and documenting the results; they were quite different from English student makers, with whom Paul had had considerable contact.

At the Rückersbach seminar, there was nearly always a presentation on the work of past masters, such as Antonio de Torres Jurado, Francisco Simplicio, Hermann Hauser III, Ignacio Fleta, Daniel Friedrich, David Rubio, Robert Bouchet and Richard Jacob Weissgerber (1877–1960), who was from Markneukirchen. Makers from many countries were included but, naturally, the lion's share were from Spain.

One notable contribution came from the Italian luthier Luca Waldner. He had recently successfully restored an important Torres guitar. Along the way, he discovered many of the different changes and restorations that it had undergone throughout its long life. Although nails are not used in the construction of classical guitars, under further examination the residue of staining, usually created from tannin in the wood when in contact with metal, indicated that at some time in the past nails had been used. This may also have been a result of using recycled wood to create their instruments. Using X-rays enabled the exploration of the instrument's interior. This and other fascinating discoveries of Torres's original work made for a memorable weekend. Many of the seminars achieved their aim and the world of lutherie gained much from these animated and informative occasions. Hogi had provided an opportunity for players and makers to benefit from a stimulating forum, something that, while common in other walks of life, was relatively rare in classical guitar making. Some of the other attendees included Herman Hauser III, Sasha Novak, Kolya Panhuyzen, Paulino Bernabé, Kazuo Sato, Gerhard Oldiges, Thomas Norwood, Michel Brück, Gernot Wagner and fellow Englishman Michael Gee. Among the guitar players attending were Wolfgang Jungwirth, Axel Wiedenfeld, Hans Michael Koch, Stefano Grondona and Carles Trepat.

The seminars were so successful that Hogi started organising two per year – the original in the springtime as well as a second in autumn – both of which Paul usually attended, not only to lecture but also to enjoy the stimulating atmosphere and the company of, by now, old friends. And there would always be new delegates as well.

Throughout the 1990s Paul continued his steady and productive work to refine his earlier work with the Taut system, but this was not the only system, and Paul was not the only one to be experimenting. Other makers with a similar pioneering spirit, and who also were not bound to blindly following tradition, developed equally groundbreaking ideas. Instruments of note that emerged during that period came from the workshops of two German makers – Gernot Wagner and Matthias Dammann – as well the Australian maker Greg Smallman (with his lattice-braced soundboards) and the American maker Tom Humphrey (with his millennium model).

One important and major fresh innovation came with the use of Nomex, a material developed by DuPont with many uses including aviation, the military and now the classical guitar. Gernot Wagner and Matthias Dammann were the first to use Nomex in classical guitar construction. When this material was used in its honeycomb form, it was found to be very effective and pointed the way forward to meeting the modern guitarist's needs. By creating a three-layer laminated soundboard – for example, a lamination of spruce, with a lamination of Nomex honeycomb, followed by a further lamination of spruce – a very light but strong membrane could be achieved. This was not unlike a normal soundboard of spruce but it provided a more efficient acoustic response through its magical combination of stiffness and lightness with a low mass.

This amazing material was used in various forms and patterns throughout the 1990s as makers explored its potential. It has now achieved not only the approval of many makers, but also players have realised and come to accept its use and benefits.

As happened in the nineteenth century with the major development from the parlour/salon guitar to what we now recognise as the concert guitar – largely through the work of the eminent maker Antonio de Torres – the late twentieth and twenty-first century is now witnessing a similar transformation of an ever-evolving instrument.

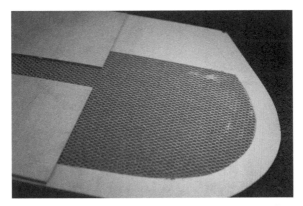

FIGURE 11.6 A Paul Fischer guitar showing a cutaway of a
Nomex laminated soundboard.
Photograph from Paul Fischer Collection.

CHAPTER 12

A New Millennium: Fresh Fields

With the passing of the twentieth century, what remained to be explored? Paul's work with Nomex was in its early stages and so there was still much to learn and discover about this fascinating material. He believed in Nomex and could see its potential, so he continued to make new instruments with fresh enthusiasm. Meanwhile, he was giving talks to colleges and the new generation of makers. Throughout his long career, Paul has held the same curiosity and enthusiasm to push boundaries and seek new experiences, very much in the spirit of the makers in earlier centuries responding to changing musical tastes and styles.

The looming age of formal retirement began to colour his thoughts as well as plans for this new century. He had no intention of retiring as such, unless health issues intervened. To carry on in his chosen career, even after more than half a century of instrument making, was his heartfelt wish. Exploring the potential of Nomex had done much to direct Paul towards a new path of discovery, and his curiosity for the changing world of the classical guitar was undimmed. His early experience in instrument making had been in the world of reproduction, though the creations of Dolmetsch and Goble were their attempts to bridge the gap between the seventeenth and twentieth centuries.

The influence of the exquisite instruments of the Baroque age had left an indelible impression and, even though most of Paul's career was focused on the guitar, this would show through in his future work. Now Paul felt less constrained by the hold of tradition, and a sense of liberation and freedom was driving his creativity.

The pressing question of using scarce and endangered wood species became more significant than ever. With each passing year, another entry

193

would be added to the database of restricted woods. In the world of the classical guitar, the impact of this was felt strongly by all makers.

Paul's adventures in Brazil had given him first-hand experience of the destruction of tropical rainforests and he was all too aware of the need to draw a line before it was too late – even though this affected his own work. The bureaucratic nightmare of the paperwork required for using endangered wood species, which was established in the 1990s, had already been confronted by makers such as himself but could only continue. Paul was very much for this approach to protecting these invaluable woods; however, bureaucracy, even for the good of the world, is still bureaucratic and time-consuming. As Paul was one of the early applicants for CITIES documentation, throughout the 1990s and the early 2000s, other makers often telephoned him for advice.

Sadly, the woods used in fine instrument making were of the rarer varieties and, as fresh species were added to the most-at-risk list, makers were forced to look even further afield for alternatives.

Woods that were already cut and in circulation before the CITES controls had been implemented could still be obtained and used but they had to be meticulously accounted for; fortunately, these stocks of wood were old and well seasoned, and so were ideal for the luthier's use. Rosewood, the premium and prized wood for guitar makers, was now very much taboo. Makers of earlier ages had used other woods in small quantities, rippled maple being perhaps the best example.

Though the current problems were pressing, they had less impact on Paul in this later phase of his career than they had on younger makers. He had the time and freedom to explore fresh woods.

Before much thought could be given to the new century and his plans for the latter part of his career, sad news came concerning the health of his former employer and mentor, David Rubio. Though only in his early sixties, Rubio had been diagnosed with stomach cancer, and by the time Paul received the news the condition was well advanced.

Paul wrote to David expressing his sorrow and sadness, which prompted a telephone response, almost by return. Forty years had passed since they had first met and much had happened to them both in their respective careers. In a quiet and soft voice, David was keen to talk, relating some of the more interesting recent incidents together with some downright unpleasant ones where previous clients were persistently demanding attention despite his obvious illness. Paul once again thanked David for the rare opportunity of working alongside him in the late 1960s, which had started him out on a path of discovery and into a fascinating career. It was a relatively short conversation but an emotional and a poignant one.

Despite David Rubio's difficult situation, he remained at his bench making beautiful instruments. Paul had made plans to visit David in Cambridge, but soon after the phone call his condition worsened and David Rubio died on 21 October 2000. He left behind many and varied instruments, which are a testament to his creative and restless energy. Paul will always have fond memories of his happy times in David Rubio's company.

***

David Linley (Viscount Linley, 2nd Earl of Snowdon, professionally known as David Linley) had the idea of celebrating the art of guitar making in an exhibition and enrolled the graphic designer and musician David Costa, of Wherefore Art?, to be its artistic director and coordinator. 'The Craft of the Luthier: An Exhibition of British Handmade Guitars' was held from 25 April–10 May 2001 in the elegant and stylish surroundings of the gallery Linley. This gallery in Belgravia, London, was a most appropriate venue for an exhibition of the work of British luthiers. In David Costa's words: 'The expertise that crafts the guitar in all its gloriously diverse and inventive forms is the true alchemy of the luthier's art.'

David Costa described the exhibition 'The Craft of the Luthier' thus: 'The luthier is quite evidently nothing less than a woodsman, a carver, a sculptor, an acoustic technician, a listener to and a maker of voices –

195

the craft of the

luthier

AN EXHIBITION OF BRITISH HANDMADE GUITARS AT LINLEY

April 25th – May 10th 2001
LINLEY, 60 Pimlico Road, London SW1

FIGURE 12.1 The poster for 'The Craft of the Luthier: An Exhibition of British Handmade Guitars' at Linley, Belgravia, London. It shows one of a pair of parlour guitars that Andy Manson made for Viscount Linley; Manson is a steel-stringed guitar and mandolin maker from Devon. This instrument has a spruce top, Brazilian rosewood back and sides and Rodgers machine heads. The bracing system Manson used was Martin style for the steel-stringed instrument and fan bracing for the nylon-stringed guitar. The scale length is 63 cm. Photograph from Paul Fischer Collection.

voices of joy, melancholy and seduction, of reflection and expression, protest and aggression.'

David Costa is well known for the design and manufacture of high-quality wooden furniture but he was also the designer of many of the iconic record covers and books from the 1970s onwards for artists such as Jimi Hendrix, Eric Clapton, Genesis and George Harrison. The sentiment behind the exhibition was to celebrate this somewhat under-lauded craft, which had many world-renowned practitioners with internationally famous clients but was less known in its own country. It included instruments demonstrating the range of styles, from copies of Renaissance, eighteenth- and nineteenth-century guitars together with twentieth- and twenty-first-century examples, showing that the luthier's imagination is alive and well and pushing the instrument to new heights in a new century. The exhibition was opened by Sir George Martin (famed, among other things, for his work with The Beatles).

Norman Charles Myall, known not only for his beautiful viola da gambas but also for other stringed instruments, offered the exhibition his exquisite copy of a Renaissance Diaz guitar, normally held in the collection of the Royal College of Music, London. This has ten rosewood fluted ribs and spruce soundboard with intricate carved pearwood/ parchment rosettes. It is a perfect example of the skill and art alive and well in Britain to this day. There were numerous other examples reflecting the ingenuity and talent of British luthiers, including a pair of parlour guitars commissioned by David Linley and built by Andy Manson and three Zemaitis guitars loaned by George Harrison. There were twenty-six luthiers exhibiting in total, with Gary Southwell exhibiting a Stauffer copy. Other classical guitar makers include Kevin Aram and Peter Barton.

Paul's own contribution was a creation showing a combination of twentieth-century exterior with a twenty-first-century interior of advanced acoustic development. A rare and unusual example of an eight-stringed guitar caught the eye of the record producer and composer Sir George Martin. He had a long conversation with Paul, who explained the reasoning behind creating such an instrument. Sir George had, in

FIGURE 12.2 Norman Charles Myall in his workshop.
Photograph © Norman Myall

fact, opened the exhibition and so attracted an impressive array of celebrities more usually seen at film premières or society events. Sir George Martin said, 'This unique exhibit sets out to celebrate a greatly understated craft, and a small section of this country's most talented alchemists.'

FIGURE 12.3 Eight-stringed guitar, Rosewood body and spruce soundboard.

Paul began a period of exploring the use of a wider variety of less-endangered wood species for his instrument making. To compensate for the justifiable downward pressure on the use of Brazilian rosewood – the luthier's first choice for guitar bodies – Paul scoured timber merchants for alternatives based on his earlier research, and for old stocks of wood as well. Fortunately, he only required relatively small amounts for instrument making. What is more, Paul had only so much working life to go and he had already begun to reduce his workload.

Some of these woods were completely new to instrument making and from which he expected surprises might spring. Other woods had been used before: for example, rippled maple, a popular wood used for bowed instruments such as the violin but less familiar in the guitar family – though, as mentioned before, Stradivari used it in his guitars. Less common variants were bird's-eye and quilted maple. Among the other woods experimented with were quilted sapele pommele, kingwood, satinwood and Macassar ebony. Even more exotic, but from Paul's ancient declining stock, was bird's-eye rosewood. This had been held back for a special instrument – his 1,000th.

Paul was looking forward to an exciting and interesting time, where he would be exploring new woods and the use of new technology materials such Nomex. The use of Nomex in soundboard laminate form complicated matters further but also gave new and very different acoustic opportunities and offer the prospect of acoustic properties to rosewood. The new woods were collected, sticked and stacked for seasoning. Although these materials would behave differently, Paul's experience had taught him that they could be accommodated by using subtle modifications in the bracing and other techniques.

Invitations to festivals kept on arriving and his annual attendance at the Guitar Foundation of America's Convention and the Frankfurt Musikmesse remained a given. These provided the opportunity to share his exploratory work to an appropriate audience and have the results evaluated.

FIGURE 12.4 Bird's-eye maple guitar sitting in lemonwood case, also made by Paul, including the quilted satin lining and a dovetailed drawer for the storage of strings and small accessories; it was built in around 2004–2005. The inlays on the headstock and the rosette are examples of the Baroque influence in Paul's work.
Photograph © Haddon Davis.

CHAPTER 13

Fifty Years an Instrument Maker and Beyond

New designs and instruments emerged as part of Paul's gentle and measured work in this latter part of his career. Although still a relatively young man of 65, Paul's fiftieth anniversary as an instrument maker beckoned. He had had the good fortune to be apprenticed at the age of 15 to the seminal harpsichord maker Robert Goble. He had started in August 1956, so 2006 was the landmark year; admittedly, there was a six-year gap, during which Paul had served in the regiment of the 11th Hussars, but fifty years had passed and a celebratory event was in order.

It was clear in the early stages of planning that a concert hall with access to gallery space for displaying his different instruments, and where guests could enjoy a glass of wine, was what would be needed. Initially, thoughts were focused on somewhere in London – the capital being ideal for attendees both from within the country and internationally. Joy, however, had an alternative idea of having it in Chipping Norton's own theatre, where she had been an assistant to the director and co-founder, Tamara Malcolm. It was a small venue but with all the necessary facilities.[71]

Paul was involved in establishing the Chipping Norton Theatre Music Society, bringing such luminaries such as the violinist Nigel Kennedy, the Danish recorder player Michala Petri and the harpsichordist Trevor

---

[71] Tamara Malcolm retired from her position of theatre director at Chipping Norton Theatre in 2002, after twenty-seven years of dedicated service. She had trained at the Royal Academy of Dramatic Arts (RADA) and worked as an actor for seventeen years before taking up the position in Chipping Norton. Joy was involved for just one year, 1979–1980, but it was a period of intense and diverse experiences.

Pinnock. Paul had hired a traditional Robert Goble instrument for the performance.

With all these connections, on reflection it became clear that the Chipping Norton Theatre was a better choice, both for the convenience of transporting a David Rubio harpsichord, which Paul had helped to build and deliver to Chadlington in the 1964, as well as a Robert Goble spinet for display, and to support the theatre that was dear to both Joy and Paul's hearts, in what had become their home town.

The chosen date of 3 September 2006 was a Sunday afternoon on a midsummer's day in the Cotswolds, close to the actual anniversary of 26 August 2006. Instruments both for the exhibition and to be played in the concert were gathered from kind and generous clients and friends from within Oxfordshire and beyond. This broad range of instruments from different centuries represented Paul's fifty years as a luthier, including copies of a vihuela from the sixteenth century, an early seventeenth-century

FIGURE 13.1 A wing-shaped spinet by Robert and Andrea Goble, with the case veneered in exquisite rippled mahogany; this instrument was loaned for the exhibition by a friend, Rose Cornwallis. Photograph by Rick Middleton.

eight-course lute, a seventeenth-century Stradivari guitar, a nineteenth-century Panormo guitar, as well as a number of twentieth-century instruments in various forms: a flamenco, a modern classical and an eight-stringed Simplicio-model guitar. There was a Robert Goble spinet and a Rubio harpsichord. The exhibition included some of Paul's drawings for his instruments.

The repertoire included a performance of Paul's commissioned piece, *The Song of Four Trees*, performed by its composer, Nicholas Hooper. Nicholas had by then moved on from being a guitarist to an internationally successful composer but, as a friend, generously offered to play one or two movements for this special occasion. John Mills, from the

Royal Academy of Music, played on the Panormo copy in duo with Cobie Smit, performing nineteenth-century works by Ferdinando Carulli (1770–1841); he also played solo on a modern Paul Fischer six-stringed guitar, performing an arrangement of J.S. Bach's Cello Suite no. 1. Alison Bendy and Gerald Garcia also performed as a duo, using both six-stringed classical guitars and then a combination of a classical guitar with a vihuela. Gerald Garcia, ever the showman, played a duet with Alison on the one guitar! Rafael performed solo on the flamenco guitar and Neil Darwent, representing the younger generation, played on an eight-stringed Simplicio-model guitar, demonstrating the benefits of the extra strings. David Taplin, from the University of Huddersfield, performed on the beautiful Stradivari guitar, a copy of the instrument held in the Ashmolean Museum, Oxford. There were also some non-professional performers playing on their own Paul Fischer guitars: Andy Daly and Warwick Mason. The keyboard instruments, both copies of seventeenth-century instruments, were not played but did show a glimpse of the work from the early part of Paul's career.

FIGURE 13.2 Paul Fischer giving the opening address at his Fiftieth Anniversary celebration. Photograph by Rick Middleton.

Paul gave an opening address telling the story of his fortuitous beginnings in lutherie and Early Music of the late Renaissance and early Baroque periods, as well as the time he served as a soldier with the 11th Hussars.

FIGURE 13.3 Paul Fischer in front of the David Rubio harpsichord, which he had worked on with David Rubio at the Duns Tew workshops/studios. Photograph © Rik Middleton.

FIGURE 13.4 Paul Fischer with the composer and guitarist Nicholas Hooper. Photograph by Colin Cooper. Used with permission.

FIGURE 13.5 Alison Bendy playing a Paul Fischer six-stringed classical guitar and Gerald Garcia playing a Paul Fischer vihuela, an instrument popular in sixteenth-century Spain. Photograph © Rik Middleton.

The instruments were all beautifully created, with exquisite detail that served to distinguish Paul Fischer's instruments.

The programme showed clearly how the development of the guitar had expanded the repertoire and served to show the scope and range of the guitar, ancient and modern. The performances came to a close with the excellent Japanese player Toru Takeuchi playing on an original instrument made by the

FIGURE 13.6 Neil Darwent playing on his Paul Fischer eight-stringed guitar, after Simplicio. Photograph © Rik Middleton.

nineteenth-century maker Juan Pagés. The headstock carries the initials FG and it is thought to have belonged to the artist Francisco Goya. Several of his paintings include this, or a similar, instrument.

After the concert, the auditorium events concluded with talks by colleagues and friends. Siegfried Hogenmüller told stories old and humorous from times in Germany. James Westbrook of the Guitar Museum in Brighton talked about a more recent collaboration on instruments of joint interest for his book, *The Century that Shaped the Guitar*.

FIGURE 13.8 From left: Colin Cooper, editor of Classical Guitar magazine, speaking with Cobie Smit and John Mills
Photograph © Rik Middleton.

FIGURE 13.9 Alison Bendy and Gerald Garcia.
Photograph by Colin Cooper. Used with permission.

FIGURE 13.7 A Paul Fischer ten-course lute – a copy of an early Baroque instrument.
Photograph © Rik Middleton.

Among the guests were fellow instrument makers, musicians, guitar enthusiasts, scholars, journalists, old school friends and Paul's whole family.

***

Anniversary Label.
The Opus Guitars

FIGURE 13.10 .

After the Fiftieth Anniversary celebration, Paul deliberately reduced the volume of commissioned work to free up time to explore new and varied guitar models. Their form and style, as with most musical instruments, is greatly influenced by history and tradition, hotly pursued by the needs of the musicians. For the guitar, this mainly falls into the sphere of the materials used in the construction of the body and its adornment.

Paul's formative work with Early Music had introduced him to instruments, even guitars, which were very highly decorated. However, in the intervening years much of this had been removed, usually for good acoustic reasons.

Paul's new project to make instruments of his own choosing, which had begun in around the year 2000, was receiving more of his unrestrained attention. Past experience had taught him that a number of musicians, once introduced to new instruments, especially those using less-endangered species of wood, were more than happy to play them. They eventually came to enjoy the fresh and original sounds of these Opus guitars, although Paul found that guitarists are generally conservative and prefer to stay with what they know. Each Opus instrument found a home with an enthusiastic guitarist as soon as it left the bench, though this had not been part of Paul's original plan.[72] Decorative features were added to most of the Opus instruments, often using less traditional woods but more adornment.

The properties of some of the new woods were already familiar but others were completely new to Paul and would have to be put to the test. It was not only their individual acoustic properties that were important to establish, but equally vital was the need to understand their working

---

[72] In around 2010 Paul received a phone call from someone in Salisbury who wanted to buy a guitar. Paul had none available because his waiting list was at five or six years. However, he had just completed an Opus guitar, which Paul said the customer was welcome to view. The customer, who was a surgeon by profession, was impressed with the unusual Opus guitar and he bought it. By coincidence, he was the surgeon who had operated on the arm of Julian Bream after his well-publicised car accident, caused by driving his sport's car too close to the wall of a narrow bridge.

properties, particularly for those with elegant and highly figured grain, such as quilted maple, sapele pommele and Brazilian lacewood. Quilted maple is particularly difficult to work because the grain is often at near right angels to the face of the wood and, as a result, might start splitting in many places, like block patterns, which just fracture; with care and special techniques, these issues could be overcome. Difficulties that could arise fell mainly into two areas: planing and bending – that is, when they were being shaped for the curved sides. Some examples of difficult woods are rippled maple and bird's-eye maple. Strikingly elegant wood grain often suggests a lot of short grain and with the thin dimensions of wood required in instrument making – for example, at 2 mm and 2.5 mm thicknesses – bending and planing can cause the wood to crack where the grain is particularly short.

FIGURE 13.11 Paul French polishing one of his guitars. Photograph by Paul Felix.

Some woods can present problems when applying varnish or French polish; not all woods accept the usual varnishes used for finishing instruments. There can also be difficulties with the varnish not drying fully as a reaction to something within the wood itself, so that the varnish remains sticky. Likewise, something known as 'fish eye' can occur, where the varnish shrinks into rings, somewhat resembling fish eyes. One further problem with the varnish can be 'crazing', which appears as fine cracks in the finish; this is the result of the varnish drying too quickly. Not all varnishes dry at the same speed and, therefore, only some are appropriate for use on musical instruments. This also occurs because musical instruments are constructed of very thin woods, which means they readily respond to changes in humidity and temperature. The extremely hard varnishes will crack and craze because of this. Of course, different woods expand and contract at different rates. It can also happen if one coat of varnish is applied too soon over an earlier layer of varnish, before it has had time to dry fully. This is where the knowledge, skill and experience of the instrument maker combine to avoid these multiple danger zones in the creation of an instrument, to guarantee that it will have a long and fruitful life.

Some of these issues have now been addressed by the development of specialist varnishes for instrument makers. These were not major issues when Paul was working on the larger instruments, such as harpsichords and spinets, as the woods in larger sections would not to be so sensitive to changes in humidity and temperature. However, smaller instruments, which use thinner woods, are much more responsive to the subtle changes in humidity and temperature. Thus, an artist moving from a green room onto the stage to perform can experience a change that requires retuning immediately.

Paul's experimentation and exploration was considerable but it was part of the plan. High quality, handmade machine heads (tuners) were the standard in all of Paul's guitars, but in these 'Opus' guitars the machine head maker, David Rodgers, was very amenable and always able to accommodate Paul's requests for variations in style. This was part of the theme of these unique and individually styled 'Opus' instruments. Paul, wishing to extend the theme of small individual details in his 'Opus'

FIGURE 13.12 Machine heads made by David Rodgers in the style of those used by the leading French guitar maker Renè François Lacôte (1785–1855) based in Paris – of course, these follow the principles of Lacôte but have been redesigned by David Rodgers with state-of-the-art precision. This guitar was created as part of Paul Fischer's Opus series.
Photograph from Paul Fischer Collection.

instruments, fitted some with the creations of the Italian machine head maker Nicolo Alessi, who also produces fine work with a touch of Italian elegance.

FIGURE 13.13 Machine heads.
Photograph by Paul Felix.

Machine heads might appear to be a small and insignificant part of the guitar but they are vital for precise tuning of the strings. Poor or even slightly worn machine heads render the instrument untuneable and therefore unusable. In the early 1970s, when the engineer David Rodgers was approached at the David Rubio workshops to consider making high quality machine heads (see Chapter 4), the wheels were set in motion that continue to this day, through the capable hands of his son, Robert. These gems of engineering precision and elegance are possibly the finest machine heads in the world. Though, in the intervening years, other makers have approached the issue with genuine flare and skill, David Rodgers set a high standard fifty years ago, which was a great leap forward, and his work provided the level that others have had to strive to emulate.

Among the familiar woods was maple, a popular wood used since the days of Stradivari, though the quilted and bird's-eye variants were less so and required special care in preparation. A less familiar but very beautiful wood was Brazilian lacewood. This is much like our native lacewood (London plain); but with a bold character figuring, it was light and strong and ideal for musical instruments. Paul cannot find sufficient words to describe his excitement for lacewood.

Other woods, some mentioned earlier in Chapter 8 on the Churchill Fellowship, worked, including kingwood, satinwood, sapele pommele and Macassar ebony, and a surprise set of bird's-eye rosewood rescued from old stock. This was a most rare and beautiful wood, which Paul had acquired back in the 1970s and reserved for a special instrument – instrument number 1,000 was to be that one.

Another interesting source for wood came from much closer to home. In the 1990s Martin Jarret, a neighbour and friend in Chipping Norton, who was the forester for David Astor's estate, Bruern Estate, provided maple, sycamore, cypress wood and willow – though these were not 'new' woods. Willow is a wood commonly used in violin making and guitar making but only in small proportions for internal components. Be aware, on inspecting old violins, that willow was also enjoyed by woodworm, who eat away at the willow and leave the other woods intact. In Brazil Paul found that certain termites would even eat the extremely hard rosewood, leaving logs with a hollow centre.

CHAPTER 14

A Visit to the Antarctic

In 2009 Paul finally realised his childhood dream to visit the Antarctic. Paul had been searching for a like-minded companion for this daring adventure for a number of years. He finally found a friend with the enthusiasm and the time: a musician friend of his, Micky Ballard, who was curious and adventurous enough to accept the challenge at the end of the Austral summer (February), when the maximum amount of ice has completed its annual melt, making access easier – just as the young penguins are beginning their moult. Flying via Buenos Aires, they reached Ushuaia, on the tip of Argentina.

FIGURE 14.1 Ushuaia, on the tip of Argentina. In the background is the tail end of the Andes mountain range in Chile. Photograph by Paul Fischer.

There, in Ushuaia, they joined an ice-strengthened Russian ship to journey through the Drake Passage and out into Roaring Forties, which were really 'roaring'! This is called the convergence, where the colder Antarctic waters meet the warmer waters of the southern oceans, with the colder water being driven down by the warmer water, thus creating extreme turbulence at the surface. All the passengers were issued with seasickness tablets. The ship, although fitted with stabilisers, still suffered from the chaotic fury of these waters and was tossed about in a white-water crescendo of foam, which remained at a furious climax point for two days. Many passengers were laid low; Paul, luckily, does not suffer from seasickness and, even in these extreme conditions, managed to keep his balance!

Then, escaping from the turbulence of the Roaring Forties, the ship sailed into the calmer waters surrounding the snow-flecked outcrops of the Antarctic Peninsula.

FIGURE 14.2 The taming of the Roaring Forties as the Antarctic Peninsula comes into view. Photograph by Paul Fischer.

Easing its way between the ever-increasing cluster of small islands, the ship continued its journey along the western edge of the Antarctic Peninsula, ever southwards and ever colder. The passengers responded by adding more layers of thermal clothing each time they ventured on deck to view the ever-changing scene of solitude and the dramatic ice creations of nature. One in

FIGURE 14.3 As the ship sailed into the calmer waters surrounding the snow-flecked outcrops of the Antarctic Peninsula. Photograph by Paul Fischer.

particular caught the attention of Paul. An iceberg hollowed out in the centre through wave action had trapped a seal in a private swimming pool; unable to escape from the polished sides of the 'pool', the seal remained imprisoned as the ship passed by.

FIGURE 14.4 An iceberg hollowed out in the centre through wave action had trapped a seal in a private swimming pool. Photograph by Paul Fischer.

The ship slowed to allow the passengers to observe the full scene: the drama of the seal in contrast to the magnificently sculptured icebergs, glaciers and the clarity of the turquoise water, as well as the surprisingly blue ice. Booming reverberant explosions could be heard when large sections of the glacier calved, sending gigantic portions of ice crashing at a majestic pace into the water, revealing a sheer wall of ice strata, formed over decades.

FIGURE 14.5 After the glacier calves, a sheer wall of ice strata is exposed. The pink colour results from the penguin droppings, which are not only odoriferous but also pink in colour – a result of their diet of krill.
Photograph by Paul Fischer.

The ship anchored in the calmer waters of the Antarctic, first at Port Lockroy, Goudier Island, in the Palmer Archipelago. In the mornings, following breakfast, there were excellent lectures about the fauna and flora of the Antarctic and its geography, history, its explorers and research stations – all given by experts in their fields. The small party of around fifty passengers from many parts of the world made it even more interesting, particularly at the evening dinner of international cuisine, where the conversation was fascinating always.

Each afternoon, those wishing to be more adventurous would venture forth in semi-rigid inflatables, called Zodiacs, which were raised from the hold of the ship each day and lowered gently into the freezing waters using a crane. This was a dangerous procedure. Once the Zodiac was in the water, the passengers would have to jump from the end of the ship's gangway into the Zodiac, which rose and fell with the movements of the ship. One false move and one could land in the freezing waters, which humans can only withstand for a few minutes before fatal results! A noble

212

Russian crew member in waterproofs would stand at the bottom of the gangway to help – sometimes with the swell rising up waist high.

The British have a research station at Port Lockroy, which was established on 11 February 1944, when the British first opened research stations in the Antarctic. Of course, Scott's hut still stands on the shore of Cape Evans on the other side of the continent and similar artefacts remaining at Scott's hut can be seen at Port Lockroy.

Since November 1996, when the station at Port Lockroy was declared a historic site by the UK Antarctic Heritage Trust, it has functioned as a museum, holding many of the original artefacts, including the tinned food in the galley Smedley's Peas, Horlicks and Quaker Oats, now in rusting tins – and on a table in the crew room was a popular weekly British magazine, *Tit-Bits*,[73] announcing the successful journey by tracked vehicle, under the leadership of Sir Vivian Fuchs; this historic British Commonwealth Trans-Antarctic Expedition in 1957–1958 was a completely fresh attempt at

FIGURE 14.6 These semi-rigid inflatables, called Zodiacs, were lifted out of the hold of the ship each day and lowered into the cold waters using a crane. A noble Russian crew member would stand at the bottom of the gangway to help passengers into them.
Photograph by Paul Fischer.

FIGURE 14.7 Rusty tinned foods remain neatly stacked on the shelves of the galley at Port Lockroy. These were typical 1950s tinned foods, which could be found in some British homes. Photograph by Paul Fischer.

---

[73] The weekly British magazine *Tit-Bits* ran from 1881 to 1989.

crossing the whole Antarctic continent, which still had not been achieved. It seemed a foolhardy approach, as they were using a heavy tracked vehicle especially designed for the expedition; it proved to be both reliable and safe and was a success.

FIGURE 14.8 An announcement of the successful British Commonwealth Trans-Antarctic Expedition in 1957–1958, under the leadership of Sir Vivian Fuchs. Photograph by Paul Fischer.

This research station held a particular appeal for penguins and they formed an honour guard for the adventurers who came ashore. The very friendly penguins with their rapidly moulting young, who were curious about the tall, unbeaked penguins (humans), would come very close, even standing on people's toes and gaping up curiously into the humans' faces. Although visitors were advised not to approach the penguins, close contact was unavoidable when large numbers of penguins would make their enthusiastic approach.

The young penguins were desperate to set out in the world, unaware of what lay ahead: their parents were constantly having to face the dangers of the deep in the form of awaiting leopard seals, who were patrolling just offshore. As the human group were travelling in the Zodiacs, they often saw penguins being attacked and eaten by the leopard seals. This was not a pleasant sight: the leopard seals would first toss their penguin/victim into the air and skin it alive with their razor-sharp teeth before eating it! The whole process took a few minutes and was very painful to observe. Leopard seals meted out their aggression even towards the Zodiacs and stories were told of the outboard motor being attacked.

The crystal-clear water meant the sea life below was easily observed. Sea leopards, whales and Adélie, Macaroni and Chinstrap penguins, as well as the diving sea birds – you could see them all swimming in the azure blue marine wonderland below. On land there were hundreds, if not thousands, of penguins with their young, accompanied by non-aggressive sea lions,

FIGURE 14.9 A sea leopard approaches the Zodiac. One should not be fooled by their calm face; they have a mouth full of razor teeth ready to attack, with the same speed and skill as their land brothers, the leopards, who never change their spots, whether on land or sea! Photograph by Paul Fischer.

who gave the impression that they preferred to be left alone.

At a latitude of 65 degrees south, it was cold, but the clarity of the unpolluted sky enhanced the shape and form of large icebergs, the number of which was an indication of the effects of global warming. While enjoying the incredible experience of the Antarctic, one was constantly aware of not wishing to spoil it in any way. The rule was that whatever one took ashore, one had to take back again – literally, everything. Unfortunately, previous visitors had left some items behind, either accidentally or negligently, such as small camera batteries, which would occasionally be seen on the ground.

FIGURE 14.10 Paul's group travelling by Zodiac to observe the icebergs and wildlife. The bluer the iceberg, the older it is; the blueness results from having the oxygen squeezed out of the ice. Photograph by Paul Fischer.

FIGURE 14.11 This is an example of one of the largest icebergs, which they encountered in the freezing waters of the Antarctic, beyond 65 degrees south. Photograph by Paul Fischer.

Totally absorbed by the magical scenery, Paul's group enjoyed the final days of their two-week trip before they would be heading back northwards to Ushuaia, which required yet another gruelling journey through the Roaring Forties. On the final evening, there was a fitting 'last supper' in the company of this charming international group of adventurers.

Paul has fond memories of this second 'journey of a lifetime' – his first being his Winston Churchill Trust Research Fellowship to Brazil. He has always been fascinated by the Antarctic and its explorers, such as Captain Lawrence 'Titus' Oates (1880–1912), who was also a cavalryman in the 6th Inniskilling Dragoon Guards. Paul has also read widely on the travels and expeditions of Captain John Franklin (1786–1847), Captain Robert Falcon Scott (1868–1912) and Ranulph Fiennes (b. 1944), another cavalryman of the 2nd Royal Scots Dragoon Guard, the Scots Greys. However, other ethical issues about the preservation of the Antarctic have added to Paul's concerns – that is, the question of whether non-research visitors should be allowed on the Antarctic continent.

CHAPTER 15

The Dawn of
Another Decade: 2010s

Without music, life would be an error!

Friedrich Nietzsche

Paul has always felt that his life has moved in roughly ten-year increments. As the next decade was about to begin, he was looking forward to the new challenges and developments that would come his way and the continuing work on his beloved Opus series guitars, which were each exciting in their own right. Retirement was never one of those 'developments' he envisaged at all!

Returning from the Antarctic, Paul only took a few days to recover and then was back at his workbench. Within a few weeks there would more travel, this time to Frankfurt for the annual Musikmesse on 1–4 April 2009. As always, this included meeting up with friends and colleagues, which was equally pleasurable and productive. He would once again be attending the Rückersbach Seminar, where much would be gained from the lectures and the exchange of ideas with the international gathering of luthiers. Sadly, while writing, we heard that the fine American luthier Thomas Norwood, who lived and worked in Paris, passed away on 14 February 2021. He was often at Rückersbach, and his range of work both in making and restoration was considerable. There were many other visitors to Rückersbach who inspired Paul, but to mention just a couple, the historian, researcher and guitarist Christof Hanusch and the very talented young maker Angela Waltner (see Chapter 10).[74] They added

---

[74] Christof Hanusch specialises in the research of Richard Jacob Weißgerber (see www.christofhanusch.com). Angela Waltner has worked as an instrument restorer, specialising in nineteenth-century French guitars, and has also participated in a study project on Richard Jacob 'Weißgerber' (see www.waltnerguitars.com).

much to the discussion and animated sessions. Rückersbach also offered the opportunity for a catch-up with Kazuo Sato from his David Rubio days, who had settled in Germany many years before. It was always a pleasure to meet up with the pioneering German maker and long-time friend Gernot Wagner, who is driven and inspired to keep searching for new refinements to improve his already outstanding guitars; this is a spirit Paul identifies with.

Paul made one of his Opus series guitars – but in a nineteenth-century form – for the Austrian guitarist Wolfgang Jungwirth, who is a nineteenth-century guitar specialist. The guitar body was made with Macassar ebony, which gave it a sweet, singing quality, which pleased Wolfgang enormously. Heinrich Zur is another player whom Paul met at Rückersbach, and he made him a very special Simplicio-style guitar. Its body was in quilted maple.[75]

Some of the other attendees at Rückersbach included Herman Hauser III, whom Paul had got to know very well over a number of years at the Musikmesse, Sasha Novak, Kolya Panhuyzen, Paulino Bernabé, Gerhard Oldiges, Michel Brück and fellow Englishman Michael Gee. Among the guitar players attending were Axel Wiedenfeld, Hans Michael Koch, Stefano Grondona and Carles Trepat (see Chapter 10).

When Paul and Joy went to Berlin at Christmas time in 2011, they met up with two friends from Rückersbach: Christof Hanusch and guitar maker Norbert Ulrich. Visiting Christof's house, they were updated on his further research and presented with a copy of his recently published book on Weißgerber,

FIGURE 15.1 This is a Paul Fischer copy of a late nineteenth-century guitar with a body made of Macassar ebony. Photograph by Paul Fischer.

---

[75] Instrument number 1,158 was made in around 2004–2005.

Weissgerber: Gitarren von/Guitars by Richard Jacob.[76] It was a short visit but it was a joy to meet up with them.

This was the first time Paul had returned to Berlin since his army days in 1965. In 2011 he was surprised at the winter colours of the city; the low clouds blocked out the panoramic views of the city that he had so enjoyed almost fifty years earlier. This did not stop them from enjoying the Christmas spirit of Berlin with its colourful Christmas markets and beautiful music in the churches and cathedral. Part of the closed-in and very dark atmosphere was the result of the sudden appearance of a black spot in the centre of Paul's right eye, which persisted.

Upon his return to the UK, after some tests at the Oxford University Hospitals, the doctors diagnosed that the spot was the result of him having suffered a TIA, sometimes referred to as a mini-stroke.[77] They recommended that a stent be inserted into the basilar artery in his head; the advice came with the warning that this was a relatively new procedure being undertaken in very few hospitals in the country, so a cardiac stent would have to be used. The black spot remained until Paul had the stent fitted at the John Radcliffe Hospital in Oxford. He was fascinated by the procedure and asked for many details, which the German consultant was more than pleased to provide. He was able to watch some of the preparation procedures on the screen. This was the first time Paul had had a TIA – but sadly not the last.[78]

While he was waiting on the hospital ward, the patient in the adjoining bed, who had been a soldier he discovered, said he had been run over by a tank. Paul, having spent six years in British Army tanks was incredulous

---

[76] Published by Association of Friends and Supporters of the Musikinstrumenten-Museum Markneukirchen e.V.

[77] A TIA is a transient ischemic attack, which is sometimes referred to as a mini-stroke.

[78] More recently, Paul has discovered that the stent is blocked, so the body has created new pathways in the brain; the stroke was on the side of the head that controls the eyesight. The wonders of adaptability of the human body, in combination with modern medicine, never cease to fascinate.

and said that he could not have been run over by a 50-tonne tank. Realising his need to clarify his 'tank', the soldier explained that he meant a rubber-tracked snowmobile vehicle had run over part of his body, whereupon many army stories passed between them. Confronted with the debilitating nature of his accident, he asked Paul what he could do with his life after being demobbed from the army. Paul, taking into account the bleak situation of his disability as well as his admirable confident personality, suggested that he become a teacher and inspire young people.

Paul, stoic as always, returned to work. He was busy working on the Opus guitars – a project he had started in the year 2000 – and despite his continuously busy schedule, he was managing to create at least one Opus guitar each year, along with his other regular guitar making. While on one of his full-day visits to Newark and Lincoln College, during the lecture Paul began to feel peculiar and excused himself in order to get some fresh air. He returned to complete the lecture but while driving back to his hotel, he felt that the cars driving towards him were floating above his car as they passed. Paul now realises that his eyes were working independently, delivering this confused picture to his brain. Once he had settled back at the hotel, he asked the reception to call an ambulance. Paul had had another TIA – a mini-stroke – and was in hospital for about three days. It was a slight warning but there was nothing Paul could do about it and so he continued working, after some rest and being prescribed the appropriate medicines.

In 2012 Paul received a phone call from Henry Astor, who needed some advice regarding his guitar. Henry Astor was from Bruern, a few miles from Chipping Norton, and although repairs were not part of Paul's normal work, in this case, as he had been referred by the composer and guitarist Bill Lovelady, Paul agreed to help if he could.

Paul knew the name Astor from the time he had obtained rippled maple from the Astor estate. When Henry arrived with his guitar, on close inspection the problem was only a minor issue with the action of the guitar and could be fixed while he waited. While Henry observed the adjustments to his instrument, he explained that he was a film-maker, and the conversation flowed along with potential ideas for collaboration.

Following his trip to Brazil, Paul had proposed the idea of making a film for Alan Yentob of BBC Four covering the destruction of the rainforests of Brazil and the ever-pressing problem of obtaining the precious rosewood for the making of high-quality musical instruments – in Paul's case, the classical guitar. Paul proposed the inclusion of the music of the composer and guitarist Nicholas Hooper (see Chapter 8). Unfortunately, Paul's proposal coincided with the BBC's decision to cut funding for Arts documentaries, so nothing came of it – but the idea lingered.

The visit of Henry Astor rekindled Paul's earlier proposal to the BBC film project of the collaboration of different art forms in the creation of music. After their exchange of ideas, Henry proposed making a documentary film along similar lines, which would combine the art of the luthier and a composer. Paul agreed and proposed that a performer should be included as well; he suggested the outstanding Chinese guitarist Xuefei Yang, who lives on the edge of Oxfordshire. Bill Lovelady was the natural choice for the composer and so the trio was complete after Xuefei's enthusiastic agreement, so completing the trio of Oxfordshire artists for the film.

A central theme of the documentary would be the making of Paul's last guitar, hence the documentary title: *Aubade: The Last Guitar. Aubade* was the name of the piece Bill Lovelady composed for Xuefei Yang to première on this 'last' Paul Fischer guitar. The director of *Aubade: The Last Guitar*, Henry Astor, described the project thus: 'The story unites Fischer with two other great contemporary talents, William 'Bill' Lovelady and Xuefei Yang, on a truly creative journey that culminates in a celebratory performance at the historic Hagley Hall!'

The whole process lasted around three months, beginning in January 2013. Henry would visit the workshop at regular intervals to film the specific stages of creation. In the meantime, Bill Lovelady was composing *Aubade* for solo guitar. The guitar was being made with exquisite Brazilian lacewood back and sides, a spruce top, with elegant Landstorfer-style machine heads by Nicolò Alessi.

The concert was set for April 2013, with Xuefei Yang performing on this new guitar by Paul Fischer and premièring *Aubade* by Bill Lovelady at Hagley Hall. This grand historic house near Birmingham, where many concerts are held, is an ideal venue for classical guitar performances because of its size and excellent acoustics. Although the concert was held as planned and the work was premièred and filmed, Paul's life took an unexpected turn at this point, as we will see in the next chapter.

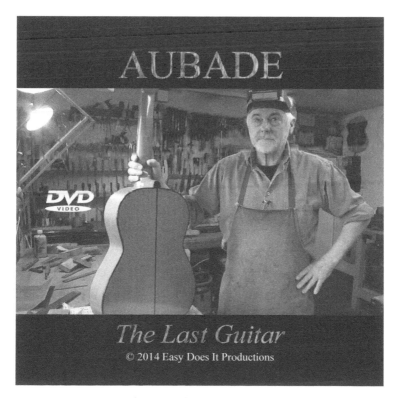

FIGURE 15.2 The DVD release Aubade: The Last Guitar.
Source: Copyright © Easy Does It Productions.

CHAPTER 16

Stroke and Recovery
'I May Be Some Time.'

By spring 2013, the majority of the film was complete; only a small amount of editing remained. On the last day of filming, as the director, Henry Astor, left the workshop, Paul became aware of an unusual sensation in his body accompanied by a mild but insistent headache. Turning to the departing Henry, he said, 'I think I need to lie down. I may be some time.' The feelings persisted after he had retired to bed and, feeling concerned, he grabbed the mobile phone and called his GP. Although he was feeling confused, Paul explained his symptoms to the doctor, and to his surprise he prescribed medication for seasickness!

Paul was alone at home, as Joy was away visiting their daughter in Kent, but he phoned his son, Scott, to ask him to pick up the prescription for him. It was mid afternoon and he slept fitfully while awaiting the arrival of his son, still very bemused by the diagnosis – even the Roaring Forties had not given him seasickness. The pills were delivered by Scott but he had to go straight away to collect his children from school. Paul took two of the pills but they didn't stay down for long. Returning to bed, he drifted in and out of consciousness without being aware of anything until he awoke two weeks later in the John Radcliffe Hospital in Oxford.

It turned out that, worried about his father, Scott had returned to check on him in the evening and found him unconscious; an emergency call summoned paramedics and an ambulance. On arrival at A&E, five hours after the original call to the GP, it became clear that Paul had suffered a serious stroke. So much for the 'golden hour' – treatment in the first hour offers the best chance for survival and recovery.

Scott's recollection of seeing his father after the stroke:

I reached the hospital and it all become a bit of a blur with lots of ambulances and dozens of medics dealing with many people in a similar state. I was shocked to see Dad plugged into many machines and remembered the Monty Python reference to the machine that goes ping. The doctors made it clear that they could really only monitor the situation and, to some extent, let nature take its course. They were pretty certain he had had a stroke but it was several hours before a scan could be done to confirm exactly what had happened and where.

I sat there for ages hoping for a change in Dad's state. He remained unresponsive for a long time but the professionals told me this was normal and was actually a good sign; it meant his body was attempting to fix itself. One of the medical staff asked me to accompany him to the family room. He warned me that things could easily go either way and the next twelve hours were critical. He also suggested I go home and get some sleep.

Because the stroke was serious, Paul was moved to intensive care and placed in an induced coma. Eventually, sometime after the coma-inducing medication was discontinued, Joy and Paul's children were able to get a response from him and answers from the doctors to their questions.

Joy's recollections of her first visit to the hospital:

My immediate thought on seeing Paul was one of surprise! He was sitting up in bed looking relatively perky. However, as soon he opened his mouth, it was obvious something was wrong. His sentences were totally and utterly confusing, talking about the army, the Isle of Man and the children, all in one sentence but making no sense at all. The following day, Paul was pretty much in the state I had expected to see him in: lying down and with very little speech.

The children and I were very worried but we were told by the consultant that this was all very usual with a stroke to this particular area of the brain.

Paul was unaware of these early responses, which still remain very much a mystery to him, and it was another week before non-family visitors were allowed and before the recollection of coherent responses took place. Regaining proper speech and mobility were not so easy: his mouth remained distorted, his limbs were immobile and his mind made little sense of anything. Although he was aware of visitors, he was unable to respond to them. With everyone's encouragement, simply through their presence and smiles, he slowly recovered the use of his limbs; it took about four or five weeks in total.

Gerry Garcia remembers:

Paul had already been in hospital for a couple of days. He was lying on the bed and awake and tried to speak when I said hello, but he struggled to get any words out. I am not sure if he recognised me. Halfway through my visit, he seemed to have an attack of pain and started kicking as he lay on his side. A nurse came in and helped calm him. He seemed to have lost his speech capacity and motor control. I left the hospital feeling less than hopeful at his chance of recovery. However, more than one year later I was amazed at how Paul had regained the use of all his faculties – with a difference! He says it is as if his brain cells were tossed in the air and re-formed themselves in a different order – he is now more outspoken and outgoing than before and was even able to drive for a while and tell jokes. His recovery is a remarkable demonstration of the resilience of the human body and spirit and determination.

Paul's condition improved and after two weeks he was well enough to be moved to the rehabilitation unit at the Horton Hospital in Banbury, which was a little closer to his home in Chipping Norton. One day, when

Paul was exercising, he walked past a group of nurses seated at their staff table and, walking with the support of a Zimmer frame and using the words of Captain Oates, he said, 'I am just going outside and I may be some time.' Of course, there was no response; these nurses were too young to know he was referring to the final words of Titus Oates as he left his tent in the Antarctic in 1912.

When the day came for Paul's discharge, walking stick in hand he made every effort to march out of the hospital in the manner of a soldier. Once home, and pleased to be so, Paul could relax in familiar surroundings with his new nurse, Joy. No more early morning 5.30 hospital regime surprises, waking up to find nurses very close at hand!

The seriousness of his new circumstances still hadn't fully registered, though the long period of rest had provided time to ponder such matters. The nursing, rest and constant badgering for exercise while in hospital had achieved a surprising amount, so his time at home could be spent out of bed. To aid his recovery and hopefully his return to full fitness, he signed on at the local gym. Just half a mile from home, he could make his own, wobbly, way there three times a week with relative ease.

The result of his hospital reflections was that he would bring down the curtain on fifty-seven years of crafting the beautiful creations that are musical instruments. With restricted mobility and a head that was to him in a 'grey zone', he could wait. Despite this, once Paul had returned home and was in familiar surroundings, with the smells of cedar and rosewood drifting through from the studio, the temptation to venture and test his possibly reduced skills was too great. Everything was as he had left it two months previously – a veritable *Mary Celeste* in workshop form. He picked up a well-honed and familiar chisel and set to work carving the heel of a guitar neck. The attempt was not a total failure, but the effort and concentration needed told him it was too soon, possibly forever, to return to his work of over half a century.

His early attempts at driving had exposed problems that had not been evident in his normal home routine; driving a manual car, Paul soon discovered that his left leg would jump uncontrollably off the clutch, resulting in constant stalling of the car, and his left arm could not operate the gear shift. These were problems encountered only when driving his classic car, a Morgan sports car, which sadly had to go. Then the DVLA rescinded his driving licence, for obvious reasons.

In the months following the stroke, emptiness filled each of Paul's days. Thoughts of returning to instrument making were, for the time being, not even considered, though fate would take a hand in the form of David Nickson, a friend and client of Paul's. David asked Paul if he would teach him how to make a guitar and this proved to be an inspired idea. There were also some residual physical handicaps, but not enough to dampen Paul's enthusiasm for the prospect of teaching.

David's idea could help fill the void; if not full time, at least for three days a week there would be a reason to get up and see how things went for them both. Six months passed in what turned out to be a happy and productive arrangement. In fact, they went on to make three guitars together, one being a particularly beautiful bird's-eye maple instrument and another being a flamenco guitar. The benefits of this were twofold: David, not only made his own instruments but it made a great contribution to Paul's recuperation.

FIGURE 16.1 David Nickson working on a soundboard in Paul Fischer's workshop.
Photograph by Paul Fischer.

Whether or not word had got out about Paul's teaching into the wider community is unknown. No sooner had David finished his first guitar and was back home enjoying playing it, another potential student appeared on the scene. Dr Martin Harris telephoned Paul to ask if he would teach him to make a guitar. Knowing nothing of his talents, Paul invited Martin for coffee and a chat. Martin, a retired GP, had a passion for things made with wood. As a hobby, he made very beautiful jewellery boxes. Over coffee, it became obvious that any technical limitations Martin had would be easily overridden by his passion for wood.

As with David, a three-day week was agreed and, although he had to be more hands-on with the detailed work, Paul found the conversation and companionship to his liking. That Martin had also been a GP was reassuring, though matters medical were not laboured.

Steadily and methodically, they jointly worked through creating a beautiful rippled maple classical guitar that was destined for Martin's grandson. Without previous experience of making a musical instrument – or even playing one – it was regarded as a tremendous achievement and was greatly admired by Martin's extended family.

FIGURE 16.2 Dr Martin Harris with Paul Fischer in the workshop.
Photograph from Paul Fischer Collection.

CHAPTER 17

Not Quite the End:

Meeting the Queen

The wood of the guitar is from a tree that died in sleep, and felt no pain,
To live in happier form again. Only the most skilful hands can release the
harmonies of nature preserved within the instrument,
and it keeps its highest holiest tone
for our beloved Jane alone.

Percy Bysshe Shelley

In the fifty years after the death of Winston Churchill and the founding of the Winston Churchill Memorial Trust, over 5,000 fellowships had been awarded, giving the recipients a once-in-a-lifetime opportunity to travel and study overseas and expand their knowledge. To mark this half-century, the Trust held many events in the semi-centennial year celebrating Churchill's life and legacy. One of the first events was a reception at Buckingham Palace, held on 18 March 2015, hosted by Her Majesty the Queen, patron of the Trust. This was a huge and signal honour for the Trust and included 300 Fellows, who were individually introduced to the Queen and then to the trustees, council and staff.

As one of the 300 guests, Paul joined Churchill Fellows from all parts of the UK, covering every decade since the 1960s, together with representatives from the Australian Winston Churchill Trust and the US Winston Churchill Foundation. Guests were requested to arrive at the front gates between 5.30 and 5.50 pm and were then ushered into a long gallery. Surrounded by the large portrait paintings in elaborate gilded frames, which adorned the walls of the gallery, they immediately joined in the lively conversations and achievement to look back, over canopés.

The Master of the Household
has received Her Majesty's command to invite

Mr. Paul Fischer

to a Reception to be given at Buckingham Palace
by The Queen and The Duke of Edinburgh
for the Winston Churchill Memorial Trust
on Wednesday, 18th March, 2015 at 6.00 p.m.

A reply is requested to:
The Master of the Household
Buckingham Palace
London SW1A 1AA
Email: master.household@royal.gsx.gov.uk

Dress: Lounge Suit / Day Dress

Guests are asked to arrive between 5.30 and 5.50 p.m.

FIGURE 17.1 The invitation to Buckingham Palace on 18 March 2015.

Each Fellow was given a badge with their name and the title of their Fellowship, providing an instant introduction to facilitate conversation. The distinguished guests included the Trust's director general, Jamie Balfour, and his predecessors, Sir Richard Vickers, Henry Beverley and Air Vice-Marshall Nigel Sudborough, and the very hospitable Trust staff.

At the appointed hour, the Fellows were directed from the long gallery into an adjoining, elegant reception room, where they were each presented to Her Majesty the Queen first, and then to HRH Prince Phillip, before moving to another long gallery for more champagne and conversation. In this gallery, Paul was pleased to encounter Prince Michael of Kent, who had served in the same regiment and squadron in the 1960s – the 11th Hussars. They recalled their time representing the regiment in winter sports events: Prince Michael of Kent was a bobsleigh competitor and Paul was a langlauf skier.

This very special evening ended at 8 pm, when Paul returned to his hotel, where Joy was waiting to have dinner with him and savour the details of his experiences – sadly, partners and families were not invited to join in this Royal occasion.

FIGURE 17.2 Paul Fischer is presented to HRH The Queen on 18 March 2015.
Photograph from BCA.

Another of the events to mark the fifty-year anniversary was a full day of celebrations at Churchill's birthplace, Blenheim Palace, Woodstock, Oxfordshire – a magnificent palace with extensive grounds, where both Fellows and their families were welcomed. Some Fellows gave presentations on their individual Fellowships, outlining the benefits to their lives, careers and the wider community. The Sir Winston Churchill Fellowships are for life, and Paul, as with the other Fellows, continues to pass on its benefits and opportunities through teaching and talks. The day ended with a single Spitfire flying past, accompanied by the ceremonial Beating of the Retreat.

***

After the severe stroke in 2013, Paul worried he might not be able to make any more instruments. The long hours spent lying in a hospital bed provided perhaps too many hours to ponder and reflect on his future and the unpredictable nature of post-stroke recovery. A career that, apart from a period of military service, had been driven by a lifetime's commitment and passion to create beautiful musical instruments would not be easy to relinquish. The unexpected requests from David Nickson to teach him to build a guitar, followed by a further request from Dr Martin Harris, each provided Paul with the support and stimulation he needed in that post-stroke period. It offered a perfect opportunity he could not have planned better himself, as it guided him gently back to his creative passion.

A further surprise came when Paul received yet another request for teaching, this time from a guitarist with a range of woodworking skills. Another coffee-and-chat session was called for before this new pupil, Julian Roach, who had recently settled in Chipping Norton, came on board. Julian had considerable knowledge of the classical guitar world and of woods used in guitar making. With this background, it was relatively easy for Julian to decide on the model of instrument and the materials he would like to use. Paul, who was still in post-stroke recovery mode, was feeling the considerable benefits of being occupied and also of sharing the company of people with a passion for craft and music. Under Paul's guidance, another excellent and attractive classical guitar was created, with an elegant Indian rosewood body (Figure 17.3).

FIGURE 17.3 Julian Roach varnishing his first classical guitar. Photograph by Paul Fischer.

So pleased was Julian about having completed his first instrument, that one instrument was no longer enough for him. A writer and scriptwriter by profession, Julian had written a book about the English Romantic poet, Percy Bysshe Shelley (1792–1822), *Shelley's Boat: The Turbulent, Tragic Last Weeks of Percy Bysshe Shelley* (see Julian Roach's article in Appendix I).[79] Towards the end of his life, Shelley had bought a guitar for a close friend, Jane Williams. This instrument is preserved with the Shelley Manuscripts and Relics at the Bodleian Library, University of Oxford. With Julian's enthusiasm and Paul's experience of creating copies of nineteenth-century instruments, they decided to request access to the 'Shelley' guitar to prepare drawings to build a copy; this would make a viable and fascinating project. Fortunately, the answer to their request was yes, but it was only under the close supervision of the Bodleian Library curator, Bruce Barker-Benfield, that they were able to enter the hallowed portals of the Bodleian and the rooms housing the Shelley collection. Shelley had included a light-hearted poem with the guitar, which he gave to Jane Williams in around April 1822 – 'With a Guitar, to Jane'.[80] The guitar is housed in a traditional coffin-shaped wooden case.

On first inspection, they soon realised the guitar had been little used, so its fine condition impressed them both, particularly Paul, who knew from experience that guitars of that age were not always well looked after. It was an elegant instrument of the period and well worth the effort needed to make a copy. The Shelley guitar's original body, unusually, was made of exquisite mahogany; all the other parts used woods that were common for instruments of that period: for example, a mahogany neck, an ebony fingerboard, a spruce soundboard and, below the bridge, a finely crafted floral ebony overlay was glued onto the soundboard. The label inside said 'Ferdinando Bottari, Pisa, 1816'. On their visit, Paul took

---

[79] Julian Roach, *Shelley's Boat: The Turbulent, Tragic Last Weeks of Percy Bysshe Shelley* (Whitstable: Harbour Books, 2005).

[80] For images of the guitar and Jane Williams, see Stephen Hebron and Elizabeth C. Denlinger, eds., *Shelley's Ghost: Reshaping the Image of a Literary Family*, exhibition book (Oxford: Bodleian Library, 2010), 96–97.

FIGURE 17.4 Paul was also allowed to take photographs of the Shelley guitar on their visit. Here we can appreciate the rich colour of the mahogany back and the craftsmanship and precision of the purfling decoration. Photograph by Paul Fischer.

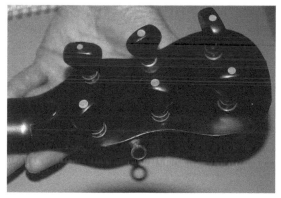

FIGURE 17.5 In this photograph, we can see the unusual tuning pegs from both sides of the headstock. The brass ring at the side of the headstock was quite common; presumably, it was used for tying a ribbon through so that the guitar could be supported around the neck of the player. Photographs by Paul Fischer.

notes, an outline profile of the body of the guitar and measurements of the instrument with an engineer's vernier gauge, including an inspection of its internal construction using a specialist telescopic mirror. With all of this information, Paul was able to draw up plans when he returned to his workshop. The string length was 65 cm.

The Shelley guitar was complete with strings in place; it had nylon strings on the instrument but the original gut strings were in its string box within the guitar's case. The tuning pegs were fascinating, particularly for the period; they were a design which brought together brass friction tubes, passing through the headstock with wooden buttons made from ebony. This is a type of tuning device that is still in common use on other instruments today. In creating the copy instrument, Paul endeavoured to use exactly the same style of tuning peg; however, those of modern manufacture are not of the quality he preferred to use, thus they used high-quality ebony violin pegs on the copy instrument, which Julian accepted.

Using his small telescopic mirror, Paul found the interior construction of the guitar to be reasonably conventional for the period, including the single diagonal bar reaching from the upper bass to the lower treble side of the soundboard. This was a relatively common practice on guitars of the time and a thicker soundboard was used to compensate, as there were fewer braces. One must remember that the standard pitch of the day was lower than the modern-day pitch, and with the strings made of gut, there was less stress on the soundboard.

Quite by coincidence, Paul had mahogany in his wood store, which had been rescued from an old square piano of the 1820s – the exact period of the Shelley guitar. Though that piano had been damaged beyond restoration, the mahogany proved ideal. When it was first planed, he discovered beautiful bird's-eye figured mahogany of an extraordinary golden colour. This wood, by now well seasoned, was of the fine quality required by a luthier.

Although this was Julian's second guitar, Paul had to be even more hands-on during its construction because practically everything Julian had learnt while building his first guitar did not apply to an early nineteenth-century instrument; in particular, it was the bending of the mahogany sides and the creation of the completely new purfling for this instrument that was more complicated than other early instruments Paul had worked on, and therefore required his full assistance.

Teaching activities after the stroke proved very useful and served to rebuild his skills while working with his students. Once the Shelley guitar was well on its way, Paul felt inspired to work on a new guitar for himself. At that point, in 2016, he had made 1,199 instruments. The Henry Astor film, *Aubade: The Final Guitar*, filmed the construction of instrument number 1,199, which at that time Paul had decided to call his last instrument. Now it seemed an untidy number to stop at. One more heave would bring it neatly to 1,200 in the sixtieth year of his profession. He spent quite a lot of time pondering the form that this instrument number 1,200 should take, thinking back over all the instruments he had made, from harpsichords to fretted instruments – such as vihuelas, lutes, citterns, pandoras, early guitars, nineteenth-century and modern guitars in their fascinating varieties – which are recorded in his maker's logbook.

As this would not be a commissioned instrument, Paul finally settled on a fantasia of a guitar, which would incorporate details taken from many of the instruments he had made throughout his sixty years in lutherie. Starting with the seventeenth century, he took the profile of the viola da gamba and incorporated the shoulders of the C-shape of the 'waist', instead of the more usual gentle curves of the modern guitar. Taking the more decorative approach of the Baroque period, he would use the highly decorated parchment insert in the soundhole and an equally decorative rosette. Other small details in this adventurous process included a bridge in the style of a nineteenth-century instrument and the headstock design of the guitar from the twentieth century. The body was made of exquisite bird's-eye maple with a cedar soundboard – another twentieth-century touch. Another twentieth-century aspect was in the bracing: the Taut system, of course. The machine heads were the finest model made by Thomas Rubner, from Markneukirchen, Germany.

With Paul's enthusiasm for these projects, he suggested holding a concert – with period music and words of Shelley's own composition – to celebrate the creation of this copy now known as 'Shelley's Guitar', as well as his own new guitar. Once again, Chipping Norton's charming theatre provided the perfect venue and the date was set for Sunday, 3 July 2016. This neatly

FIGURE 17.6 Paul with his instrument number 1,200 – Opus X. Photograph by Glenda Jane Wilson.

coincided with Paul's last personal project. Having the last Fischer guitar – guitar number 1,200 – along with the Shelley guitar, would make for a broader range of musical styles and a more appealing concert.

John Mills, a long-term friend and guitar maestro, expressed his enthusiasm for the concert in the theatre. The Chipping Norton Theatre accepted the event and plans were put in place. John and his charming wife, the guitarist Cobie Smit, would perform appropriate solos and duets, including Romantic-era pieces that would have been known to Jane Williams.

FIGURE 17.7 This is Paul Fischer's guitar number 1,200 – Opus X – and Julian Roach's Shelley guitar (right), built with considerable input by Paul Fischer. Though the elaborate inlay was mostly prepared for the Shelley guitar copy, they ran out of time before this concert and thus the soundboard remained undecorated.

In the sixtieth anniversary year of his instrument-making career, Paul Fischer created his final guitar, which gave him great pleasure and fulfilment. In writing this book, he has been able to review the joys of his life and he hopes it offers some insight for others who might be interested or inspired to be involved in such a wonderful profession. The making of this last guitar was a fitting and appropriate culmination of his life's work as a luthier – one that he is content with and, despite the stroke, has not left him with any regrets.

FIGURE 17.8 Paul with his grandson Charlie.

He has held on to this last instrument for posterity and as an example of his work for his grandchildren.

Afterword

In 2021, as Paul Fischer celebrated his eightieth birthday, he looked back to consider the modern history of classical guitar making. When he began making guitars in the late 1960s, there was no identifiable school of British guitar making. Was such a school established by that 'Englishman in New York', David Rubio? Surely, he was just following lessons learnt from the Spanish makers he so carefully observed and copied, and, of course, Antonio de Torres.

At the time David Rubio established his studios at Duns Tew, there had been some successful makers of classical guitars, such as A.A. Jones in Norwich, who made many guitars for Adele Kramer and her students; R.E. Spain, initially selling his guitars through the Ivor Mairants Music Centre; and, of course, the Danish maker Harald Pedersen (1910–1969), living in Cumbria, who sold his guitars through Len Williams's London Spanish Guitar Centre. Arnold Dolmetsch also made some classical guitars, which were not so refined and had little impact. However, when David Rubio began making classical and flamenco guitars, the impact internationally was almost immediate.

By the early 1990s, when Paul was organising the first British guitar makers' exhibition at the Classical Guitar Festival in West Dean, bringing together the then young, and now internationally renowned, makers, was that the first public acknowledgement that a school of British guitar making had evolved? The fresh and youthful faces of Gary Southwell, Michael Gee, Simon Ambridge, Kevin Aram, Trevor Semple and Christopher Dean have gone on to become the artisans we now respect for their art and knowledge built up from decades of dedication to their craft.

Paul's own lineage as an instrument maker traces back to Robert and Andrea Goble, and through them to Arnold Dolmetsch, all of whom were connected strongly with the Arts and Crafts movement, a connection Paul Fischer still identifies with today. Paul, however, has always been an enthusiastic seeker of knowledge and collaboration with others, always willing to share his knowledge and time, and his regular and long-term engagement with the international seminars organised by Siegfried Hogenmüller in Rückersbach, Germany, have been an important part of his life as an instrument maker.

In his brief biography, Paul has tried to bring some perspective on his lifetime's work as an instrument maker in the context of his being an Englishman, an army man in the 11th Hussars, a craftsman trained in the most traditional and thorough manner of apprenticeship, and as a family man, who has extended his sense of family to all those who have had the good fortune to know him as their maker, teacher and friend.

Thérèse Wassily Saba
London
December 2021

Appendix I

Sérgio Abreu

SÉRGIO and EDUARDO ABREU

FIGURE AI.1 Sérgio and Eduardo Abreu. Photograph from Sérgio Abreu Collection.

Dearest friends, Paul and Joy,

I remain extremely grateful for your warm friendship through so many years, for so much that I always learnt from you and, not least of all, for your superb guitars, which my brother and I were proud to use during the peak of our very short career. You remain a great reference both as a luthier and as a human being!

Not very long ago, some video recordings my brother and I recorded in France – in around 1974, I believe – have been rediscovered in the French television archives. We used your guitars for those videos, and the sound of the instruments is really quite stunning on these videos. I send below the YouTube links in case you have not seen these videos before:

Duo Abreu playing Rameau:
https://www.youtube.com/watch?v=5Z3YV4Ab-18

Duo Abreu playing Granados:
https://www.youtube.com/watch?v=ViQF-qk5Umk

Duo Abreu playing Manuel de Falla's *La Vida Breve*
https://www.youtube.com/watch?v=YO1J-KiOVdY

The video below was recorded in Rio de Janeiro in 1974:
https://www.youtube.com/watch?v=S_2Gy_Z20n4

For this video, I used a David Rubio 1965 guitar and Eduardo used the 1972 guitar made by Paul Fischer, which he used on all the videos.

My warmest best wishes,

Sérgio

A letter from Sérgio Abreu in celebration of Paul Fischer's eightieth birthday.

Badi Assad

FIGURE AI.2 Badi Assad (playing a Paul Fischer).
Photograph © Felipe Fittipaldi. Reprinted with permission.

When I was born, my two brothers Sérgio and Odair already played the guitar. It took me fourteen years before I also started to play this instrument. I got started the same way my brothers did: by accepting my dad's invitation to accompany his mandolin. However, when this happened, my parents and I were far away from my brothers, who had already started their international career, so I didn't have a good guitar that was handy and learnt to play with a very ordinary instrument.

Even so, in just a year I had mastered my father's musical style, the chorinho, a typical traditional genre of music from Rio de Janeiro. I had also learnt to read sheet music and was able to play a few pieces from the classical repertoire. However, I was taken by surprise when a letter from Sérgio arrived asking me how I felt about entering my first guitar competition. He thought I was already prepared to face the challenges of the 'Young Instrumentalists Competition' in Rio de Janeiro and encouraged me to give it a try. I remember that I immediately started to ask myself how I was going to prepare for the competition without a coach and which guitar I was going to perform with. The first problem was solved when Sérgio started sending me scores, where he carefully wrote down the fingering of both hands as well as all the dynamics I should apply on top of each musical note and phrase. Odair generously lent me one of his best guitars, for my practice and performance, and that's how a genuine Paul Fischer came to me.

I got ready, went to the contest and brought home my first prize. The Paul Fischer guitar came up on that stage along with me, lending its lightness, naturally (and beautifully) amplified sounds and its resonance that responded to my emotional commands. If I wanted a strong sound, it would give it to me; if I wanted delicacy, it would respond as well; and if I vibrated its strings, it would return in sonically balanced waves. Since that day, the Fischer guitar has been accompanying me. Now, in 2021, it has been forty years! Of course, the guitar today is mine! I insist on saying ☺ [*sic*].

Since then, the Fischer and I have won a few awards – such as the best Brazilian guitarist in the Villa-Lobos Guitar Competition and best CD of the year (*Rhythms*) by North American *Guitar Player* magazine – and has entered the list of the best 100 albums of the year with the CD *Wonderland*, and so on. It has kept me company for thousands of hours while I learnt and practised so many songs. It has been my faithful companion on all twenty studio CDs I have ever recorded.

I once had to change the top's varnish but I made sure that the mark Odair had left before lending it to me was not removed. It's a dark spot left by his beard when resting his chin on the wood while practising. That spot is still there today, along with other small scars that accidentally happen through time and a lot of use. Paul Fischer, this incredible and inseparable instrument has been part of my journey as my first and eternal guitar.

Sérgio Assad

GHA / LIVE IN BRUSSELS

Odair & Sergio
ASSAD

THE DEBUT CONCERT — BRUSSELS 1983

FIGURE AI.3 Assad Brothers record cover, with artwork by Anne Denis.
Reprinted with kind permission of Françoise-Emmanuelle Denis, GHA Records.

The GHA recording of 1983 was made with the first pair of Fischer guitars we had. We kept playing the new ones we got from Paul until 1986, when we changed to the Humphreys. The first Fischer from the 1983 recording, I gave to Badi. She has made all her albums with that guitar. She plays guitars like Takemine, or similar guitars, in concerts, but when she records, she always uses the Fischer. I still have the second Fischer I bought and play it from time to time. It is a wonderful instrument.

Christopher Dean

It was a privilege to have been given a place on the three-year course at the London College of Furniture to study musical instrument technology. There I specialised in modern fretted instruments under the tutelage of Herbert Schwarz. This was in the late 1970s/early 1980s. While there, I met Paul Fischer, once on a visit to his workshop and once when he visited our college.

Around a year after leaving, I contacted him to see if there was a possibility of working alongside him. To be accepted, for a trial period initially, was the greatest honour and gave me the grounding in the real world of making guitars that I could only have dreamt of. Although my time at college was extremely useful, I feel I learnt more in the first three months of working with Paul than I did in the whole three years of that course.

I relished there being an English school of guitar making and was determined to proudly continue that line when I imagined venturing into my own independent making. I was aware of the great works of David Rubio, in whose workshop Paul had learnt much of Rubio's craft, and this made me so want to be a part of this lineage. I went on to work with Paul for over two years and took priceless knowledge with me when I began working on my own.

I recall that I began my time there by helping make a series of eight guitars from woods that were potential substitutes for Brazilian rosewood (*Dalbergia nigra*), which was becoming harder to obtain. Paul had recently returned from Brazil with these woods and wanted to test their qualities. They were demonstrated in a blind testing to an audience in London. It was a wonderful experience and I felt proud to have been a part of it.

Paul could see I had learnt much prior to my working alongside him and felt comfortable tasking me with the overall production of his Fischer Lutherie-labelled guitars. These were made solely by me but with his input in checking or amending the soundboards to his own liking. The differences lay in their being made with Indian rosewood (rather than Brazilian, which was used on the Paul Fischer guitars), slightly less-perfect soundboards and less-expensive tuners. These guitars were sold across the world. Occasionally, I come across one and it can take me back to that workbench on the other side of our – quite small – workshop.

Despite it being a small (but organised) workshop, we got along very well. We sometimes went to the pub for lunch together and often travelled to concerts and occasionally sat over a pint of an evening. There were many work-related outings too; I would often accompany him to buy wood, which I found fascinating and educational.

Of course, we were often visited by many players. I recall meeting for the first time the Assad brothers, Forbes Henderson, Gilbert Biberian, Eduardo Fernández, and many others. It was a very exciting place to be!

In time – as was bound to happen – I grew restless and wanted to make my own sound, my own aesthetic, my own guitars. That came to pass in the autumn of 1985. Over the previous two and a half years, while I was working there, we had made great progress in reducing the long waiting list (around six years when I had begun) but the time had come for me to branch out on my own. This I did in October of that year. Even so, Paul helped me greatly. I still recall him helping me put in stud partitions in my first workshop. He gave me work, on a part-time basis, which was very helpful considering I was newly married and we had a child, and so starting a business from scratch was not easy. He also allowed me to use some of his contacts – an immensely generous deed.

Since then, for the past thirty-five years, I have been making my own guitars. The foundation he gave me has proved invaluable, and I am eternally grateful. I too have given tuition to aspiring makers: some as paying pupils, others as paid assistants. Oren Myers worked with me for some reasonably long periods and has gone on to produce excellent professional guitars. Guitar making is a rather solitary, and possibly selfish, activity, so I have first-hand experience of the pleasures, and frustrations, of having someone alongside you who wants to learn. It has, though, proved to be a rewarding experience for me. I hope the same is felt by Paul when he looks back on our time together. I feel confident enough to suspect so!

Siegfried Hogenmüller

Paul Fischer – A Man and his Guitars

FIGURE AI.4 Siegfried Hogenmüller in Rückersbach.

At first glance, it seemed to be quite easy writing about a now almost-four-decade-long friendship between Paul Fischer and me. There were so many different occasions, events and experiences we shared together that they could already fill up a little book. But then, sitting at my desk with paper and fountain pen, waiting for the right words to come, I must confess that bringing all these facts into a serious form causes some problems. Finally, it led to the decision to separate my little story into two parts: Who is the 'man' Paul Fischer to me? And his guitars?

Who is the 'man' Paul Fischer to me?

An open-minded personality, interested in all kinds of human cultures he had discovered from the Far East of Japan to the deep south-west of Patagonia – a real 'world citizen'!

A tough character, never losing his will to fight against all difficulties, always believing in himself!

A reliable human being, for whom the sentence 'A word is a word!' is part of his personality. Whatever he promised, he fulfilled!

And a modest, likeable companion, treating the persons opposite himself in a fair, open and friendly way!

So, on the one hand, Paul represents to me the ideal image of what I would call an 'English gentleman', and, on the other hand, a 'true friend'!

And his guitars?

I have been in the lucky position of accompanying Paul's career as an independent maker from the beginning of the 1980s up to his retirement. There were examples of many different tonewoods – like rippled and bird's-eye maple, satinwood, tulipwood, tigerwood, kingwood, cypress and the most spectacular Brazilian rosewood one could imagine. They all were executed with an extremely high quality of craftsmanship, expressing in every detail the love of the *guitarrero* (guitar player) for the beauty of wood and for his profession. Together with fantastic spruce or cedar tops, necks of cedar and ebony, and, finally, with David Rodgers' fabulous tuners, Paul combined all these different parts into wonders of sound and aesthetics.

Apropos sound! The Fischer guitars are full of power, rich in their colours and dynamics and extremely easy to play. But, last, there is a special element living in all of them: they always sound in the same high-quality way, in all kinds of climates, twenty-four hours a day. They are not like nervous 'race horses', who are sometimes fantastic, sometimes sullen. One can always rely on them – just as it is with their 'father'!

At the 2006 festivities celebrating Paul Fischer's 'fifty years of instrument making', I had been allowed to say some words. And the final part of this little speech I would like to repeat here:

In my German mother tongue there is the adjective *sicher*. It means that one could feel himself being in good hands, in a good atmosphere, well equipped. And, related to Paul's guitars, I allowed myself to form a little English–German proverb:

'Feel *SICHER* with a FISCHER!'

Hogi
Karlstein, Germany
18 May 2020

Siegfried 'Hogi' Hogenmüller

Born in 1949, Hogi is a guitar historian researching on the life and work of the great *guitarreros* from Antonio de Torres to the end of the twentieth century. In 1980 he was the founder and organiser of the Aschaffenburger Gitarrenwoche (today the Aschaffenburger Gitarrentage), one of the oldest and continuing guitar festivals worldwide. In 2002 Hogi was the initiator of the Rückersbach Seminar, a meeting for guitar makers, players, collectors and aficionados normally taking place twice a year. Over the years, he has given many lectures and published on Spanish guitar history in different European countries. He lives in Karlstein (former Dettingen, the battlefield, where the famous G. F. Haendel 'Dettingen Te Deum' had its origin).

Thomas Liauw

For My Friend and Buddy for Many Years: Luthier Paul Fischer

FIGURE AI.5 Paul and Thomas Liauw. Photograph from Thomas Liauw Collection.

There are just too many things and events to mention in this short passage, so I am going to keep it as precise as possible.

First, I started playing the guitar as an accompaniment instrument. It was in 1985 that I began to be serious on the classical guitar at the age of 24. During this time, I was introduced to the guitar made by luthier Paul Fischer via my instructor. Ever since I bought it, I never have regretted it at all and started practising on it all the time. At times, I spent more hours on it than other things, and even the entire day enjoying it. Since then, I started taking examinations and improving myself, although age is catching up, but I never see it as a problem.

Something about this guitar I have is that it gives clarity, precision and accuracy on every note I press and pluck. This guitar will just show your technique if you can control it, and this is something you cannot. It is a simple instrument, yet when played it gives out sonority and projection you cannot find in many instruments.

Throughout the years of playing, I became a guitar instructor and attained all basic grades plus diplomas. Thereafter, I decided to pursue my degree in Kingston University London (1991), and that is where I met up with Paul Fischer for the first time. He treated me well during my first visit to his home in Oxfordshire, UK (a 500-year-old house, I believe). When I finished my Bachelor of Arts with Honours, I gave solo concerts in the UK, Iceland, Italy, Poland, Asia, etc. using his guitars. In addition to my performances, I wrote five arranged books for guitars and recorded with Paul Fischer's guitar on my two albums (sold out and later converted to CDs: *Time for Romantic Guitar – Love Songs*; and *Thomas Liauw Plays A. Lauro, F. Tarrega, A. Barrios, H. Villa-Lobos and F. Martin*).

The national radio station Media Corp Radio (FM 99.5) also invited me to give a thirteen-part series on guitars and their characteristics, which of course I used Paul Fischer's guitar for. It was so successful that I was invited to do another thirteen-part series.

In 1999 I was given a research scholarship for a Master of Arts, 'Tonal Production on Classical Guitar', where I focused between a simple guitar and a handcrafted one. Paul Fischer assisted me in the research and also recorded my interview with him during those times. Paul is not only a luthier but is always advanced in knowledge and research on this craft. We also travelled to Germany to meet and discussed guitar development of today. He makes wonderful musical instruments with thought and research, and not just merely following the book.

One part of my career is organising concerts and events. In 2000 I started organising the Singapore International Festival and, of course, Paul Fischer was my guest luthier, alongside artistes like Kazuhito Yamashita, Jorge Morel, Flavio Cucchi, etc. He not only makes guitars but also taught many up-and-coming luthiers in Asia during that time. He further returned with a warm welcome for his new findings in guitar making in 2006 for the sixth Singapore International Guitar Festival, alongside Oscar Ghiglia, Juan Martín, Marco Pereira, etc.

In addition to the above, I also started the retail shop, which sells quality musical instruments, books and accessories. Of course, Paul Fischer's guitars belong to the exclusive list of instruments I have. Still today, his guitars just sell by themselves, without any publicity. It is extremely sad that in recent years he could not carry on making them due to unforeseen circumstances.

Finally, I must say that the one thing that sparked off my career was the guitar made by Paul Fischer, which I am still using and playing today, and loving it. This is the only instrument that has stayed in my bedroom for past thirty-five years of my life and has never left me.

Juan Martín

My Paul Fischer 1972 Flamenca Nigra

I visited and spoke to Paul Fischer in his workshops in Oxfordshire with regard to a concert flamenco guitar. We decided on Indian rosewood for the back and sides and a spruce top; I also asked for pegs rather than machine tuners, to retain a flamenco look rather than a classical one. When I played the finished instrument, I was immediately impressed by its volume and depth of tone combined with a percussive 'flamenconess' for rhythmic playing.

I used it straight away in a concert at Sussex University and, after a few more performances, in a solo recital at London's Wigmore Hall. In Madrid I used the guitar to accompany the gypsy cantaor Rafael Romero, and subsequently for certain pieces, like the *Tarantas* in my video series *Solos Flamencos*, where its wonderful bass resonance enhanced my sound.

In my 1984 concert at Wigmore Hall I began the programme with my old war horse, the *Tarantas*, and without a microphone the instrument effortlessly filled a packed auditorium, which of course is more difficult than when one is playing beforehand in a resonant empty hall. I followed with my *Zapateado* – 'Taconeos' – and I remember Ivor Mairants enquiring, 'What guitar is that you're playing?' He was clearly impressed. In Holland I played at the Royal Concertgebouw, the Utrecht Arts Centre and Haarlem Hall with this '*pedazo de nigra*', and everywhere its sound travelled to the last row of the concert halls.

On my *Serenade* recording, which I made with the Royal Philharmonic Orchestra, conducted by Louis Clark at Abbey Road Studios, I played it for the pieces *Cavatina* and *Romance Anónimo* and *Love Theme From The Thorn Birds*. I also featured Paul's guitar when I appeared on *Top of the Pops*, *Wogan*, and many other television programmes. The guitar remains with me still today, sounding better than ever. My profound thanks to you, Paul.

Julian Roach

The Making of the Shelley Guitar

FIGURE AI.6 My Shelley guitar.

In my teens I borrowed, from a Liverpool Public Library, a book that told you how to make a Spanish guitar. I even bought plans of a guitar made by Torres, the nineteenth-century creator of the modern 'classical' guitar. Going on sixty years later, I still had the plans in their cardboard tube but hadn't made a guitar and, by now, it was beginning to sink in that I never would. What I did have was a classical guitar that needed a small repair, and it so happened I was living a few hundred yards from a certain world-renowned luthier. All the pictures I'd ever seen of Paul Fischer made him look, well, frankly, a bit forbidding, but my guitar was a respectable instrument by a good luthier. Maybe it would not be an insult to Paul Fischer to ask him to repair it. It turned out he wasn't forbidding at all. Perfectly amiable, in fact. But he wouldn't repair my guitar. On the other hand, after we'd talked a bit, he offered something much better: he would stand at my shoulder and teach me to repair it myself. And from these beginnings, under Paul's patient tutelage and with the repair finished, I went on to make a whole guitar from the raw timber. It was, as far as I was concerned, one giant leap for mankind. You have to remember that I first hatched my plan about the same time NASA started to plan the moon landing ...

I believe I was Paul's final pupil. Session after session in his workshop, and step by step, he taught me how to make a classical guitar. That guitar is beside me now and I'm still in love with it.

Over the cups of coffee, we talked about those eighteenth- and early nineteenth-century instruments often called the 'Romantic guitar'. Your interests in life often cross in odd ways and I had an interest in the life and death of the poet Shelley. And this has something to do with guitars? Yes, with one otherwise unexceptional guitar made by Ferdinando Bottari of Pisa in 1815 or perhaps 1816. It's hard to say, as Ferdinando's handwriting was smudged on the label. No other Bottari instrument is known, and had the poet Shelley not bought this one, the name of Bottari the Luthier would have vanished from history.

Three months or so before the abrupt end of his short but intensely complicated life – his love life being far from the least complicated part – Shelley made a gift of this little guitar to the beautiful Jane, wife of his devoted admirer, Edward Williams. The four of them – Shelley and Mary, Jane and Edward – left Pisa to spend the summer in a rented house at the sea's edge near Lerici. The house was a ruin, but the setting idyllic, and an idyll needs music. Jane was the one who could play and sing, and so the gift of a guitar from Shelley, and a poem to go with it. Out on their terrace, the sea waves murmuring just below, Jane would sometimes massage the poet's inspired temples as he lay with his head in her lap (they all thought she had 'healing fingers'), and sometimes she would take up Bottari's little guitar and play and sing for them all. The truth was that she had enchanted Shelley before she played a note. The poem had been – no two ways about it – a love letter.

The music and the idyll at Casa Magni came to an abrupt end when Shelley and Edward Williams drowned, caught by a sudden storm while sailing their little boat back to Lerici from Livorno. Mary and Jane came home to England and the guitar came with them, in the little wooden case that Shelley, in the poem to Jane, had likened to a coffin. Eventually, it ended up in the vaults of the Bodleian Library in Oxford, at the heart of the same university that had kicked out the undergraduate Shelley for being an atheist just eleven years before his death and cremation – on a sort of oversized barbecue – on the sands of Viareggio.

So, having made a classical guitar, what could I do for an encore? What else but a replica of the guitar Jane had cradled in her comely lap and played to Shelley under the purple sky of the Italian night? Paul was all for it. He could even supply a fine board of old mahogany that was about the right age: the remains of the carcass of a rectangular, long-dead piano Paul had kept for many years – it was too good a piece of timber to let go.

This was an altogether different challenge. Dr Bruce Barker-Benfield, Keeper of Western Manuscripts at the Bodleian Library, generously gave us permission – under his watchful eye – to measure and examine what the library calls 'Shelley Relics No. 1'. The first time I took this little object from its case, held it and turned in my own hands, I was piercingly aware that the first time he saw it in Pisa, Shelley must have picked it up and turned it and looked it over in this same way, possibly asking, 'How much?' Jane would have held and turned it like this, too, though with more delight. It is what you do. I had known the poem 'To Jane: With a Guitar' for many decades. To be holding that same guitar was something of a woozy moment.

We weren't there to hold a séance with the thing, though, but to inspect it more intimately than either Shelley or Jane ever did. All measurements taken – and recorded by Dr Barker Benfield – we examined the interior with a telescopic mirror. It was no surprise to find that Bottari's handiwork precisely followed the practice of his more famous contemporary, Fabricatore. Much less complicated than the Torres pattern that created the modern concert guitar, these guitars have just two bracing bars and no fan struts. They are structurally simple. I could copy this with little difficulty.

In just one significant detail of construction would my guitar differ from the original. The practice then was to join neck and body with glue and one big nail. Glue, fine. But a nail? This kind of square-edged nail was used by carpenters, I knew, because it had a reduced tendency to split your floorboards. I was not going to trust that whacking in a nail would not split my laboriously but exquisitely – if I say it myself – crafted neck and heel. And how do you whack away at a nail and still contrive to keep that very precise angle between neck and body? We used, invisibly, a more modern method – a mortise and tenon joint.

Replicating the basic structure, then, was straightforward enough. What wasn't in any way straightforward was replicating the fioritura, that decorative wreath or garnish that is often a feature of these guitars and most conspicuously a feature of Shelley's.

Paul had made many guitars and, in an earlier life, many a harpsichord with fancy-work, but decoration of this kind, and these proportions, even he had not tackled before. Many hours of thought and labour were wasted because all kinds of bright ideas simply didn't work and we were running short of time before the planned concert. Once the concert was over, I returned to the task at home. What did work was taking a photograph of the original, correcting the orientation in Photoshop and expanding it to the right size, to produce an image that could be printed out for one half of the decoration and turned mirror image for the other half. From there, the technique of transferring the pattern to the material was exactly the same as the 'cartoon' technique used by Renaissance artists like Leonardo and Michelangelo – pin pricks and chalk then lots of very careful work with a surgeon's scalpel. The first idea that seemed good was to use two layers of black veneer glued cross-grain. A lot of work went into this to no avail. The veneer breaks up, the glue makes it curl and the stuff just won't behave. The final solution, which in some ways I feel I ought to keep a secret or a mystery of the craft, was to use black card impregnated with resin. I'm sure that Bottari bought his in from a specialist. I'm also sure the specialist had a much better and quicker method than mine, or his children would certainly have starved.

Two things are surprising about the Shelley guitar. Its scale length is exactly the same as a standard modern classical guitar. The fingerboard is a little narrower but to a modern guitarist the 'feel' of the fingerboard and movement of hand position is just what he or she is used to. The second surprise is that, while the instrument looks as if it will be demure and simply not very loud, the sound is actually sweet but perfectly robust. Less reverberant, certainly, just as a fortepiano is less reverberant than a modern grand, but that lends a certain 'open' clarity to chords and arpeggios that is perfectly suited – unsurprisingly – to its own contemporary repertoire. John Mills thought it sounded just as such a guitar was supposed to sound. That was a pleasing endorsement of the idea that we had, in effect, made a real Bottari. A somewhat double-edged endorsement that we have recreated the original can be seen if you examine the bridge and saddle. On Shelley's guitar, in the style of the times, the bridge is narrow and the section of ebony supporting the saddle is really insubstantial. On the original, the tension and pressure of the strings has pushed the saddle towards the soundhole and opened up a crack in the ebony. The replica has precisely the same affliction. As I say, we must have got it right then

The journey Paul Fischer started me on and guided me through – from that first step of do-your-own repair, that led me in the end to think that, in another life, I might have been a half-decent luthier – has been as enriching as any journey I have ever, or could ever have, made. It is hard to express my gratitude. It is enough, perhaps, to say that I sat at the foot of a master and am proud to have done so.

Julian Roach

The Shelley Guitar: Concert Programme

Chipping Norton Theatre
Sunday 3 July 2016
'Guitars, yes. But not (quite) as we know them ...'

Two new and unique instruments, played in public for the first time by John Mills. Music by Bach, Schubert, Sor, Giuliani, Pujol, Aguado and Piazzolla.

John will play the only replica of the beautiful, sweetly musical and really rather sexy instrument that Shelley gave to the fascinating Jane Williams, about whom he said pretty much the same things, but in verse. Jane played it and sang for him beneath Italian stars until, just three months later, Shelley drowned, shipwrecked in a thunderstorm, and the music stopped. A luthier's label is an instrument's birth certificate. The label in Shelley's guitar, now a mute treasure in the Bodleian Library, tells us it was born in Ferdinando Bottari's Pisa workshop in 1816. The presentation of this re-creation, by Julian Roach in the Chipping Norton workshop of Paul Fischer (with lots of his help), therefore comes as a Two Hundredth Birthday party. You are invited to hear music from Shelley's world and with it something of the rebel poet's strange journey through that world – and even stranger departure from it.

While Shelley's guitar was much like many a guitar of its time, the second is like no other, of this or any time. It is, says Paul Fischer, the last he will make. It brings his catalogue to a well-rounded 1,200, the output of a lifetime that has made him the undisputed doyen of English luthiers. You could call it a fantasia of a guitar that tells the history of the instrument, with accents drawn from the lute, the viol and the Baroque guitar combined with techniques and unique methods Paul has evolved over decades. Unfamiliar to the eye it may be, but the characteristic warmth of its sound is familiar enough to the ear. It is Paul's farewell to the art and craft he has practised and adorned for sixty years.

A double – and doubly unique – musical celebration.

Jasper Sender

My journey through the world of guitar making and luthiers has not at all been an obvious one. It is the fruit of a youth spent mainly avoiding scholarly responsibility. I couldn't wait to leave the confined spaces of study and get into the world and discover for myself. And so, at 18 years old, I travelled. It was what I had been seeking, an expanding of the possibilities, purchasing camels and travelling for months though the Rajasthan desert, motorbike expeditions, and meeting human nature of every kind, from the saint to the cannibal. It was a wild time and this continued for about four years until the desire to create something concrete started to manifest itself in me. I was growing tired of consuming experiences and wanted to become involved in making them.

By chance, a friend of mine showed me a website for the Newark and Sherwood school of instrument making. My ignorant self, having addressed no consideration to the way instruments came into being, was instantly fascinated. I didn't come from a musical family and had no experience as a woodworker, and so in my mind, not only would I learn to use tools and make something beautiful, but even if I didn't like the course, I would at least have a guitar to play. In fact, I was so naïve, I assumed that with the skills acquired it wouldn't be a giant leap to make wooden furniture, fittings and even a house perhaps. It is still amusing to me now how little I knew.

On the opening day of the term, I was given a toolbox and rough-sawn timber, which was destined to become my first guitar. The colours and smell of the rosewood and cedar struck me. The weight of the ebony, and the glassy resonance of the alpine spruce. It was a feeling of immense excitement, privilege and responsibility to have been entrusted with these most precious of natural resources. The toolbox, on the other hand, was filled with objects I had no vocabulary for. The learning curve would be steep.

Despite having no experience, I took to the course with a passion I had never experienced previously in my academic life. Working was easy when it was so engaging and magical. Like phoenixes, instruments were being born from fiery coloured piles of wood shavings on benches all around me until finally my own original guitar was also born. One might think that this was a benchmark moment for a luthier, and in many ways it was, but my overriding emotion was the desire to make another one – a better one! This feeling has never left me.

About halfway through my second year in the school, there was a talk given by Paul Fischer about his philosophy and his life as a professional luthier. He was beguiling, a smart and very English gentleman with bright eyes and half a smile as he was presented to us. Paul hadn't come with any finished instruments but his obvious passion and generosity painted a beautiful picture of his years of research and experience, meticulous attention to detail and his inclination to share the treasure trove of his years. I was also struck by his modern approach and desire to embrace contemporary methods to expand the tradition without sacrificing its artisanal roots. It was captivating. I had to see his finished instruments and my appetite to learn more from him was thoroughly whetted.

I finished my final year at Newark with a French violin-making girlfriend (later to become my wonderful wife), a certificate of distinction and, to my surprise, I had also won the annual prize for most outstanding student. Despite these accolades, I knew I was still a sapling and was hungry to learn more. The notion of earning a living through guitar making really hadn't entered my mind. I was simply living with a kind of compulsion to keep making and advancing. I needed to know if this was folly. The next step in my evolution seemed self-evident: I had to meet Paul again.

I called Paul with a certain sense of trepidation. I was acutely aware of my shortcomings as a maker and was afraid of being woefully out of my depth. When Paul answered, my fears were very quickly allayed. He was as warm and generous as he had been in Newark. He invited me to bring a guitar to his West End Studio workshop for a critique.

On arriving at the atelier, the familiar sights and smells birthed a feeling of belonging to a certain kind of tribe of artisans. It felt like home.

I could see myself filling these shoes. Paul welcomed me and we quickly turned to the guitar I had made. Paul was complimentary, but I never much cared for compliments; they don't help one move forward and the only thing that mattered to me was the development of my instruments. I told Paul not to pull any punches. He obliged.

On a deeper level, I think what I was looking for was more than an evaluation; I wanted to know if he thought my talent and motivation had the potential to warrant a more profound dedication to the art. I think Paul was sufficiently impressed because he proposed a short apprenticeship with him. I couldn't believe my luck and, in the few weeks I spent with him in his workshop, I was once again filled with those same emotions of privilege and wonder. The magnificence of those Brazilian rosewood backs and his use of snakewood as ornamentation, watching his adroit manipulation of tools and his unselfish sharing of techniques he had devised and the suppliers he used. My head span at the end of each session, and I have been drawing on those experiences since my time there. I was also fortunate to acquire a certain quantity of splendid wood from Paul, from which I preciously draw on to this day.

Without Paul's encouragement, I almost certainly wouldn't have pursued this path. I was the only student in my class to continue making guitars.

Years have now passed and I have continued to forge my own way. I have since moved to France with my wife, who makes Baroque violins and viols. I have continued to be influenced by many other luthiers, each with their own philosophy. My own approach is really an amalgam of the very precise woodworking of French traditional guitar makers, German double-top innovators, the mastery and flourish of the Baroque influence from my wife and, of course at the root of it all, my time with Paul. It is an honour to be included in this book and I cannot thank Paul enough for his influence and guidance. By virtue of him, my attitude in this domain has always been one of generosity towards young makers and my confrères, humility in the face of how much there is to learn and a lasting sense of wonder.

Xuefei Yang

Aubade

Figure AI.7 Xuefei Yang with composer William Lovelady during the filming of Aubade; Henry Astor is the cameraman and John Taylor, assisted by Judy Taylor, is the sound engineer. Photograph from Xuefei Yang Collection.

I think it was in 2012 that Paul got in touch to moot a project that had been brewing in his head. Paul had been doing some guitar repairs for a local, Henry Astor, who turned out to be a film-maker. He became a regular visitor to Paul's studio and became interested in making a video based around Paul. From their discussion, the idea arose to involve a composer (Bill Lovelady), and a guitarist (me!). The video would follow the triple strands of the building of a new guitar, the composition of a new piece and the learning and performance of that piece on the new guitar, culminating in a live concert performance at the historic Hagley Hall. There was also some local interest, as we were all based in and around Oxfordshire.

The construction of a guitar takes many hours of skilled work, so Henry and his camera were regular fixtures at Paul's studio over several months. Little did we know that the drama of real-life events was about to cast a shadow over the project. On the very last day of this filming, just hours after Paul had finished the guitar and Henry had packed away his camera, Paul suffered a major stroke that left him in hospital for several weeks and rehab for several months. Henry, presumably in conjunction with Paul and his family, decided that this aspect of real-life events wouldn't be covered in the film, other than in the title – subtitled 'The Last Guitar' – but the uncertainty about Paul's wellbeing cast a dark shadow over the filming Bill and I were involved in over the subsequent months. Looking back, I suppose it added an extra poignancy to the project during those months – it became all the more vital for our own efforts to showcase the full glory of Paul's craft. In the early days of Paul's recovery, it became clear that he believed the stroke would mark the end of his career – he thought that this guitar, his 1,199th, would be his last. However, people's characters do not change. The orderliness of his workshop, and structured military background, tell us something about Paul's psyche. A few months into recovery, with improvement in his condition, the untidiness of finishing at 1,199 must have been gnawing away at the back of his mind. Once recovered, he made one more guitar – to bring his lifetime tally up to a nice round 1,200!

Both instruments were very special. I recall visiting Paul's workshop to be introduced to guitar 1,199 for the first time. The guitar had a beautiful spruce top with lots of cross-grain, and a very unique back and sides from lacewood, which true to its name made it look as if the guitar was dressed in fine lace. The neck dimensions were the same as a previous instrument Paul had made for me, so as well as being a beautiful instrument to look at, I found it particularly comfortable to play and make music with. The sound of the guitar was quite open, right from the start, with a clear focused tone. I don't know all the technical details, but I know it was built using a lot of Paul's own ideas and experience from a lifetime in lutherie – a special instrument for sure, and worthy of a modern-day concert performer.

I also had the privilege to play Paul's very last guitar – guitar 1,200. This one is very different too, both in look and character. The appearance of the guitar pays homage to the string instruments of centuries past. The shape is slightly different to a traditional guitar, with a shoulder on the upper bout, rather like a member of the viol family. The guitar had many historically informed small details, as well as a Baroque-style ornate inlay, made from parchment, inset in the soundhole. Despite all the visual references to a long history of string instruments, this cedar-top guitar was a modern concert instrument with a full-bodied projecting sound. The acoustic design and interior of the guitar were probably as modern as one could imagine, with Paul putting his lifetime's experience into making this instrument fit for the demands of a modern-day concert guitarist.

Two very different guitars, but both wonderful instruments in their own right and worthy of a place on the concert stage.

In March 2013, while Paul was still recovering, the video production continued with Henry filming myself and Bill, both separately and jointly, to pull the three strands of the story together.

We had one lovely day all together at a large barn just north of Chipping Norton, near Bill's home, where I played sections of the piece for Bill, with sound engineer John Taylor on location too, to record the sound. It was an exciting day, as it was the first time the new guitar and the new piece of music came together. To keep Paul involved with the progress of the project, we forwarded some photos from the day, some of which are shared here. This part of the story is documented on the final video too.

Just one month later, with Paul still too ill to join us, the team from that day were all back together again at the historic Hagley Hall to film and record a concert in front of a capacity audience, where I would give the première of Bill's piece on the new guitar in live concert. It was a special evening. The audience were aware of the story of the new piece being played for the first time on a new guitar. To add some further interest, and as a tribute to Paul, I used my own Paul Fischer guitar for the first part of the concert and switched to the new instrument for Bill's piece. The story around the instrument and the piece certainly added to the audience's anticipation, and I think this is captured very nicely on the finished video. The applause that evening was a clear appreciation of the efforts of everyone involved in this endearingly unique project.

In February 2014, with Paul well enough to participate, we all came together for a special event at the wonderful theatre in Paul's hometown of Chipping Norton. Family, friends, acquaintances, local dignitaries, guitar lovers and music lovers all turned out to fill the theatre in this charming market town and celebrate the achievements of one of the country's finest instrument makers. It was an evening of film and music to celebrate Paul's lifetime of world-class achievements. As well as the first public screening of the video, I also performed a handful of pieces on Paul's guitar that evening, including *Aubade*, and a small collection of his instruments, borrowed back from past clients, was on display in the theatre's upper gallery.

As a performer, having a comfortable instrument is a necessity. From early on in my career, I had often used nuts with a narrower string spacing I found more suited to my left hand. In an early visit to Paul, we discussed some of the physical things I was looking for in an ideal instrument: for example, the size and shape of the neck, string spacing for both hands, and other variables that came up in the discussion. The first guitar he built for me was very different to any I had played before; the slight variations in these physical aspects gave it a distinct feel. In short, it was an instrument custom tailored for me. Naturally, I find it very comfortable to play, and I feel that this liberates my music making even more.

FIGURE AI.8 Xuefei Yang with her Paul Fischer guitar.

Appendix II
Articles by Bernard Richardson

Guitar Acoustics at Cardiff
Bernard Richardson

After graduating in physics in the mid-1970s, I moved to Cardiff University to undertake PhD research on the acoustics of the classical guitar under the guidance of Professor Charles Taylor. This work was motivated by my interests in music and musical instrument making. I'd kept asking why and how, until all the answers ran out and I realised I would have to find out for myself because at that time there was almost no literature on the acoustical function of the guitar.

Guided by the more-extensive research available on violin acoustics, I set up a holographic system for the 'visualisation' of the modes of vibration of the guitar body. Holographic interferometry produces beautiful pictures of the guitar overlaid with 'optical fringes', which can be read like contour lines mapping out the displacements (see Figure AII.1). Each instrument has many modes, which together create the 'acoustical signature' of the instrument (see Figure AII.2). It is these modes that govern how readily the string is able to pass energy to the body and subsequently how efficiently the body radiates sound to the outside world; they ultimately govern the 'sound quality' of the instrument. Because of my interest in guitar making, these studies focused on instruments in various stages of construction, as well as completed instruments, with the long-term aim to investigate quantitative relationships between the construction of instruments (their materials and shape) and their perceived tone qualities. The work has all sorts of challenges; the physics of sound production by musical instruments is surprisingly intricate at times, and for the results to have any real meaning, they must be interpreted sensitively in a musical context. But perhaps the biggest challenge of all is conveying meaningful physical ideas, concepts and practical help to musicians and musical instrument makers. From an early stage, Paul was very interested in this work and graciously loaned various instruments to assist in our studies.

Over the years, I have been joined by like-minded research students and research assistants, setting up a centre for the study of guitar acoustics. As we built a better understanding of the mechanics of the acoustical function of these instruments through measurements, we applied various theoretical techniques, such as finite element analysis and the boundary element method, to calculate the vibrations and sound radiation fields from instruments. This sort of work allowed sounds to be calculated purely from data relating to the dimensions and construction of the instrument, allowing a systematic approach to investigate the important features of its acoustics. Some of our 'simplified models' allowed us to generate sounds to be used in psycho-acoustical listening experiments, and it is these sorts of tests that have been employed to relate constructional parameters with perceived sound quality with the potential to establish acoustical criteria for use by instrument makers. There is, of course, no substitute for making real instruments, but this sort of knowledge allows more-informed decisions to be made at an early stage of construction or even to explore new sounds.

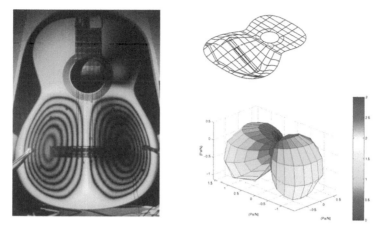

FIGURE AII.1 Left: a guitar mode visualised using holographic interferometry. The very bright lines (around the perimeter of the guitar and down the centre line) are nodes (stationary regions) and the 'fringes' can be read like contour lines mapping out the soundboard's displacement. The small inset cartoon shows a wire-frame representation of the same motion. Right: the sound field radiated by this mode. The instrument would sound equally loud if you were to walk around this 'dumb-bell' surface. Note that because this particular mode exhibits equal and opposite motion of the two halves of the soundboard, it is a very poor radiator to the front of the instrument. Other modes radiate more omnidirectionally. Photograph from Dr Bernard Richardson Collection.

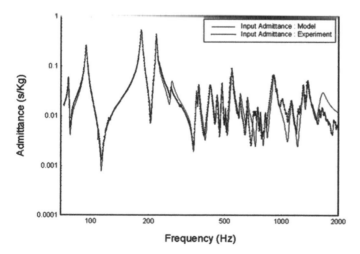

FIGURE AII.2 An input admittance (velocity per unit force) measured at the bridge of a guitar. A different mode is found at each peak. Note that the response of this instrument varies over several orders of magnitude. This is the 'acoustical signature' of the instrument. Photograph from Dr Bernard Richardson Collection.

PhD Theses from Cardiff University

1. Richardson, Bernard, 'A Physical Investigation into Some Factors Affecting the Musical Performance of the Guitar', 1982.
2. Roberts, Gareth, 'Vibrations of Shells and their Relevance to Musical Instruments' 1986.
3. Walker, Gordon, 'Towards a Physical Model of the Guitar', 1991.
4. Brooke, Matthew, 'Numerical Simulation of Guitar Radiation Fields Using the Boundary Element Method', 1992.
5. Wright, Howard, 'The Acoustics and Psychoacoustics of the Guitar', 1996.
6. Pavlidou, Maria, 'A Physical Model of the String–Finger Interaction on the Classical Guitar', 1997.
7. Lewney, Mark, 'The Acoustics of the Guitar', 2000.
8. Richardson, Stephen, 'Acoustical Parameters for the Classical Guitar', 2001.
9. Perry, Ian, 'Sound Radiation Measurements on Guitars and Other Stringed Musical Instruments', 2014.
10. Roberts, William, 'Physics and Psychophysics of Plucked String Instruments', 2015.

Suggested Publications by Bernard E. Richardson of Interest to Guitar Players and Makers

The following are arranged in order of general interest. Note the '*Catguts*' can be obtained online (from Stanford University), as can the two '*Second Vienna Talks*'. The others are books or journals – all available from publishers.

1. Richardson, Bernard E., 'The Acoustical Development of the Guitar', *Journal of the Catgut Acoustical Society*, series II, 2/5 (1994), 1–10.

2. Richardson, Bernard E., 'Simple Models as Basis for Guitar Design', *Journal Catgut Acoustical Society*, series II, 4/5 (2002), 30–36 [see erratum in *Journal Catgut Acoustical Society*, series II, 4/6 (2002), 75].

3. Richardson, Bernard E., 'Science and the Guitar Maker', John Morrish, ed., *The Classical Guitar: A Complete History* (London: Outline Press, 1997), 94–95.

4. Richardson, Bernard E. and Roberts, G. W., 'The Adjustment of Mode Frequencies in Guitars: A Study by Means of Holographic Interferometry and Finite Element Analysis', *SMAC '83*, vol. II (Pub. of the Royal Swedish Academy of Music), 46/2 (1985), 285–302.

5. Richardson, Bernard E., 'The Influence of Strutting on the Top-Plate Modes of a Guitar', *Catgut Acoustical Society Newsletter*, 40 (1983), 13–17.

6. Hill, T. J. W., Richardson, Bernard E., and Richardson S. J., 'Acoustical Parameters for the Characterisation of the Classical Guitar', *Acta Acustica united with Acustica*, 90 (2004), 335–348.

7. Richardson, Bernard E., 'Guitar Making: The Acoustician's Tale', *Proceedings of the Second Vienna Talk* (2010), 125–128.

8. Richardson, Bernard E., 'Mode Studies of Plucked Stringed Instruments: Application of Holographic Interferometry', *Proceedings of the Second Vienna Talk* (2010), 129–132.

9. Wright, Howard A. K., 'The Acoustics and Psychoacoustics of the Guitar', PhD thesis, Cardiff University, 1996.

Dr Bernard Richardson,
School of Physics and Astronomy, Cardiff University

Bernard Richardson's acoustical research was forged from an early interest in playing and making guitars. Over the last forty years, along with his research students at Cardiff University, his primary objectives have been to study the fundamental physics of sound production on classical guitars and to determine quantitative relationships between the construction of instruments and their perceived tone and playing qualities. These studies have necessarily been multidisciplinary, involving cooperation between the physical and perceptual sciences as well as significant input from musicians and makers.

Appendix III

Articles by Paul Fischer

Report to the Churchill Trust Fellowship
Paul Fischer

The purpose of my visit to Brazil was to study first and foremost the supply situation of Brazilin rosewood (*Dalbergia nigra*), and, secondly, to seek alternatives to this traditional wood used in musical instrument manufacture.

The classical guitar is the most important instrument using rosewood, and on my return from Brazil I will continue the study by manufacturing at least six instruments, each made of different woods considered the most suitable for the project. It is important to start and complete this research before current stocks are exhausted.

Brazilian rosewood has for at least 150 years been used for the highest quality classical guitars. For the past ten years, it has been extremely difficult to obtain in Europe, and naturally the price has risen accordingly. This problem has not been helped by Brazil's inflation of over 100 per cent and their insistence to trade in US dollars.

Many guitar makers have changed to the well-established alternative of East Indian rosewood (*Dalbergia latifolia*), which has proved most satisfactory, but while recognising its undoubted suitability, I feel it should not be considered the only alternative.

With the ever-increasing problem of dwindling supplies of Brazilian rosewood, it seemed an appropriate time to undertake a serious study in Brazil and establish once and for all the true situation and, while there, seek suitable samples for further study upon my return to the UK. Bearing in mind the great range of species and similarities, and success of the work I have already done in this direction, I considered it worth continuing the study of South American tonewoods.

I travelled widely throughout Brazil, starting first in São Paulo, where I sought expert guidance as to the most important and useful regions to visit, then onto Belém on the equator and the Amazon region. Belém is the most important port for the export of timber from the state of Para and the Amazonas. It was also an opportunity to attend the thirty-fifth meeting of the Brazilian Society for Science at the Universidade Federal de Para. Under discussion at this meeting was the future of the rainforests, zoology, botany and geology. Arriving in time only for the last three days of this seven-day meeting, I was fortunate to catch a lecture given jointly by Henry van der Slooten, Flavia Silva and Mario Rabelo. Henry van der Slooten is a wood utilisation consultant working on behalf of the Brazilian Food & Agriculture Organization, which also includes forestry. His recent work included a study of wood from the Amazon for use in musical instruments. Flavia Silva is a coordinator for the arts, which includes musical instrument making. His specific task was to encourage the manufacture of instruments in order to extend the range of uses of their vast natural resource.

Professor Mario Rabelo is researching acoustics at the Laboratorio de Produtos Florestais in Brazil. The lecture was given in Portuguese but I was given a brief translation at the end. Unfortunately, their work is still in its early stages and is handicapped by a shortage of good luthiers to take their work to fruition. Naturally, they found my reason for visiting Brazil most interesting, not to say coincidental, as my own work fills the gap sadly lacking in their own. They hope to complete their research by 1985; a copy of the results will be sent to me, and likewise the results of mine to them, I hope by mid-1984.

While in Belém I took a short boat trip up the Guamá River in order to see the forests of that region. We travelled about 10 km upstream, the river passing through dense young forest. A few mature trees broke through the younger canopy but quite obviously this was not an area for timber extraction; this took place further inland. However, the importance of timber in the economy of this area was much in evidence. Along the shoreline, timber mill after timber mill converted the logs shipped down from the Amazonas for domestic use and export from this this major port. The smell from sawing filled the air with the scent of cedar, a popular wood for the necks of guitars.

I later visited the main docks and, with the help of a hired guide, visited two very large timber merchants, both supplying mahogany (*Swietenia macrophylla*) and cedar (*Cedrela odorata*) to the USA and Europe. Directors of both companies informed me that mahogany from the Para region would be finished within three years and that preparations were underway to go over to plywood production. Both mahogany and cedar are woods commonly used in the manufacture of guitars.

After four days in Belém, I flew to the state of Bahia to meet up with Dr Eugen Follmann, an acoustics expert and timber merchant. With his help and guidance, I travelled widely in the forests around the town of Itumaraju, central Bahia. This whole region is engaged in the timber trade, felling, converting and transporting timber to the ports and cities of the south. There being no railway in this area, all timber is transported by road, and very bad roads at that. It was not uncommon for sections of the road to be washed away. With very little forest remaining in Bahia, the light soil was easily washed away, taking the roadway with it. I travelled the whole length of the state of Bahia and the picture was the same throughout: vast areas of barren hillside with nothing but solitary, dead, burnt tree trunks remaining as testimony to the once-flourishing forests and their fiery destruction. Forests did exist, but only as small pockets of a few square kilometres, quite often on difficult ridges or terrain.

Talking with merchants, as well as seeing the evidence for myself, I gathered that the system of extraction was to cut only the mature trees, perhaps 30 per cent of the forest, and for the remainder to be burnt to clear the land quickly for cattle rearing or growing sugar cane. Much of the forest is owned by peasant farmers and they have a duty to replant three trees for each one cut down. Because of the remoteness of many of the farms and poor communications, this policy is rarely complied with. Their wish is to use the land for a purpose that will provide them with a regular income. In all my travels, I saw no indication of replanting, a failure made more urgent because of the destruction of future supplies by fire, not to mention the ecosystem destroyed along with it. Talking with others involved in timber in São Paulo and Rio, I discovered that burning was not confined just to Bahia. It is quite a common practice throughout Brazil.

The main purpose for my study being centred in Bahia was because rosewood only grows in that state; also, a number of other interesting species are to be found in that region. After visiting many mills and timber merchants, it was clear that rosewood had not passed their saws for a very long time. The sawyers and merchants just shook their heads to my enquiries after rosewood and indicated that to continue in this search would be pointless. I eventually came to the conclusion that, commercially at least, rosewood was extinct.

I saw a number of very large saw mills in the throes of closing and even some of the smaller ones were short of work – a very clear indication of the depletion of the forest of that region. Much of the work remaining was converting timber for domestic use – for example, doors, housing joists and rafters, floorboards, door frames and general utility furniture – and for this purpose any tree was used. There appeared to be no selection in order to use the most suitable tree for a specific purpose – even ebony was used for railway sleepers.

The mills themselves were particularly primitive, there being very little lifting gear. Most of the logs were manhandled, even the largest at 4–5 feet in diameter. Large crowbars and simple winches moved logs from truck to saw carriage, a very dangerous operation. The saws themselves were equally primitive and would have four or five large belts totally exposed, with no guards around the blades.

The most common was the frame saw, which, although of vintage manufacture and design, was particularly suitable for cutting some of the extremely hard woods of that region. Ironwood was one such tree, and pernambuco, the traditional violin bow wood.

The practice of using the common names, of which there can be three or four for each tree, can cause confusion; therefore, in the interest of accuracy, I will use the Latin names.

Of the woods I eventually decided worthy of further study, most were native to Bahia, but not all.

After nine days in the region of Itamaraju, I left by bus with Dr Follmann. Our destination was Vitoria in the state of Espirito Santo. The purpose for stopping in Vitoria was to visit Atlantic Veneers, a factory manufacturing veneer and plywood. This German-owned factory was extremely large and very efficient, employing about 400 people. The equipment used for conversion was of the latest design, reducing logs of three to four feet diameter to veneer 1 mm thick in about half an hour. Laminations of 3 mm were rotary cut from logs of similar dimension and fed through a continuous automated system to produce high quality plywood, glued, sanded and polished, eventually to be spewed out at twenty sheets a minute. An order for 40,000 sheets could be prepared, packed and ready for shipping within two hours, an example of the production capacity of Atlantic Veneers. The processes within this factory were 80 per cent automated and produced equal quantities of veneer and plywood. Much of the raw material came from Amazonas, but wood from the USA and Europe were also converted, only to be re-exported. Atlantic Veneers also holds a wood stock of domestic timber in log and plank form, this being for general sale. We were shown much of their stock, which included six small logs of rosewood of about 15 cubic feet. The price quoted for this was £8,000. I studied three other woods of interest in their yard. Colour, weight and tonal qualities indicated their suitability for further study. Unfortunately, the company refused to sell me sufficient for my work, being interested only in selling large quantities. The three woods of interest were:

Macacauba (*Platymiscium*)
Cardinal wood (*Brosimum paraenses*)
Sabourana (*Swartzia laevicarpae*)

While in Vitoria, we also visited the Brazilian branch of Theodor Nagel, another factory of German parentage. This was a comparatively small concern preparing pernambuco for violin bows, ready for dispatch to the parent company in Hamburg, an important source of tonewoods in Europe.

Upon my return to São Paulo, I made an appointment to see Dr Chimelo at the Institute de Pesquisas Technologies. The Institute holds over 2,000 samples of native species, although as I was soon to discover that classification is a very difficult task and many trees of Brazil remain without title. The conditions within the forest, such as density and lively insect activity, stimulates cross-pollination to such a degree as to produce many trees with very similar characteristics. The Institute put all their facilities at my disposal and I spent one full day studying the samples and narrowing down the possibilities for my work down to ten. They were as follows:

Caesalpinia ferrea
Swartzia fasciata
Astronium fraxinifolium
Coniorrhachis marginata
Dipladenie macrocarpa
Machaerium villosum
Astronium macrocalyx
Dalbergia frutescens
Ferreira spectabilis
Caesalpinia scleroxylon

Although most of the specimens selected may prove suitable for making guitars, some are, or will be shortly, as difficult to obtain as rosewood. Because of the close appearance to rosewood, they have been sought as substitutes and used in the manufacture of veneers and furniture.

As relief from the intense study in Bahia and the IPT in São Paulo, I visited the guitar factory of Tranquillo Giannini. Unfortunately, because of a recent fire, part of the factory was not in operation and the remainder on limited production only. I was escorted about the factory by Sérgio Abreu, Brazil's leading concert guitarist; he is called in by the company as a consultant in order to improve their instruments to meet the needs of the professional guitarist.

My visit to the research and development department stimulated much discussion, particularly on the use of new woods. The company had experimented with one or two new species with some success but cracking had created some delays. Humidity in Brazil is extremely high, particularly in the south; I therefore suggested that humidity control within the workshops was a must, as I had experience in that direction.

Another visit took me to the workshop of Japanese guitar maker Shiguemitsu Suguiyama, an ex-employee of the Giannini company and married to a Brazilian girl. Common to many solo instrument makers, his studio was small, but in true Japanese fashion, extremely tidy and well organised. The walls of his studio were covered with plans, templates and moulds, the usual paraphernalia of the dedicated luthier, a dedication clearly reflected in his work. Although Japanese, he is by far the most respected maker in Brazil – a respect I readily shared. Curiously, Suguiyama purchased all his materials from Japan and showed little interest in the woods of Brazil. I sensed a reluctance to experiment, a feeling later confirmed by guitarists in Rio and São Paulo.

My last few days in São Paulo were spent in the workshop of Dr Follmann, looking through his extensive stock of tonewoods. As an acoustics and wood expert, his travels in Bahia enabled him to gather an extraordinary variety of woods suitable for a whole range of musical instruments: woodwind, percussion, bowed, plucked and keyboard instruments.

With the knowledge gained in Bahia, and later at the IPT, I felt confident in selecting a final seven woods to make into guitars upon my return. Although not all have the rich colour and beautiful grain pattern of the true Brazilian rosewood, the weight, density, flexibility and tone match sufficiently to give me the greatest chance of success.

Temperature, Humidity and the Guitar[81]

Paul Fischer

Guitar makers and musicians alike are only too familiar with the effects of temperature and humidity on guitars. Changes in the action, cracking and tuning are perhaps and most familiar problems. Keeping in mind the fact that wood *is* never and *can* never be a consistent and stable material, how can these problems be kept to the absolute minimum? What can the makers do and guitarists contribute to help this process?

The process of seasoning timber is well understood and goes a long way to reducing distortion and cracking but cannot be the whole answer to the problem. Even if wood has been well stored and seasoned for many years, this process alone cannot prevent the wood taking in or expelling moisture under what may not always be extreme circumstances. A change of 15–20 per cent relative humidity may be all that is required to create problems. Even the hard exotic woods used in a guitar can generally cope with changes of 20 per cent either way, as long as this happens over a long period. A rapid increase or decrease in humidity, associated generally with temperature, is where trouble can begin. As an example, severe frost in the winter does not alter the humidity outside greatly, but in response to that frost, central heating within a building may remain on longer and consequently dry the interior air more than usual.

England has a generally mild climate, with humidity averaging between 60 and 80 per cent in the winter and 45 and 65 per cent in the summer. Central Europe, on the other hand, can go as low as 15–20 per cent in the winter, where frosts are considerably more severe than ours and the air very much dryer. Dryness is always a serious condition to be aware of. Moisture can, of course, present difficulties. As the wood expands, it may create distortion. The neck may move forward a little and raise the action, but all this will return to normal as the atmosphere

---

[81] An earlier version of this article appeared in *Soundboard*, summer 1985.

dries, hence the importance of well-seasoned wood. Poorly or unseasoned wood is inclined to remain in the new, distorted shape.

In order to obtain a better understanding of the conditions that normally exist in the UK, two graphs were prepared covering a period of three-and-a-half months: one details the change of temperature and humidity outside and the other shows the changing conditions inside.

The inside test area was the workshop in which guitars were made. The room was heated by a radiator, with the thermostat set at 68°F (20°C). For the first sixteen days, humidity was left to control itself. After that period, a humidifier was set at 50 per cent in order to control humidity and determine its effect in relation to conditions outside. It will be seen from the graphs how the conditions varied over that period and, of course, the effect this would have on the wood before, during and after completion of an instrument. These conditions will, therefore, have great bearing on how the instrument will perform once it has left the workshop and been put through a whole range of temperatures and humidity levels. This exercise relates only to the conditions of central England and will vary according to the geographic location. But the parameters were such that it will provide a useful guide for most of the instruments constructed here and in other areas of the world.

The control of workshop humidity is determined by the range of countries to which instruments may be sent, but on average this should be between 50 and 60 per cent, which means a fair amount of control is needed in the case of the UK, as the average humidity is rather high.

Unlike related professions, such as cabinetmaking and so forth, musical instrument makers cannot compensate for the expansion and contraction of wood through the traditional methods of construction. A musical instrument is a fixed unit with all of its components solidly glued one to the other, moving in some cases in unison and in others against its neighbour. The degree of stress created by the latter is determined by the species of adjoining wood and the quality of seasoning: for example, hard ebony of the fingerboard glued to the moderately soft mahogany or even softer cedar of the neck. These three woods move at different rates with changes in humidity, and will, unless steps are taken to reduce this conflict to an absolute minimum, cause warping or cracking.

The absolute minimum is achieved by choosing wood that is straight grained, free from knots or blemishes. This is quartered out and seasoned, and finally the instrument is assembled in a humidity-controlled environment. It is an advantage to use wood that is on the dry side, a lesson drawn from the experience of harpsichord makers, who for centuries have shrunk their soundboards before insertion. This reduces the amount the wood may contract in the future, which is potentially more dangerous than the wood expanding.

Expansion will be most obvious with the back and soundboard; they may arch and distort. The neck may also move forwards or backwards and upset the action, making it more difficult to play and increasing the risk of buzzing. Shrinkage can cause cracking, as well as distortion, although the latter to a lesser degree. The frets may protrude from the edge of the fingerboard, and here again the action might be affected.

What can guitarists do to prevent or reduce the risks of these problems? First of all, be aware of the effects of changes in humidity and temperature on wood. As little as a 10 per cent increase or decrease will affect the instrument. The degree of change will be determined by the condition of the wood (seasoning) and the rate of humidity change. A drop of 10 per cent within one hour will have a greater effect than 10 per cent over six hours. Wood expands and contracts at different rates according to the species. The soft woods such as spruce and cedar (soundboards) are elastic and will generally expand and contract with ease, whereas the hard and more brittle rosewoods respond very slowly; therefore, damage can occur if the change in humidity is too rapid. The neck, which may be mahogany or cedar, falls somewhere between the soft and hard woods mentioned above, and the ebony fingerboard is definitely of the brittle variety.

So, to the practical considerations for guitarists. Avoid passing the instrument through rapid humidity or temperature changes if possible. Reduce the effects of rapid change by the use of 'dampit' or silica gel crystals within the case. Do not place the instrument, whether in or out of the case, in direct sunlight, remembering that most guitar cases are black and will get very warm. Do not place it near a radiator or convector-type heater or expose it to the dry conditions generally associated with central heating.

It is well worth investing in a humidity gauge for the guitar case and aiming to keep it within the 45–50 per cent range, although this will depend to some extent on the maker's advice. It should be emphasised that conditions can go below or above these figures with little risk, so long as it is not rapid – that is, 5 per cent per hour either way.

Journal Articles By and About Paul Fischer

Cooper, Colin, 'Interview: Paul Fischer – Leading Luthier', *Classical Guitar* (November 1986), 13–15.

Cooper, Colin, 'Interview: Paul Fischer – Leading Luthier Part 2: The Problem of Volume and Other Matters', *Classical Guitar* (December 1986), 17–21.

Cooper, Colin, 'Paul Fischer's New Guitars', *Classical Guitar* (January 1985), 33–34.

Fischer, Paul, 'David Rubio – Obituary', *Classical Guitar* (December 2000), 28–29.

Fischer, Paul, 'The Effects of Temperature and Humidity on Guitars', *Classical Guitar* (September 1985), 43–44.

Fischer, Paul, 'Les effets de la température et de l'humidité sur les guitarres', *Les Cahiers de la Guitare* (1986), 1st trimester, 28–29.

Fischer, Paul, 'Temperature, Humidity and the Guitar', *Soundboard* (Summer 1985).

Fischer, Paul, 'Winston Churchill Travelling Fellowship to Brazil: A Report by Paul Fischer', *Classical Guitar* (July–August 1984).

Saba, Thérèse Wassily, 'Interview with Paul Fischer', *Classical Guitar* (February 1999), 11–19.

Gallery of Instruments by Paul Fischer

GALLERY FIGURE 1: Fiftieth Anniversary guitar 2006, with a spruce top, traditional fan bracing, figured kingwood body (back view).

GALLERY FIGURE 2: Bird's-eye maple guitar. Cedar soundboard. Abalone decorated bridge (front view).

GALLERY FIGURE 3: Bird's-eye maple guitar (back view).

GALLERY FIGURE 4: Fiftieth Anniversary guitar 2006, with a spruce, fan-braced soundboard, with the back and sides made from sapele pommele (front view).

GALLERY FIGURE 5: Fiftieth Anniversary guitar 2006, with a spruce, fan-braced soundboard, with the back and sides made from sapele pommele (back view).

GALLERY FIGURE 6: Eight-stringed guitar, Rosewood body and spruce soundboard.

GALLERY FIGURE 7: Head of classical guitar. Inlaid sapele facing with inlaid ebony.

GALLERY FIGURE 8: Head of flamenco guitar. Macassar ebony. Ebony pegs. Bone pips.

Bibliography

Baines, Anthony, *Musical Instruments: Non-Keyboard*, vol. 11 (H.M. Stationary Office, 1968).

Baines, Anthony, *Musical Instruments* (London: Chancellor Press, 1983).

Bellow, Alexander, *The Illustrated History of the Guitar* (New York: Franco Colombo Publications, Belwin/Mills, 1970).

Buchner, Alexander, *Musical Instruments: An Illustrated History* (London: Octopus Books, 1973). [Beautiful instruments with fine illustrations.]

Clemenicic, Rene, *Old Musical Instruments* (London: Octopus Books, 1973).

Chapman, Richard, *The Complete Guitarist* (London: Dorling Kindersley, 1993).

Cooper, Colin, 'Classical Guitar News: Song of Four Guitars', *Classical Guitar*, 7/1 (September 1988), 6.

Cooper, Colin, 'Paul Fischer's New Guitars'. *Classical Guitar*, 5/3 (January 1985), 33 34.

Evans, Tom and Mary Ann, *Guitars: Music, History, Constructions and Players – From the Renaissance to Rock* (New York: Paddington Press, 1977).

Fiennes, Ranulph, *Living Dangerously* (London: Macmillan, 1987).

Grondona, Stefano, and Waldner, Luca, *Masterpieces of Guitar Making*, To the Memory of David Rubio, L'Officina Del Libro, 2002. [Superb book for guitar makers and those interested in its history; includes a CD.]

Grunfeld, Frederic V., *The Art and Times of the Guitar* (New York: Macmillan Publishing, 1969).

Hebron, Stephen, and Elizabeth C., Denlinger, eds., *Shelley's Ghost: Reshaping the Image of a Literary Family*, exhibition book (Oxford: Bodleian Library, 2010).

La Guitarra Espanola (Madrid: Opera Tres). [For the exhibition held at the Metropolitan Museum of Art in New York in 1991–1992, and at the

Museo Municipal in Madrid in 1992, as part of the activities for the Quincentennial of the Discovery of America ('The Meeting of Two Worlds').]

Lewis, C. S., *Surprised by Joy: The Shape of My Early Life* (London: HarperOne, 2017) (originally published in 1955).

Mairants, Ivor, *My Fifty Fretting Years* (Gateshead: Ashley Mark Publishing, 1980).

Martin, Jason, 'A Guitar Maker's Musical Journey', *BBC Oxford* (10 August 2009).

Milanese, Diego and Piazza, Umberto, *Francisco Simplicio: Luthier* (Milan: Edizion 1, 2010). [A very fine book with beautiful photography.]

Milnes, John, ed., *Musical Instruments in the Ashmolean Museum: The Complete Collection* (Berkhamsted: Oxford Musical Instrument Publications LLP, 2011).

Munrow, David, *Instruments of the Middle Ages* (London: Oxford University Press, 1975).

Paul, John, *Modern Harpsichord Makers: Portraits of Nineteen British Craftsmen and Their Work* (London: Victor Gollancz, 1981).

Roach, Julian, *Shelley's Boat: The Turbulent, Tragic Last Weeks of Percy Bysshe Shelley* (Whitstable: Harbour Books, 2005).

Russell, Raymond, *The Harpsichord and Clavichord* (London: Faber and Faber, 1959).

Saba, Thérèse Wassily, 'Letter from London', *Gendai Guitar* (April 1992), 128–130.

Saba, Thérèse Wassily, 'Letter from London', *Gendai Guitar* (November 1992), 130–133.

Shaw, Robert, *Hand Made, Hand Played: The Art and Craft of Contemporary Guitars* (New York: Lark Books, 2008).

Whiteley, Jon, *Stringed Instruments* (Oxford: Ashmolean Handbooks, 2009).

Index

Lightning Source UK Ltd.
Milton Keynes UK
UKHW050902080223
416625UK00016B/226